British Columbia's

Premiers in Profile

the good, the bad
and the transient

British Columbia's
Premiers in Profile

the good, the bad
and the transient

William Rayner

Heritage
House

Copyright © 2000 William Rayner

Canadian Cataloguing in Publication Data

Rayner, William, 1929-
 British Columbia's premiers in profile

 Includes bibliographical references and index.
 ISBN 1-895811-71-6 (bound)   ISBN 1-894384-06-7 (pbk.)

1. Prime ministers—British Columbia—Biography.
2. British Columbia—Politics and government—1871-
I. Title.

FC3805.R39 2000   971.1'03'0922   C00-910114-4
F1086.8.R39 2000

First edition 2000

    Heritage House wishes to acknowledge the financial support of the British Columbia Arts Council and of the Government of Canada and Heritage Canada through the Book Publishing Industry Development Program. Heritage is also grateful for the collections at the British Columbia Archives and Records Services (BCARS) and extends thanks to the staff for their help.

Design and layout by Darlene Nickull

Front cover: The old and the new. A host of premiers overlies the last of the original nineteenth-century "Birdcages" legislature buildings in Victoria and the successor structure that has accommodated B.C. politicians for more than a century.

HERITAGE HOUSE PUBLISHING COMPANY LTD.
Unit #108 - 17665 66A Avenue, Surrey, B.C. Canada V3S 2A7

Printed in Canada   Canadä

This One's For Melba

Politics is the science of who gets what, when and why.
—Sidney Hillman, 1944

I tell you folks, all politics is applesauce.
—Will Rogers, 1924

CONTENTS

The Corner Office

The office of the premier of British Columbia is the font from which all the political power in this province springs.

Within the framework of the constitutional monarchy that is Canada, the office—like that of the prime minister in Ottawa—is the apex of a pyramidal structure that paradoxically gets weaker as its base gets broader. In descending order from the premier are the cabinet, the party caucus, the legislative assembly itself, the bureaucracy and—at the bottom—the electorate.

Strictly speaking, the premier is not chosen by the voter. He or she is simply elected as a Member of the Legislative Assembly (MLA) from a slate of candidates in a particular riding. Since 1903, when political parties began contesting B.C. elections, it has been the party that has chosen the premier. Canada's parliamentary model is unlike the republican form of government in the United States, where presidents and state governors are elected separately from other representatives. Another difference from U.S. practice is that the premier almost always has the support of the governing body in the House.

To be sure, when British Columbia voters mark their ballots for a politician who is also a party leader, they can be reasonably confident that their MLA will be sworn in as premier should that party form the government. Not infrequently, however, an MLA can be made premier without the electorate having any prior inkling. This happens when the incumbent first minister resigns or dies while in office. Four recent examples of immaculate succession are Bill Vander Zalm, Rita Johnston, Glen Clark and Dan Miller.

Studiously casual, an early legislature formed after the union
of B.C.'s two colonies in 1866 poses in front of one of the
five Birdcages buildings that stood beside Victoria's harbour.

Vander Zalm was chosen party leader and premier at a Social Credit convention in 1986 after Bill Bennett abruptly walked away from the job. Johnston succeeded Vander Zalm in 1991 in similar fashion after he stepped down, just as abruptly, in the midst of scandal. After Mike Harcourt quit because of another scandal, Clark took over but was forced to resign himself in 1999. He was replaced by Dan Miller. Financial ineptness, rampant patronage and a rapid-fire series of political disasters made Clark's premiership one of the most controversial since the office was first filled in 1871.

British Columbia's transformation that year from colony to province was an abrupt departure from the status quo on many fronts. Under the old system, the absentee landlord was Great Britain's Colonial Office in distant London. Its man on the scene—the governor—ran the colony as he saw fit without worrying much about input from the locals.

For years, the Hudson's Bay Company played a major role in how the territory was governed, because anyone of any consequence was connected to the firm—including, for many years, the governor. When the first house of assembly was formed in Victoria in 1856, the means test for entry to the legislative lodge was so strict that few qualified. For a time, some members were appointed and some elected (bearing in mind that the privilege of voting was a long, long way from being universal). They had limited input into the conduct of the Colony of Vancouver Island and, after 1858, the newly formed Colony of British Columbia on the mainland.

The two colonies were combined into one, British Columbia, in 1866, and entered Confederation in 1871, giving the new legislative assembly of 25 freely elected members a new absentee landlord: Ottawa. The assembly could pass laws, formulate budgets, hire a civil service and collect taxes. The autocratic governor of the HBC days had been replaced by a lieutenant-governor who (as an appointee of the Governor General of Canada) was the representative of the Crown. This was part of the British parliamentary tradition going back to Saxon times, when the king called on leading citizens to advise him. The fiction of giving "advice" to the monarch still persists, which is why parliamentary jurisdictions in the Commonwealth submit legislation to the Governor General or lieutenant-governor for formal approval.

The Vancouver Island colonial assembly had moved into a new set of administrative buildings on the south shore of Victoria's Inner Harbour in 1859. Because of the pagoda-like roofs, the balconies and brickwork "fancifully painted in various shades of red," a newspaper christened the complex the "Birdcages," and the name stuck. The first premier, John McCreight, and his little band of MLAs took them over for the 1872 legislative session. Although increasingly inadequate as the administration of the province became more intricate, the Birdcages were not replaced until 26 long years had passed.

The new Parliament Buildings of British Columbia were officially opened by Lt.-Gov. Thomas McInnes on February 10, 1898. As the contemporary press put it, the new structure was "a marble palace." In accordance with architect Francis Rattenbury's original design, the premier's office occupied a choice location on the main floor at the southwest corner. "The room of the chief minister, though perhaps not excelling others in any detail of appointment or of furnishing yet seems in its richness and comfort beyond them all," the *Victoria Times* enthused. "This may be an impression due to the knowledge that this is the most important room of all."

More than 100 years later, the first minister's office (it is actually an extensive complex) is still the focal point of government. However, the premier's precincts have expanded over the years as the direction of B.C.'s affairs has become more labyrinthine and time-consuming. Back before the Great War, Richard McBride employed noted archivist and historian Richard Gosnell as his secretary. Gosnell authored several of McBride's key policy speeches on railroads and natural resources, and so influenced government policy to some extent. In the latter decades of the twentieth century, the power wielded by the principal secretaries and deputies to the premier became so pervasive that they were perceived as trigger men for their boss. One of them became so addicted to meddling that he precipitated a cabinet revolt against Bill Vander Zalm in 1988.

The new Legislative Buildings, close to completion in 1897, loom over the Birdcages, where the provincial government had been housed since colonial days.

Moreover, the influence of the premier's office has been deliberately shifted away from its headquarters in the west wing of the Legislative Buildings. Premier Glen Clark conducted much of the province's business out of the cabinet offices in downtown Vancouver.

A first minister's control over the cabinet—both by the choice of ministers and by how the ministries are then allocated—can make his or her authority almost absolute. The premier also selects the deputy ministers, who are the senior civil servants, as well as the bosses of the Crown corporations, and either appoints or approves other key public sector personnel. Premiers can also have considerable influence over the party caucus, which is composed of all government MLAs. They manipulate committee selections and agendas, and indeed chair the most powerful committees themselves.

This legacy of power evolved dramatically in the final 30 years of the twentieth century. W.A.C. Bennett's Social Credit government replaced the consensual politics of the 1941-52 Coalition, which in turn had succeeded Duff Pattullo's one-man show of the Thirties. Like Pattullo, Bennett preferred the hands-on approach. It seems that for 20 years he ran the province out of his back pocket and juggled elections, scandals, megaprojects, unions, big business, budgets and the media without recourse to any elaborate support mechanism.

When his son, Bill, took over from Dave Barrett in 1975, the business of government had become too big for one person to handle, and Bennett the Younger redrew the organizational chart of the premier's office so that committees and trusted senior bureaucrats handled many details under the overall direction of the chief executive (himself). Bill Vander Zalm made the roles of deputy ministers and principal secretaries even more powerful in the Eighties. By the mid-Nineties, a top-heavy executive committee structure had evolved, and the potent cabinet policy and communications secretariat became the central authority representing the power of the premier. Called CPCS (or "Cupcakes," as irreverent media insiders dubbed it), the secretariat was headed by Glen Clark's top deputy until it was disbanded after Clark's resignation.

The governance of British Columbia had come a long way since 1872, when Lt.-Gov. Joseph Trutch postponed the opening of the first legislature for one day because the premier and the legislative assembly had forgotten to choose a Speaker of the House.

Before the advent of formal party structure in Victoria in 1903, keeping the office occupied was a nagging problem. In the first 32 years of B.C.'s existence, from Confederation in 1871 to the ascension of Richard McBride in 1903, the province tested and discarded fourteen of its premiers. In the 96 years up to 1999, there were just seventeen more.

Part of the problem was the anarchical political climate of those formative years. British Columbians, already bloody-minded about anything originating east of the Rockies, didn't pay much attention to the political structure of the House of Commons. (Actually, the Commons itself was rather fragmented, with such parties as Liberal, Conservative,[1] Reform and Liberal-Conservative all grinding their own particular axes.) After all, the Dominion of Canada was only four years older than B.C. in 1871, so who's to say they got it right by adopting a party system? Without the discipline of a party apparatus, however, premiers were at the mercy of their colleagues in the legislature. Personal loyalties often foundered on that barrier reef called self-interest. Thus, B.C.'s first ministers came and went with distressing frequency.

And of the fourteen who had somewhat more than a cup of tea in the corner office, only two had any positive impact. One was George Walkem, who governed for two separate mandates (the only premier to do so),[2] and the other was William Smithe, who managed during four years at the helm in the 1880s to bring some stability and prosperity to B.C. Alas, he died suddenly, so his potential had little chance to reach full flower.

With premiers falling regularly on the swords of their fellow MLAs in those early years, the temptation to take a more direct hand in the affairs of the legislature proved irresistible for two of our lieutenant-governors. The first

All is calm inside the legislative assembly in 1900, before turmoil erupts over
the firing of Premier Charles Semlin by Lt.-Gov. Thomas McInnes.

representative of the Queen, Joseph Trutch, was more powerful than the
politicians in those chaotic months following Confederation. Because the
province had to have a first minister for the parliamentary model to work
properly, and because the voters (having not yet cast any ballots) hadn't indicated
their preference, McCreight was chosen after consultation between Trutch and
Prime Minister John A. Macdonald. Because McCreight was safe, sober and a
barrister, he got the nod. In hand-picking the first premier, Trutch was running
the show in the manner of the old colonial governor. He even sat in on cabinet
sessions until the second premier, Amor De Cosmos, curtailed the practice.

At the turn of the century, another vice-regal inhabitant of Government
House moved from dabbling to direct interference. Lt.-Gov. McInnes first
removed Premier John Turner from office in 1898, without benefit of an election,
then did the same thing with Charles Semlin in 1900. McInnes's preferred
successor to Semlin, Joseph Martin, lasted only five months (the shortest tenure
of any B.C. premier), and McInnes himself was eventually fired by Prime
Minister Wilfrid Laurier. (Today, apart from myriad ceremonial duties, the

vice-regal appointee confirms which political party will form the government—without fail, the one with the most seats—gives Royal assent to all legislation and rubber-stamps the party's choice as premier.)

Even without outside interference, being the premier of British Columbia is not an easy job. In addition to William Smithe, several died while on duty. Smithe's successor, Alexander Davie, became so exhausted by the post that he had to take a leave of absence after less than a year. He died within months. John Robson crushed his finger in the gate of a hansom cab while visiting London and succumbed to blood poisoning. Harlan Brewster contracted pneumonia while returning by train from an Ottawa conference and passed away in Calgary. John Oliver, after long service in government, fell victim to cancer after nine years as premier. A few more of our chief ministers were forced to resign while still in office, while two of them, as we have noted, were summarily dismissed by the lieutenant-governor.

When not distracted by the bumpy path of power, all the premiers embraced favourite causes, from agriculture to unionism. In addition, there has been one common theme over the years: Ottawa-bashing. The true Canadian national sport is federal-provincial relations, and B.C. has been a major player since Confederation. Victoria's 130-year quarrel with the uncaring East has spawned many slogans: Fight Canada, B.C. First, Better Terms—and even Separation.

From the very first day the terms of union were signed, B.C. started complaining. Ottawa's foot-dragging over construction of the transcontinental railroad—one of the key inducements for the colony to join Canada—was the first indication that this marriage would not be a peaceful one. George Walkem pursued the matter vigorously, to the extent of going to London to push B.C.'s position. Later, the Esquimalt graving dock (another term of union) became a further source of irritation.

In the twentieth century, the "railway belt," freight rates, fisheries and transfer payments took their turns as headline-friendly issues. While his cabinet was preparing to defy him in 1941 by making a coalition overture to the opposition, Pattullo was back east, obstinately trying to dredge a better deal out of Ottawa. In recent years, Clark took Ottawa-bashing to another level over the salmon issue by also attacking both the state of Alaska and the U.S. federal government in Washington.

Often, attacks on Ottawa and other outside interests peak when the populace begins muttering about the inadequacies of the incumbent premier. The final humiliation, as always, comes from the ballot box. On many occasions after the introduction of party politics, premiers with seemingly comfortable majorities found themselves relegated to opposition benches, if they weren't bounced out of the legislature entirely.

There have been good premiers, bad premiers and just plain run-of-the-mill premiers. Some were colourful bordering on the eccentric, some were bullies and some were even loved. Amor De Cosmos, with his strange name and high-profile career as a newspaperman, drew lots of attention from historians. Their treatment of his eccentricities probably generated the perception in many quarters that the office of the premier has often been populated by off-the-wall occupants. A hostile mainstream press and at least one historian transformed B.C.'s most effective premier into "Wacky" Bennett. In spite of how he was portrayed in the brilliant cartoons of the *Vancouver Sun*'s Len Norris, "Wacky" wasn't wacky at all.

Even with occasional lapses, B.C.'s leaders were more normal than aberrant. Edward Prior let a company he owned bid on a government contract, then wondered why he got sacked. McBride wrote a cheque for $1.15 million of the province's money to buy two submarines at the outset of the Great War. In a Vancouver hotel room, Wilhelmus Nicholaas Theodores Maria (Bill) Vander Zalm found himself in possession of a plan brown envelope stuffed with $20,000 in U.S. hundred-dollar bills.

Starting with John McCreight in 1871, British Columbia has witnessed the arrival of premiers whose political leanings and personal philosophies have been as disparate as their physical dimensions and their backgrounds. W.A.C. Bennett, prior to becoming an MLA was in hardware. De Cosmos was an itinerant photographer and journalist. Oliver was a farmer. Several were lawyers, but since William Bowser in 1916, only one other premier had formal legal training during the rest of the twentieth century. The point is, the worth of a premier doesn't depend on his or her background.

A good premier and leader is someone who is credible and who can grasp complex issues. The challenge is to make sure the public understands the issues, no matter how complicated and apparently insolvable they may seem. As Kim Campbell said in 1986, when she was unsuccessfully seeking the Social Credit party leadership, "A great political leader is not someone who has all the answers [but] is someone who understands the questions." Exactly what constitutes a good premier will be discussed in more detail in a later chapter. For now, we can point out the obvious: A good premier must be able to lead.

He or she also has to connect with the public—at least well enough to get elected. Policies are important, as is the need to articulate them. Ideology didn't mean much back in 1871, although it gained in importance during the twentieth century. The emergence in the Thirties of the Co-Operative Commonwealth Federation, dedicated to its own brand of socialism, polarized B.C. politics for evermore. The fuzzy distinctions between the Liberals and Conservatives got even fuzzier as they tackled the left-wing menace (leading to a Liberal-Conservative hybrid government in the Forties), but the NDP enters the 21st century as a directionless bastard offspring that bears no relation to its parent CCF.

During B.C.'s first 50 years, premiers used land as the currency of progress. Early governments spent real estate like play money, granting huge chunks of it to railway developers and vested interests. As late as the W.A.C. Bennett dynasty, progress was measured in dirt. Premiers trying that in the latter years of the twentieth century have been eaten alive by the eco-warriors. Similarly, the earlier politicians would be puzzled by our preoccupation with equality—racial and otherwise. Their simplistic view of race and class distinctions made governing a lot easier.

The aroma of power emanating from the corner office adds an extra twist to the equation. Ask any premier or lesser mortal inhabiting any legislative chamber in the land why they are there and you'll surely get the standard litany of altruistic homilies: A desire to change things for the better, working toward the common good, I'm here to serve my fellow man, whatever. But when many of them discover what a rush it is to control the destiny of others, altruism is replaced by patronage and cynical manipulation. As one smug NDP cabinet minister said in the mid-1990s, "Don't forget that government can do anything."

Another factor is added shortly after an election, especially for those MLAs in government. This is the need to get re-elected. For most parties and premiers, this last imperative colours every action they take and decision they make

A subjective analysis can grade each premier's performance while in office into one of three categories. Eight of the premiers have been Good, ten I have ranked as Bad. The remainder are classified as Transient because, in my view, their imprint on our affairs is too faint to register.

Good, bad or merely transient, not all the premiers are equal. The longevity of Bennett, Oliver, McBride and Pattullo is contrasted by the brief reigns of several others. While length of term in office has contributed to perceptions of a premier's worth, brevity of tenure does not limit the good, or the damage, a politician may do.

During the past century, the premier's precincts have blossomed and shifted away from "the most important room of all," as originally included in Francis Rattenbury's design. Change walks hand in hand with the passage of time. That all of our premiers—whether competent, bumbling or just passing through—even made it to those precincts is a noteworthy achievement in itself. However, mere ascendancy does not guarantee success. The individual profiles in this book will help place each premier's contribution in context.

John Foster McCreight

(November 13, 1871– December 20, 1872)

I n the year 1870, the Crown Colony of British Columbia peered cautiously toward a decade that promised upheaval and change. For this fractious amalgam of isolated outposts, footloose miners, transplanted Yankees, outcasts of Empire, subjugated aboriginals, bickering journalists and dedicated secessionists, it was a sobering prospect.

The union in 1866 of the two existing colonies on the far western rim of North America—Vancouver Island and B.C.—had sharpened this mood of uneasy expectancy rather than softened it. There were more than a few in these sprawling precincts of rock, rain and forest who were casting their eyes either to the south or to the east.

The standard model of no-nonsense British colonial rule, epitomized by Governor Frederick Seymour, was becoming increasingly burdensome to those trying to carve a living out of the wilderness, and there were many anxious discussions about the future. That this future might include union with the fledgling Dominion of Canada was occupying Dr. John Sebastian Helmcken's thoughts on a chilly day early in the new year as he hurried toward a meeting of the colony's executive council at Government House.

Helmcken, a surgeon with the Hudson's Bay Company and one of Victoria's most influential citizens, was an anti-Confederationist. He had once supported union with Canada, but then backed off. "The absence of communication governed me much," he told his grandson, Ainslie Helmcken, many years later.

Architects of Confederation Dr. J.S. Helmcken (upper left), R.W.W. Carrall (upper right), J.W. Trutch (lower left) and Prime Minister John A. Macdonald (lower right) were instrumental in making B.C. part of Canada.

"There could be no immigration from Canada, there being no means of travel."

The meeting Helmcken was rushing to attend had been called by Governor Anthony Musgrave to thrash out the issue. Musgrave had succeeded Seymour, who providentially died suddenly only months before. Seymour had been an avowed foe of Confederation, but Musgrave took the opposite tack. Great Britain's official position was to encourage B.C.'s entry into Canada, and he endorsed it wholeheartedly. Many British Columbians saw Alaska, which had been purchased by the United States in 1867, as the top half of a giant American sandwich, the juicy filling of which would soon be their unfortunate selves.

The prospect did not daunt Helmcken, who thought B.C. should reject both Canada and the Yankees and remain "proud Englishmen." What changed his mind once again that day in January was a lunchtime conversation with colleague Joseph Trutch.

The council had been discussing a wagon road eastward from Kamloops as one of the terms of union. Trutch, however, had a grander vision. "Suppose I propose that there shall not be your little difficult road, but a railway all the way East—will you assist me?" he asked Helmcken in the hallway. "Yes Trutch, with both hands," the doctor responded. During that brief encounter, Helmcken changed from an opponent brimming with skeptical questions to an advocate hammering out conditions favourable to B.C.

Meanwhile, as the capital city's chosen few pondered the relative merits of statehood, provincehood or the continuing embrace of Britannia, a barrister named John Foster McCreight was practising his profession and living quietly on Michigan Street, not that far from Government House. Neither he nor those at the fateful meeting with Governor Musgrave had the faintest clue that

McCreight would, inside the span of two years, become the first premier of the province of British Columbia.

The tide of events that would eventually engulf the Irish-born lawyer began with selection of the delegation to argue B.C.'s case in Ottawa. Several weeks after Trutch and Helmcken introduced their railway plan at the executive council meeting, Governor Musgrave appointed the two of them along with R.W.W. Carrall. When the trio arrived in the Dominion capital prepared to haggle with the feds, they were astonished to learn that Canada desired the union as much as the colonists from the Coast. Until then, B.C. had not fully appreciated Ottawa's unease over the "Manifest Destiny" expansionism of the United States. Prime Minister Sir John A. Macdonald considered a full-fledged Canadian province on the Pacific rim as much more desirable than a half-forgotten possession administered by the far-off Colonial Office in London. The terms of union, which included a transcontinental railway, were finally agreed upon June 25, 1870, and British Columbia became Canada's sixth province on July 20, 1871.

Although there were "manifestations of great joy" reported in Victoria that day, there were as yet no faces to accompany this historic event. John McCreight was still diligently sifting through the legal dross that occupied a frontier lawyer's time in the 1870s. Constitutional reformers Amor De Cosmos and John Robson were still better known as sharp-tongued journalists. Helmcken and Carrall returned home to virtually no public acclaim.

On August 14, Joseph William Trutch was sworn in as B.C.'s first lieutenant-governor. It seems Trutch did not confine his activities to negotiating while a member of the Ottawa delegation. The former road contractor, civil engineer and colonial land commissioner also assiduously tilled the fertile soil of federal politics, impressing along the way none other than the prime minister himself. Perhaps what tipped the scales in Trutch's favour was a speech he made in Ottawa on April 10, 1871. Responding to a toast at a banquet honouring British Columbia's acceptance into Canada, he remarked that the Dominion's commitment to build a railway "was not an iron-clad contract" as far as B.C. was concerned. This flexible approach marked Trutch as the sort of politician Sir John could work with, and he duly recommended to the Governor General of Canada, Lord Lisgar, that he be appointed to the crucial post.

With an election still to be called, Trutch tapped McCreight as attorney-general in his provisional executive council. "I have been fortunate to get Mr. McCreight the leading barrister here—a gentleman who commands the respect and confidence of the Community to a greater Extent than any other member of the profession—although he has hitherto consistently abstained from politics," Trutch wrote to Macdonald later in August.

Trutch's reference to political abstention was not strictly true. McCreight was in fact a member of De Cosmos's Confederation League—a quasi-political party—although not an active one. His interest in Confederation was not as a reformer but as a lawyer who realized a strong constitutional government would bring stability to the colony.

Polling for the first legislative assembly of the province of British Columbia took place between October 16 and December 15, 1871. Eventually, 25 members were elected from among 46 candidates. McCreight, the reluctant politician, harvested more votes than anyone else: 373 in the four-member Victoria City district. Prior to the voting, however,

D.B. Ring was one of many early B.C. lawyers who ran afoul of Judge Matthew Begbie.

Trutch and Macdonald realized that parliamentary tradition called for a premier to be in place as soon as possible. They settled on McCreight. (Although November 13 has been recorded as the date of his swearing in, it is open to interpretation. Under early voting legislation, members appointed to the executive council after their election were legally required to run again in a byelection to confirm their cabinet job. McCreight did not have to suffer through such a confirmation vote, which suggests that Trutch named him to the premier's post before October 16.)

The exact date of John Foster McCreight's entry into this world is also obscure. It is known that he was born in County Tyrone in 1827 as one of four children of James and Elizabeth Foster McCreight, but the precise day is buried in the dust of vanished parish records. McCreight's father was an Anglican clergyman who named him John Foster in honour of his great-uncle, the legendary last Speaker of the Irish House of Commons. The family was also related to Major Rudolph de Salis, who rode with the Eighth Hussars in the Charge of the Light Brigade at Balaclava in 1854.

McCreight was called to the bar in Dublin in 1852, but his father's untimely death helped provoke the young barrister's emigration to Australia soon after. He set up practice there and had reached the heights of Crown prosecutor in Melbourne before severing his six-year connection Down Under. On June 16, 1860, McCreight was admitted to the bar of Vancouver Island and settled in on Michigan Street in Victoria (where he lived until 1880). He was admitted to the British Columbia bar November 30, 1862, but his practice in the mainland colony was short-lived. On December 17 of that year, he and compatriot D.B. Ring ran afoul of Judge Matthew Begbie. After the autocratic Begbie abruptly dismissed an Assize Court jury in New Westminster, Ring demanded of the court registrar: "Then please dash your pen across my name" on the list of barristers. According to an account of the incident in the *British Columbian*, McCreight made a similar demand (which meant both had effectively resigned from the mainland bar until union of the two colonies).

McCreight considered Begbie to be unreliable and slipshod, basing many of his decisions on whims of the moment. Even though McCreight would later join Begbie on the Supreme Court bench, they remained uncomfortable with each other because of their earlier disagreements.

The premier-to-be was a thoroughly honest but shy man who was necessarily regarded as aloof and distant by his contemporaries. He did not have the popular appeal or political initiative of the more colourful characters shaping the destiny of the colony. McCreight distanced himself so much from family and friends that there is virtually no surviving correspondence in his name.

Although no marriage record has been found, press accounts and gossip from the 1860s onward mention a Mrs. McCreight—including "the astonishment of everyone" at her separation from her husband in 1867. There is some evidence to suggest John met his younger wife-to-be in Australia and that they were married in San Francisco. By the time he achieved political office, she had left Victoria.

When John McCreight ventured onto centre stage in the former colonial administration complex overlooking Victoria's Inner Harbour, he was the most unlikely instrument of Joseph Trutch's grand design. There were other choices for premier that seemed much more suitable, but were discarded for one reason or another. Trutch's eyes first fell on John Helmcken, but the surgeon quickly declined. He felt he had been neglecting his medical practice during the many months of Confederation debate and would accept no more public offices.

Both John Robson and Amor De Cosmos (who were elected to the House in the 1871 election) were ardent Confederationists as well as strident editors who used their newspapers as pulpits for their radical opinions. They were not the type to be lorded over by a former colonial contractor. Carrall, another possibility, was an upcountry physician from the Cariboo who would soon accept an appointment to the Canadian Senate. As Trutch wrote to the prime minister, the available prospects were mostly "kittlecattle—a wild team to handle..."

So the barrister from Michigan Street was the answer. As Trutch once remarked, he was first drawn to McCreight "on account of the profundity of his legal erudition." Of more importance to the post-colonial agenda of the new lieutenant-governor was McCreight's apparent malleability. Besides, Trutch was beholden to Sir John for *his* job, so he was receptive to the prime minister's views about choosing a safe appointee.

It was assumed by some that McCreight and Trutch were friends, or at least knew each other reasonably well. In the words of one observer, however, Trutch "had but a bowing acquaintance at the time" with the man he chose to be premier. Moreover, observed Victoria's *Colonist* newspaper tartly some months later, Trutch chose "one whose history in this country has been chiefly remarkable for the uniformity of his shrinking from every public movement..." (It should be recorded that the writer of the editorial was the spurned John Robson.)

The flowery hand of an anonymous legislative clerk records opening day, February 15, 1872: "On this day being the first session of the first Parliament for the despatch of business pursuant to a Proclamation hereunto annexed of His Excellency Joseph William Trutch, Lieutenant-Governor of the Province of British Columbia, His Excellency entered the House of assembly attended by his Private Secretary and took the chair at three o'clock p.m."

However, Trutch didn't stay long. McCreight rose and noted that His Excellency would not continue until a Speaker had been chosen. With Trutch absent, James Trimble was elected. Everyone came back the next day, and Trutch's inaugural Speech from the Throne promised, among other things, that a "non-sectarian" system of free schools would be a priority of the new government, and that road tolls would be abolished.

From the beginning, there was little flamboyance from the government side of the small chamber. McCreight proved to be a steady and learned lawmaker, content to establish the statutory framework of the province and leave the rhetoric to others. Within two months, the legislature debated and passed 36 bills dealing with such fundamental aspects of governance as free public schools, revenues, roads, municipalities and registration of voters. On April 11, 1872, 32 bills were given Royal assent by Trutch, including "An Act to remove doubts as to the jurisdiction of the Supreme Court of British Columbia, and of the Judges thereof, over the pensions and estates of Idiots and Lunatics."

The joker in this precarious house of legislative cards was J.W. Trutch. His opening speech, while touching upon some of the government's goals, also noted that the "state of transition in public affairs...compelled me to take for a while the direct charge" of provincial business. To this end, Trutch unabashedly sat in on McCreight's cabinet meetings. Colonial administrative habits die hard, and the lieutenant-governor was loath to become a mere figurehead reduced to ceremonial duties.

That McCreight allowed Trutch to participate in executive council deliberations (and even chair meetings) is less a reflection on his weak character than on his single-minded pursuit of legislative truth. Political machinations and the pursuit of power were well below lawmaking on the premier's list of worthy objectives. This attitude would cost McCreight his job.

"NOVEMBER, 1871.

Honest John—Can you get me and my man a place in your house, Sir? Will clean your boots,
brush your clothes, Sir; find us very useful, not particular as to kind of work, Sir.

David—(in a whisper)—Lay on the polish thick, John!

P.M.R.—I have half a mind to try you, if your character suits."

John Robson (kneeling) and D. W. Higgins try to influence Premier John McCreight's thinking.

The premier's first few months at the helm did not go entirely unchallenged.
"Bad-tempered and queer" was one assessment of his conduct, with the added
complaint that he was either too credulous or too suspicious. However, MLAs
Robson and De Cosmos, who were not part of McCreight's four-man cabinet,
were content to wait. They confined their opposition to their respective
newspapers (De Cosmos was editor of the *Standard*). There were no formal
party loyalties, and factional politics ruled. Although both Robson and De
Cosmos were heavily involved with the Confederation League, its raison d'être
disappeared on July 20, 1871. Besides, as feuding editors, they didn't really get
along with each other.

The picture changed shortly before the second session of the legislature was
called in December. De Cosmos, who had been in Ottawa in his other role as a
Member of Parliament, patched up his differences with Robson, and they stitched
together a united opposition to Trutch and McCreight. Trutch hastened a
showdown by specifically alluding to the government's progress during the first
session. He taunted the opposition MLAs in his Throne Speech on December

17 by bragging "that far from the prognostications of the failure of Responsible Government," the people of B.C. were satisfied.

The De Cosmos-Robson clique quickly retaliated. After Simeon Duck, in moving acceptance of Trutch's speech, repeated his self-satisfied phrase, "the administration of public affairs has in the main been satisfactory," they moved an amendment December 19 altering it to read, "has not been satisfactory." The amended statement, which was essentially a motion of non-confidence, passed by eleven votes to ten.

McCreight's government had been defeated on what was really a minor point. Nevertheless, he resigned December 20 "in consequence of the adverse vote of yesterday."

It's not hard to understand why McCreight folded. He had many supporters and could have fought on, but the alacrity with which he accepted defeat strongly suggests he was waiting for just such a setback. Unable to escape his distaste for raw politics, and uncomfortable with Trutch's heavy-handed, colonial mindset, McCreight quit while he was ahead. In his mind, he knew he had fulfilled a barrister's dream: to lay down a bedrock of law for a new government.

Trutch swallowed hard and told De Cosmos to form a new cabinet. Only a few days earlier, De Cosmos had snarled in an editorial that the lieutenant-governor's original choice of McCreight was "one of those official blunders which admitted of no justification." Now he was premier himself, and McCreight moved to the backbenches.

Before declining to seek re-election, McCreight added one more historical footnote. Chairman of the committee on privileges in 1873, he recommended that a law be framed exempting members from being sued "in respect of words spoken during the course of debate" in the House. The law was duly passed and is the basis for the "privileged" utterances that still bounce about the chamber to this day.

On January 4, 1881, McCreight was sworn in as a B.C. Supreme Court judge. His first assignment was the Cariboo, and he travelled between Victoria and the long-forgotten community of Richfield, near Barkerville, until November 1883, when he was appointed permanent judge for New Westminster. McCreight was widely respected during his career on the bench. His personal library of ink-stained, heavily annotated law volumes at the Royal City's courthouse attests to his shrewd understanding of the statutes he helped draft.

The good judge retired from the court November 17, 1897, at the age of 70. By then, the *Colonist* had forgiven McCreight his trespasses of 1872 and commented that the former premier was "fine-looking and athletic and of a high determined character...a learned, bold, conscientious, successful lawyer and a thoroughly honest man." Shortly after, McCreight returned to the Old Country. He died November 18, 1913, at Hastings, England.

Amor De Cosmos

(December 23, 1872– February 9, 1874)

They sniggered when William Alexander Smith petitioned the California Senate to legally change his name to Amor De Cosmos. They even jeered a bit when Smith claimed the name symbolized "what I love most, viz: lover of order, beauty and harmony."

The year was 1854, and to the rough-hewn lawmakers of the young state, this sissy potpourri of Latin, French and Greek seemed somehow unAmerican and unmanly. They had good sport with amendments suggesting such variations as Amor Muggins Cosmos and Amor De Cosmos Caesar.

Snickering and confusion aside, the senators duly passed the new name into law on February 17. No longer plain Bill Smith, the young photographer from Canada now had a moniker that would command attention and curiosity. "Cosmos" in the original Greek means order and harmony, but De Cosmos lived a most disorderly life. Although the California statute officially prints the name as Amor de Cosmos, the former Mr. Smith soon began signing with a capital D. For a time in the 1870s, he also combined the last two words into DeCosmos.

William Alexander Smith was born August 20, 1825, in Windsor, Nova Scotia. He was one of ten children born to Jesse and Charlotte Weems Smith, whose families had come to Nova Scotia from the American colonies following the Revolutionary War. After a normal education, during which he exhibited a talent for debating, William toiled for a time as a grocery clerk before succumbing to the lure of California gold.

Plodding westward by wagon train, young Smith paused for several months in the Mormon community of Salt Lake City, where he acquired some photographic equipment. Even with the cumbersome, time-consuming ritual of early photography, Smith made a decent living taking pictures of the miners and their gold claims. After he was joined by elder brother Charles, the pair branched out into "mining speculation" and other endeavours. It was about this time that Bill began thinking about a new image. The mining camp he lived in, Mud Springs, changed its name to El Dorado, and this may have had an influence on his decision. There is also a suspicion that there were just too damn many Bill Smiths hanging about. It was an ordinary name, and the future Amor De Cosmos was not an ordinary man.

First printing press in the colony.

In 1858, De Cosmos switched countries. By June of that year, he was in Victoria, the administrative centre of the Crown Colony of Vancouver Island. There he was to stay and raise hell for a good part of the next 25 years. John Helmcken, Speaker of the colonial assembly, describes in his memoirs his first encounter with Amor De Cosmos:

> One morning, while lighting the fire...to my alarm a real expectant audience appeared, i.e. a glossy stove pipe, with a black-haired, dark-eyed, thin visaged, spare and well clothed gentleman under it, who said in measured tones, "If I were Mr. Speaker, I would soon have a decent place of meeting and someone to light the fire." This gentleman afterwards...published a newspaper called the "British Colonist," a regular spit-fire, which made things lively and set people by their ears.

This confrontation took place in dingy quarters at Judge Pemberton's Hotel, which was serving as the temporary site of the assembly. And De Cosmos, by then sporting the beard that he wore for the rest of his life, did indeed make things lively.

He founded the *British Colonist* on December 11, later claiming that it was "for amusement during the winter of 1858-59." But the rude shack on Wharf Street was really the launching pad for De Cosmos's crusade against monopoly and privilege. The *Colonist* (he dropped "British" after a while) began as a weekly, expanded to thrice-weekly and then to a daily.

The *Colonist*, Victoria's first newspaper, graduated to this solid structure (right) after B.C. joined Confederation. It began life in a much humbler shack (left).

In his second edition, De Cosmos attacked Governor James Douglas for the "toadyism, consanguinity, and incompetency, compounded with white-washed Englishmen and renegade Yankees" that infested colonial institutions. Douglas was chief factor of the Hudson's Bay Company as well as governor, and his oligarchic administration, which ignored the needs of the ordinary settler, was prime pickings for the crusading editor.

De Cosmos railed against Douglas and the HBC again and again, driving the governor to distraction and public displays of ill-temper. Douglas, seeking more than once to muzzle this free expression of the press, even resurrected an elderly British law that required newspapers to post a bond of £800. De Cosmos, relying on "the torrent of public opinion," promptly raised the money at a large public meeting and resumed publishing.

By assuming the role of advocate for the common man, De Cosmos was British Columbia's first political agitator. He believed in free will, free speech, free assembly and responsible governing by representative institutions. Although his editorials in the *Colonist* provided a handy pulpit from which to hurl thunderbolts at Douglas and his cronies, De Cosmos realized he had to take the next step: run for a seat in the legislative assembly. In the vocabulary of the day, this was the "Six by Nine" parliament—six members elected by an extremely restricted voters' list, and nine appointed by Douglas.

De Cosmos didn't think much of these worthies. "Of all the unmitigated muffs that were ever collected together, perhaps our assembly is the most perfect indeed," was one of his descriptions of the colonial legislature. Nevertheless, he ran for election in 1860—and lost after arriving drunk at a candidates' meeting in the Victoria Theatre. According to Helmcken (who was Douglas's son-in-law), "I am told [De Cosmos] always 'took a little' before appearing on a public platform." This time, apparently, he took a little too much.

After another failed try, the hard-drinking candidate finally made it to the Birdcages in 1863. Once in a position to influ-

James Douglas, the founder of Victoria, was governor of the Colony of Vancouver Island from 1851 to 1864, and governor of the mainland Colony of British Columbia from 1858 to 1864.

ence (even slightly) the official conduct of the colony's affairs, De Cosmos embarked upon his next dramatic cause: consolidation of Vancouver Island and the mainland colony of British Columbia. He introduced a resolution calling for legislative union, but it was narrowly defeated. The time for such a marriage had come, however, because the cessation of gold fever on the mainland made it economically imperative that B.C. join hands with the trade-oriented Island. In 1866, De Cosmos and other proponents of union got their way, sort of. Instead of combining both colonies, the Imperial government in London, in all its intractable wisdom, folded Vancouver Island into the mainland colony and called the whole thing British Columbia. Even more galling, New Westminster was designated the new capital (if only for a short time).

On October 6, 1863, De Cosmos resigned as editor of the *Colonist* and sold it to a group of employees. The paper had carried him into elected office, and now he could concentrate on politics. The *Colonist*, despite its popularity and ever-present patent medicine ads, never turned more than a small profit. De Cosmos was able to live quite comfortably without its income—mainly because he had quietly prospered from astute real estate deals over the years.

With the union of the two colonies in the bag, De Cosmos threw his energies into Confederation. The British North America Act had created the Dominion of

27

Canada in 1867. De Cosmos thought one Dominion, from sea to sea, with responsible government for all, was a prize worth the grasping. Accordingly, he and a group of reformists founded the Confederation League in May 1868. Its aim was "to effect Confederation as speedily as possible and secure representative institutions for the colony, and thus get rid of the present one-man government, with its huge staff of overpaid and do-nothing officials." This was undoubtedly penned by De Cosmos, for it exactly echoed the tone of his vintage *Colonist* broadsides.

A convention at Yale in September generated a manifesto favouring immediate union with Canada, and popular opinion started gravitating toward the League. De Cosmos was momentarily sidetracked that year by losing his seat in the assembly, but he returned in 1869 via a byelection and participated in the debates leading up to the formal representation to Ottawa in 1870.

That he was not a member of the three-man delegation troubled De Cosmos considerably. Disliked by almost everybody in authority (Helmcken, who had flip-flopped outrageously on the desirability of union, called him "a bad smell in a high wind. You got him from every direction but you never knew where he stood"), De Cosmos was ignored by Governor Anthony Musgrave in favour of Joseph Trutch, Helmcken and R.W.W. Carrall as bearers of the colony's terms eastward. De Cosmos was so perturbed about being shut out of the loop that he started another paper, the *Standard*. In early issues, he concentrated on the need for responsible government, then switched to criticism of the new provincial cabinet.

When B.C. joined Canada on July 20, 1871, there was need for a premier to lead the 25-member legislature. Trutch, the province's first lieutenant-governor, rejected De Cosmos. Although the outspoken editor, elected in Victoria District, was undoubtedly the single person most responsible for keeping Confederation on the front burner, Trutch went with John McCreight, a pedestrian barrister. To Trutch and his mentor, Prime Minister Sir John A. Macdonald, De Cosmos was a loose cannon who was perhaps too emotionally unbalanced to occupy the premier's office.

When the new province opened for business February 15, 1872, the 25 MLAs had formed no firm affiliations. The four-member cabinet bore the heavy stamp of Lt.-Gov. Trutch upon it, and those opposed to the conservatism of Premier McCreight were continually shifting ranks and forming new allegiances. John Robson, by now the editor of the *Colonist*, was another firebrand journalist with strong views. He attacked De Cosmos with the same regularity that he did the government. United in approach, the two editors might have accomplished much, but for most of 1872, it was not to be.

De Cosmos was absent from the legislature for several months. He had spent barely a week debating the province's business in February before entrusting the *Standard* to brother Charles and decamping for the federal capital. As well as being elected MLA, he had gained one of the new B.C. seats in the House of Commons, so while McCreight drafted the laws necessary to govern Canada's latest province, De Cosmos was at the other end of the Dominion. It appears his heart was elsewhere: in Ottawa, perhaps, or lost in new visions of windmills to assault. Did thoughts of "Prime Minister De Cosmos" dance through his brain, or was he still pining for the premiership?

When De Cosmos returned to Victoria in July, his first priority was to get re-elected as MP in October. That accomplished, De Cosmos finally turned his attention to provincial matters. When the legislature reconvened in December, De Cosmos and Robson laid aside their sniping pens and collaborated on a strategy to unseat McCreight. Their chance came when Trutch's self-satisfied Throne Speech mentioned "satisfactory" progress in B.C.'s affairs. De Cosmos and Robson pounced on the government's reply to the speech, which repeated the phrase, and forced through an amendment that stated the administration had not been satisfactory.

McCreight resigned December 20, the day after losing the vote, which he accepted as a non-confidence motion. Barely thirteen months after spurning De Cosmos because of his volatility, Trutch called on the leading champion of Confederation to form a government on December 23. Trutch and Macdonald needn't have fretted. Although finally offered the office he thought was his due, De Cosmos became strangely disinterested in his new job. His cabinet, as unremarkable as that of McCreight's, was only distinguished by the retention of the solid George Walkem as attorney-general and the exclusion of the captious Robson.

De Cosmos did severely restrict Trutch's dabbling in cabinet business, thus putting B.C. truly on the road to self-governance. But otherwise, the great agitator was notably quiescent at the helm and did little more in the way of legislation than continue McCreight's agenda. In fact, De Cosmos was absent from the corridors of the Birdcages even more so than in 1872. He spent most of 1873 in Ottawa and London—on provincial concerns such as the Esquimalt graving dock and the Esquimalt-Nanaimo railway, to be sure—but nevertheless, he didn't seem to have the stomach for the daily grind of legislating.

When the spring session of 1874 began, B.C. and Canada were in the throes of a depression. De Cosmos had negotiated what effectively was a trade-off in priorities on the terms of union. The federal government had agreed to give B.C. a cash grant toward building the Esquimalt drydock, on the understanding that the Island railway would not be treated as part of the transcontinental line and that construction across Canada be further delayed. On February 7, after it was proposed in the legislature that the terms of union be altered, a seething mob of several hundred protesters, fearing that any more stalling would imperil their economic future, invaded the House. Speaker James Trimble was forced from his chair, and the premier took refuge in the Speaker's chamber. The terms of union were not changed.

Two days later, De Cosmos resigned. A year earlier, Charles Semlin had introduced a "Bill to render Members of the House of Commons of Canada ineligible as Members of the Legislative Assembly of British Columbia." It was given Royal assent February 21, 1873, and De Cosmos had to decide where to sit. Recently re-elected as an MP, he chose Ottawa. So ended the provincial labours of Amor De Cosmos. And about time, said his host of enemies. There was not a man in Canada "more double-dealing and deceitful," one told the *Colonist.* Another called the former premier a "dogmatic dog—and egotistical egotist."

De Cosmos survived a royal commission inquiring into land transactions on Texada Island involving mineral deposits, and gradually faded from view. He caused a brief stir in 1879 when he moved a resolution (not seconded) calling for B.C. to separate from Canada. In 1882, De Cosmos suggested that Canada become an independent country free of the Imperial yoke, and this last bit of demagogy caused him to lose his seat in that year's election.

In 1881, while still an MP, De Cosmos accepted a commission from B.C.'s finance minister, Robert Beaven, to lobby Queen Victoria on behalf of the Esquimalt & Nanaimo Railway. "Praying that Her Majesty will be graciously pleased" to instruct Ottawa to pay more attention to its constitutional obligations, De Cosmos settled in at the Tavistock Hotel in London. His constant stream of letters and despatches on the matter finally elicited a vague Imperial promise to do something.

The deal with Beaven was for $2,500 in expenses, but De Cosmos came home expecting a $10,000 fee for his several months of work. Eventually, he sued the province for $7,773.93. On September 19, 1883, the B.C. Supreme Court dismissed his suit, saying that De Cosmos could only expect his expenses and could not seek redress because of the lack of generosity of the government.

Following the trial, De Cosmos's mind slowly slipped into the shadowy embrace of madness. Although his decline was gradual, those encountering him on the streets began to expect bursts of incoherence and outright brawling. Haggard and lost, his beard dyed black because of vanity, he still appeared in his frock coat and silk hat. But the clothes hung awkwardly on his long, wasted frame. The thunder faded from his voice and the fire from his eyes.

In 1895, De Cosmos was declared of unsound mind. He was a lifelong bachelor, so his brother, Charles Smith, watched over him until the end. Amor De Cosmos, born William Alexander Smith, died July 4, 1897. His burial in Victoria's Ross Bay Cemetery was sparsely attended.

George Anthony Walkem

(February 11, 1874–
January 27, 1876)
(June 25, 1878–
June 6, 1882)

B ritish Columbia's first professional politician showed up in the Cariboo
gold country in the summer of '62. He was George Anthony Walkem,
a graduate of McGill College in Montreal and an accredited barrister
in both Lower and Upper Canada.

George Anthony was born November 14, 1834, in Newry, Northern Ireland,
one of ten children born to Charles and Mary Anne Boomer Walkem.[1] The
Walkems emigrated to Canada in 1847. After Charles obtained a position with
the Royal Engineers, young George began preparing himself for the bar. All
seven Walkem sons distinguished themselves in careers ranging from the law to
the military, but George's accomplishments were probably the most important
of this diverse and talent-rich family.

Nonetheless, his legal career got off to a slow start in British Columbia.
Because of a prejudice against "Canadian" lawyers who had not passed the bar
in Great Britain, Chief Justice Matthew Begbie at first refused to allow Walkem
to practise. Finally, after pressure from the Imperial cabinet via Colonial Governor
James Douglas, the rules were changed and Walkem was admitted in 1864.
After this inauspicious beginning, Begbie and Walkem clashed many times (a
not uncommon occurrence where the "Hanging Judge" was concerned). Their
dislike for each other was intense, spilling over from time to time into sharp
personal attacks.

On the other hand, Walkem and the Cariboo were made for each other. The rough, tough denizens of the back country took to the convivial young lawyer, whose gregarious personality did not detract from his fighting spirit. This combination was a winner, and he represented the region politically for the better part of the next eighteen years.

In 1864, Walkem was elected to the mainland's legislative council. Like Amor De Cosmos, he supported union of the two West Coast colonies, as well as eventual Confederation with Canada. After Great Britain merged the two colonies in 1866, with New Westminster designated as the capital, it was Walkem who initiated the repatriation of the seat of government to Vancouver Island. On May 2, 1868, he moved that Victoria become capital of the combined colony, and the legislative council promptly adopted the resolution.

Walkem was not a leading figure in the debates that preceded Confederation, but he did advocate firmness in negotiations over the transcontinental railway. This was the first hint of the approach Walkem would take as premier regarding the primary terms of union. His obdurate attitude would drive federal politicians and various vice-regal appointees to distraction. However, the battle over the railway, which was to become the most important segment of Walkem's career, was still in the future. First, he had to get elected as an MLA.

No problem. In the general election of 1871, George Anthony Walkem led the polls in the three-member Cariboo riding. He did the same in 1875 and 1878. Walkem's standing on the mainland gained him a chair at Premier John McCreight's cabinet table. As commissioner of lands and works, he tended to hinterland matters while McCreight crafted the legal framework of the new province.

When the De Cosmos-Robson cabal toppled McCreight in December 1872, Walkem effortlessly moved over to the De Cosmos cabinet. With no party discipline available to ensure loyalty, an MLA was not compelled to follow his fallen leader to the opposition benches. So Walkem had no compunction about serving the new premier. He was appointed attorney-general—a post he would hold for most of the new province's first decade. Although not personally fond of the erratic De Cosmos, Walkem dutifully ran B.C. while the wandering premier spent most of the time in Ottawa as a Member of Parliament. Forced to choose between being an MP or an MLA, De Cosmos opted for the House of Commons and resigned as premier February 9, 1874. Walkem was Lt.-Gov. Joseph Trutch's logical choice, and he took over two days later.

The premier had barely settled into his new job when the Texada Scandal grabbed the attention of British Columbians. This arose from a contention by John Robson that Walkem and De Cosmos were involved in a scam to profit from valuable iron deposits on the island in the Strait of Georgia. Rising in the

Sober garb and chin whiskers predominate as members of the 1875
legislative assembly gather on the front porch of the Birdcages.

legislature February 20, Robson cited newspaper reports about questionable proceedings and demanded an inquiry. "I believe that these charges, or some of them, can be established," he told the House.

At this point, Walkem took over and tabled his own motion that a royal commission be appointed to probe the allegations. (A sentence in his motion referring to De Cosmos extorting $150,000 from the federal government was struck out before a vote was taken.)

Begbie and the other two justices on the Supreme Court were duly appointed to the commission the following month. Their hearings focussed on the contention that a "ring to acquire possession of Texada Island" had been formed in 1873. The affair involved four occupants of the premier's office—Walkem, De Cosmos, Robson and George Beaven—to some degree, but its conclusion was far less dramatic than its buildup.

Despite prodding by an increasingly hostile Robson, the inquiry could not elicit any admissions of impropriety. De Cosmos did admit he had hoped to make a 10 percent commission if Ottawa acquired the deposits, but that was about it. Walkem testified that he went to the island as part of a tour of logging camps and that the subject of iron ore was a side issue. He denied any partnership or any plan to profit from a mine. "I did not take silver for iron," he told the hearing.

On October 8, the commission reported its conclusion that no government member "has attempted to acquire possession of the whole or any part of Texada

Island in a manner prejudicial to the interests of the public." It was not a wholesale vindication, for the commission did find there were apparently suspicious circumstances involved; the general view was that Walkem and De Cosmos had been indiscreet at the very least.

Political indiscretions aside, the Texada inquiry was only a minor irritant during a very busy year for the new premier. The dispute with the feds over the Pacific railway, which had only simmered during B.C.'s first two years in Confederation, was now reaching the boiling point, and Boomer Walkem was just the man to throw some extra logs on the fire. The terms of union had stipulated that construction of the transcontinental line would start within two years and be completed within ten. By 1874, however, the route to the coast had not even been chosen.

As attorney-general, Walkem (along with Lt.-Gov. Trutch) had been involved since 1873 in an endless exchange of correspondence between Victoria and Ottawa. Later that year, Sir John A. Macdonald's Conservative government fell as a result of the bribery and corruption surrounding the formation of the Canadian Pacific Railway syndicate. This became known as the Pacific Scandal, and it led to the election of the Liberals under Alexander Mackenzie.

Mackenzie was not a bad prime minister, but he seriously mishandled negotiations with B.C. over the delay in construction. Misreading the extent of the rivalry between Vancouver Island and the mainland, he proposed that the Esquimalt & Nanaimo Railway be constructed before the main line was begun. Although it was obvious the original deal would have to be amended, Mackenzie's attempts to do so incurred the displeasure of two Lords—Carnarvon, the British colonial secretary, and Dufferin, Canada's Governor General. Carnarvon, who sought to mediate the dispute, viewed his revised "Carnarvon Terms" as immune from meddling. Dufferin, who was also committed to solving the impasse, thought Mackenzie was negligent at times in keeping him informed.

The prime minister also took a giant misstep when he dispatched Liberal hack James Edgar in March 1874 to jolly the bumpkins into a new agreement. To begin with, in a letter dated February 9 introducing Edgar, he insisted on calling the new province "Columbia." Then Walkem, who understood that any terms giving preference to the Island portion of the railway would anger his mainland power base, stalled.

While continuing to argue with Edgar over the exact meaning of the Railway Clause in the terms of union, he refused to accept him as a bona fide negotiator and demanded confirmation of Edgar's official status before considering any alterations. The premier's disdain for Mackenzie and his messenger boy soured an already tense situation, and Trutch had to intervene. Edgar, in a rage, was recalled by Mackenzie.

In this age of multiple transportation choices it may be hard to imagine the ferocity with which British Columbia pursued the railway connection. The new province needed immigrants, because population brought growth and wealth. A steel artery to the East could bring settlers here within days rather than weeks or months.

The situation was underscored by the enormous effort required to get from the West Coast of B.C. to the shores of England. A traveller had to take a steamer to San Francisco, board a train for a bone-jarring ride across America, then catch another vessel heading for Europe. So when Walkem decided he must go to England to press his government's case, it took him six weeks to reach London. After testifying at the Texada inquiry, he left Victoria on June 16, 1874. He arrived in Ottawa June 29, and London on July 28.

Walkem's formal mission was "to present to Her Majesty's Government a Petition...complaining of the breach by the Dominion of the Railway Clause of the Terms of Union, and to advocate the cause of the Province, as set forth in such Petition." During his stay, Walkem had a long interview with Carnarvon, part of which was devoted to the colonial secretary's offer to arbitrate between Canada and B.C.

Before returning home, Walkem also sought (unsuccessfully) the Imperial government's financial support for the Esquimalt graving dock, another contentious term of union. Reporting to his own legislature early in 1875, the premier noted a positive side effect of his trip: It attracted so much attention that applications for resettlement in B.C. rose markedly.

Premier Walkem had been absent from Victoria for more than half a year. His government had not yet been tested by an election, so upon his return in February, he knew he could not long avoid facing the people. Part of the problem was the Carnarvon Terms, which Walkem had accepted before consulting the electorate.

The revised terms were not much different from those of Mackenzie and Edgar, and called for rail construction on the Island, accelerated survey work, monetary guarantees and an extension of the final deadline for completion of the transcontinental line to December 31, 1890. In February of 1874, a mob's rallying cry of "The terms, the whole terms and nothing but the terms" had thrown the De Cosmos legislature into a panic when it attempted to discuss the issue. Now, as Walkem finally called for an election in September 1875, he knew he too faced a disgruntled citizenry that was also irritated by a public works program that plunged the province into debt.

Nevertheless, he managed to hang on to the premiership, with a reduced majority of supporters in the House. Within months, that support eroded even more. When the legislature returned to work January 10, 1876, his administration had only days to live. The problem was finances or, as a Victoria newspaper put it, Walkem's "extravagance, dishonesty, tyranny and arrogance."

After it was disclosed that the province was so far in debt that the Bank of British Columbia refused to loan it any more money, the government succumbed to a vote of non-confidence, 13 to 11. Walkem resigned January 27, and Trutch handed the reins to Andrew Elliott.

As leader of the opposition, the former premier hardly slowed down at all. Elliott was a nice enough chap, but no match for Walkem. He did improve the province's financial picture during his two years as premier, but the canny advocate from the Cariboo still exerted influence. Walkem's skill as a politician and a lawyer became evident during a strike at the Wellington mine on Vancouver Island. As defence counsel, he won acquittal for most of the miners, who were charged in connection with their occupation of company property. The incident bolstered his reputation as a champion of the working man.

When Elliott's shaky coalition was defeated over a redistribution bill, he resigned June 25, 1878. With a sigh at the volatility of B.C.'s politics, Lt.-Gov. Albert Richards beckoned to Walkem once more. Back in the saddle again, the born-again premier lost no time in pursuing the still-unresolved railway question. On August 29, the legislature adopted by a 15 to 9 vote a long, bitter resolution by Walkem that begged Queen Victoria "to see fit to order and direct that British Columbia shall have the right...to withdraw from the Union." In a word: Secession. The threat fell on sympathetic ears in Ottawa because Macdonald was swept back into office less than three weeks later. Satisfaction was not far away.

Walkem also had Asian immigration on his mind. Like most citizens of British Columbia during that era, the premier held views that would be considered racist today. He was part of a legislature that denied Chinese and Indians the right to vote, and which attempted to control their employment. In 1879, Walkem's report on the "Chinese Question" recommended legislation to control immigration. A subsequent bill was ruled unconstitutional.

Meanwhile, the premier was undergoing a lifestyle change. By 1879, he was 45, a middle-aged bachelor, smallish and plumpish in appearance. Some said he bore a close resemblance to Rudyard Kipling, although his surviving portraits don't bear this out. At any rate, George was attractive enough to Sophia Edith Rhodes. They were wed December 30, 1879.

The marriage of the premier naturally drew the attention of the press. "Politically we are at daggers-drawn...and we know that he heartily dislikes us as we mistrust him," wrote the *Colonist*, which nevertheless wished the premier "all the happiness that can fall to the lot of poor humanity." The Walkem union produced one daughter, Mabel Sophia.

Contractor Andrew Onderdonk (inset) used steam shovels (above) to clear the way for the transcontinental railway through the Fraser Canyon in the 1880s.

Except where Ottawa was concerned, marriage may have softened somewhat the political animal that Walkem had become. In October 1880, while on a visit to his Cariboo constituents, he paused in Kamloops for "a pleasant music evening" at the home of Circuit Judge Henry Crease and his wife. According to Sarah Crease's journal, "Mr. Walkem sang comic songs very quietly & well." (A few years earlier, Judge Crease had called Walkem "the little trickster," but this apparently did not affect their socializing.)

While the premier pondered married life, things began to happen. In October, Macdonald's cabinet approved a Burrard Inlet terminus for the railway. In December, Andrew Onderdonk was awarded several contracts to build B.C. segments of the line. In May 1880, the first symbolic blast of dynamite at Yale signalled the start of construction. A new CPR syndicate was formed in June.

Walkem, however, still had a few burrs under his saddle. One was the Island stretch of the railway, which had been downgraded to branch-line status. In

1881, B.C. sent De Cosmos to London as a special agent to lobby on behalf of the Esquimalt & Nanaimo.

The graving dock was another irritant. The terms of union had included a £100,000 loan from the Dominion to build the dock, but B.C. soon exceeded this amount and the rising cost was becoming a burden. As early as 1872, Walkem, in his capacity as commissioner of lands and works, dispatched letters to eastern newspapers and English magazines cancelling ads calling for tenders to build the drydock. This pessimism over the uncertain future of the enterprise did not go away; nine years later, Walkem's shaky reputation as a fiscal manager was damaged anew by the dock's cost overrun.

As 1881 limped to a close, Walkem's innings at bat were nearly over. The drydock, plus stalling over a promised redistribution bill (which would have increased the number of MLAs), made life in the House a succession of daily crises. Still the deft politician, he managed to muster enough support to hang on until the spring of 1882.

A painless escape presented itself when Alexander Rocke Robertson died, leaving a vacancy on the B.C. Supreme Court bench. Sir John A., who once noted that Walkem was "inclined to sharp practice," saw this as an opportunity to remove a strident critic of the federal railway policy from the political scene, while Walkem wished to avoid another defeat as premier. He resigned June 6, 1882, and Macdonald appointed him to the bench on June 12.

Walkem's career as a justice did much to dampen the negative aura surrounding his final months in office. He was as sharp on the bench as he had been as a lawyer appearing before it. He helped establish rules of practice for the court and co-existed reasonably well with Begbie, his old adversary.

Walkem also had his reputation upheld by winning a libel suit against D.W. Higgins of the *Colonist*, who had cast aspersions on his character. He participated in various commissions, and in 1898 conducted an inquiry into newspaper charges that the surveyor-general had accepted bribes. Walkem concluded that the story in the *Victoria Times* was based on hearsay and had no merit.

Justice Walkem retired October 2, 1904, and spent his last years at "Maplehurst," his mansion on Blanshard Street in Victoria. He died January 13, 1908, and was buried in Ross Bay Cemetery. Predeceased by his wife in 1902, the former premier and jurist left behind a simple will that contained one cryptic clause. He decreed that "no sum whatsoever" be given to Miss Patty Rhodes, his wife's sister, despite any claims on his estate.

Andrew Charles Elliott

(February 1, 1876–
June 25, 1878)

he careers of Andrew Elliott and George Walkem are entwined to the extent that one served as a pothole on the other's path to power. Elliott was a relative latecomer to provincial politics. He was an appointed member of the colonial assembly rather than an elected one, and he served the Crown in a number of civil posts prior to 1875.

Andrew Charles Elliott was another of those sons of Erin whose beginnings are obscured by time. He was born in 1828, and his father's name was John, but the name of Andrew's mother and the exact date and place of birth are lost. Although called by Lord Dufferin "a Dublin lawyer...of no more than respectable ability," Elliott actually passed the bar in London and practised there before emigrating to British Columbia.

In 1859, with a letter of introduction from Edward Bulwer-Lytton[1] in hand, the young barrister presented himself to Governor James Douglas in Victoria. After being admitted to the colonial bar later that year, Elliott was appointed county court judge for the district of Yale and Hope in January 1860.

After dealing with the mercurial miners along the Fraser River for several months, Elliott returned briefly to England to collect his wife, Mary (the date of their marriage is also obscure), and their daughter, Mary Rachel. Although not a particularly assiduous public servant, Elliott was elevated to gold commissioner at Lillooet in 1861. This was an important post at the time. The

The mining settlement of Lillooet (shown in 1865) was headquarters for future premier Andrew Charles Elliott when he was B.C.'s gold commissioner.

commissioner filled the roles of Indian agent, coroner and justice of the peace, as well as being responsible for the regulation of mining activity.

However, Elliott's attitude toward these new duties was as dilatory as his judging, and Douglas suspended him for a while. Elliott's upbringing as a member of the Anglo-Irish gentry probably had something to do with this casual attitude toward work, but he was also a frail man who found it difficult to cope with the vertical geography surrounding him.

Douglas's successor, Frederick Seymour, appointed Elliott to the colonial legislature in 1865, and when the two colonies were merged, made him high sheriff of B.C. Just five years later, the deck was shuffled again and most of the colonial sinecures disappeared, but Elliott landed on his feet in Victoria as police magistrate.

Elliott didn't succumb to the political fever surrounding the province's first election in 1871. Four years later, however, he did jump into the legislative waters. Called the "little giant" by a supportive *Colonist*, the diminutive candidate won election in 1875 as a Victoria MLA.

Self-described as an independent, he campaigned as an advocate of the full terms of union. Elliott's candidacy was not without controversy, because he was still Victoria's police magistrate. Despite charges of conflict of interest, Elliott refused to resign, pointing out that he was paid by the city and not the province. (Eventually, he silenced the grumblers by retaining the post of magistrate, but at no salary.)

Soon after taking his seat, the novice legislator was acclaimed leader of the opposition. As such, he led the attack on Premier Walkem for the messy state of

The Earl of Dufferin was Canada's third Governor General, from 1872 to 1878.

B.C.'s fiscal picture. When the Walkem government lost a non-confidence motion and resigned January 27, 1876, Lt.-Gov. Joseph Trutch selected Elliott as the new premier five days later. It was Trutch's last significant act before stepping down in July.

Elliott's administration had a rather crowded plate in 1876. Apart from the province's financial problems, the distrust of the Dominion government over the railway question was fuelling a vocal separation movement. Elliott, however, got the full attention of everyone with a deluge of taxes on income, real estate, schools and undeveloped land. He also briefly imposed tolls on the Cariboo Road.

The premier's doctrine of tight spending controls and increased taxation did much for the bottom line, but didn't exactly win over the voters. Even amending Walkem's self-serving voter registration legislation, which favoured mainland candidates, didn't help in the long run.

The Carnarvon Terms were the catchwords of the year, and Elliott did his dutiful best by supporting the compromise suggested by Lord Carnarvon, the Imperial colonial secretary. But the Canadian Senate had rejected this solution the year before, and the government of Prime Minister Alexander Mackenzie was reluctant to fast-track the railway.

Enter the Earl of Dufferin, Governor General of Canada. Ottawa decided that a goodwill visit by the Queen's representative would calm the troubled waters in British Columbia. It didn't.

After arriving at Esquimalt on August 16, 1876, aboard HMS *Amethyst* (following the usual protracted train journey across America to San Francisco), the vice-regal group was confronted with a cheeky arch strung across the route of its procession. The arch was emblazoned with the motto "Carnarvon Terms or Separation," and Dufferin refused to pass under it. A detour had to be hastily arranged.

An irritable sort, Dufferin did not think much of this display of independence. He later refused to see a delegation that wished to complain about Ottawa's delaying tactics. As we have noted, the Governor General's first impression of Elliott was not a kindly one. And although he defended Mackenzie to the restless colonials in Victoria, he didn't think much of the prime minister, either.

B.C.'s touchiness over the Pacific railway is
exemplified by this arch over a Victoria street.
"Carnarvon Terms or Separation," reads the banner.

During Dufferin's extensive tour of the province that summer, the anti-Dominion sentiments were always present to some degree. Although he eventually displayed some sympathy for B.C.'s plight, he did become considerably annoyed at the provincial "firebrands" and their fixation on a single subject. He returned to Ottawa with the "horrid B.C. business" still unresolved.

Elliott's four-man cabinet had too much to do and subsequently performed many duties badly. Elliott, for instance, was attorney-general, provincial secretary and minister of mines as well as being premier. The A-G's portfolio was one of unending correspondence and must have distracted Elliott considerably. And it was all couched in the stilted prose of the day.

One letter began: "I have the honor to inform you that a murder was committed...at Canoe Pass on Saturday, the 12th instant..." Another, discussing the lack of lights at Race Rocks, acknowledged "receipt of your letter of the 23rd ultimo." Meanwhile, the Indian menace was everywhere, it seemed. On August 30, 1877, Elliott sent this telegram to R.W. Scott, secretary of state, in Ottawa: "Real danger an invasion of the States Indians on our borders. No force here to repel them..."

A political novice and a poor disciplinarian, Elliott had to deal with a quarrelling cabinet split by dissension. In 1876, he had to dismiss both Thomas Humphreys, minister of finance and agriculture, because of his uncooperative attitude, and Ebenezer Brown, president of the executive council, for opposing the Carnarvon Terms.

With Lord Dufferin safely back in the frigid East, 1877 was a quieter year in B.C. The legislative load was less onerous and the contentious matter of the Esquimalt & Nanaimo Railway was put on hold with Elliott's blessing. There was a flurry of excitement when the miners at Robert Dunsmuir's Wellington Colliery went on strike. Dunsmuir's response was to ask for the militia.

"For goodness sake act promptly on this matter," he wrote to Elliott. "I am afraid that there will be blood shed among us at this time. I know the miners as well I think of anyone, and I can see that we have all a hard battle to fight." As attorney-general, Elliott dispatched 107 officers and men of the volunteer militia April 30. The problem was greatly exaggerated and the troops had little to do.

Walkem, who was still the most influential politician in the province, let Elliott cruise through '77, but was waiting for him when the 1878 session opened. When Elliott attempted to ram through a redistribution bill that would dilute Walkem's mainland power base, it foundered on the Cariboo champion's rock-hard opposition. Elliott's plan was to increase the seats in the legislature to 33 from 25. With 17 coming from the mainland and 16 from Vancouver Island, the near-equal split would mean a more representative assembly. The bill was defeated March 29. Elliott prorogued the House two weeks later and called an election for May 22.

The voters of 1878 were only slightly more sophisticated than in 1871, when B.C. began its experiment in democracy. They didn't demand much from their politicians or that they be lily-white in character or deportment. What they did expect, though, were results in the form of prosperity. The man who could stand up to Canada and finally deliver the Pacific railway was their kind of politician, never mind the warts.

Elliott was not that man. He was a gentleman with few blemishes, but his soft stance on the railway (he was called a "traitor" for it by Walkem) and the irritation factor of his taxation policy led to electoral defeat. Although there were no formal party lines yet, the official record shows 15 out of 25 seats went to former opposition members. Elliott lost his own seat in Victoria by thirteen votes.

His brief fling at provincial politics over, Elliott resigned June 25 and concentrated on his magistrate's job (and presumably started getting paid again). He sought election to the Commons later in the year and lost. In 1884, Judge Elliott was a member of the Metlakatlah commission inquiring into Indian troubles on the northwest coast.

Unsuccessful in getting a government pension for his colonial service, Elliott was in London in 1881, seeking Imperial support, when his wife died. In poor health himself, the ex-premier lived in Victoria with his daughter for a time, then moved to San Francisco in 1886 to avoid the "dangerous" northern coastal climate. On April 9, 1889, Andrew Charles Elliott died. He was buried in Ross Bay Cemetery April 17.

Robert Beaven

(June 13, 1882–January 29, 1883)

R obert Beaven, another expatriate who moiled briefly for gold before adopting more decorous pursuits, succeeded George Walkem in the premier's chair by practising the same survivalist technique as this mentor. When chosen premier June 13, 1882, by Lt.-Gov. Clement Cornwall, Beaven had held a cabinet post in every administration since 1872, with the exception of the Elliott interregnum of 1876-78.

Along with many others who settled in British Columbia, Beaven could trace his roots to the Old Country. He was born in the parish of Leigh, Staffordshire, England, on January 28, 1836, to James and Elizabeth Speed Frowd Beaven. The family emigrated to Upper Canada in 1843 when James Beaven, an Anglican clergyman, accepted an academic appointment.

After graduating from Upper Canada College, Robert tinkered with a business career before succumbing to the lure of the Cariboo gold rush. In the early 1860s, he and some adventurous buddies made their way to the diggings on Lougheed Creek. Prospecting was not for young Beaven, however, and he soon repaired to Victoria, where he became a commission agent. In 1866, Beaven returned to Georgina Township in Upper Canada, where he married Susan Ritchie on May 5. Their union produced two sons and a daughter.

Victoria, during its final decade as a colonial outpost, gradually solidified its role as the commercial hub of British Columbia. Old Fort Victoria disappeared and Vancouver Island emerged from the shadow of the Hudson's Bay Company.

Real streets and buildings replaced the tents and muddy trails of pioneer days. The tall ships, their holds full of deep-sea cargoes, crowded into the harbour. Stores, warehouses, banks and factories gave the fledgling city the aura of permanence. In a word, Victoria bustled.

Joining in this heady transformation was Robert Beaven. Along with his commission work, he kept busy as a real estate agent and insurance broker, and also established a clothier and outfitting business. Politics were not overlooked. Recruited by Amor De Cosmos, Beaven became secretary of the Confederation League. When union with Canada was finally accomplished, Beaven ran for election in the 1871 provincial election and became one of the four MLAs from Victoria City. He would hold that seat for more than twenty years, topping the polls in four successive elections.

After taking over from Premier John McCreight in December 1872, De Cosmos appointed Beaven commissioner of lands and works. Because B.C. had retained control of its land and resources as part of Confederation, Beaven had the important and pivotal task of exploiting the natural bounty of the new province. It was also a controversial portfolio. On one hand, Beaven was accused of incompetence for not opening up the land for settlement fast enough; on the other, he was criticized as a "narrow, stubborn man" for not reserving enough space for the Indians.

When George Walkem replaced De Cosmos as premier in 1874, Beaven retained his lands and works portfolio. He also got caught up in the Texada Island scandal that spring. Goaded by John Robson, Walkem was forced to establish a royal commission into charges he and De Cosmos had schemed to profit from iron deposits on the island. Beaven's role was peripheral. As land commissioner, he gave dry details about mining claims on Texada and testified that no favouritism was given to any party. The commission found no hard evidence of wrongdoing.

Beaven followed Walkem to the opposition benches during Andrew Elliott's short-lived premiership. There, he proved almost as skilful as Walkem at pestering the government ministers. During Walkem's second occupation of the premier's chair, Beaven was elevated to finance and agriculture minister. It was a tough assignment. Grossly underestimating the cost of developing the province, B.C. politicians took just seven years to get into a fine fiscal pickle. Their track record made borrowing almost impossible; revenue from development of Crown lands fluctuated wildly; and federal subsidies were inadequate.

One nagging burden was the cost of constructing the Esquimalt graving dock, which Beaven had earlier initiated as works minister. Despite being called "tight as bark to a tree" by government contractors, Beaven only managed once to match revenues with expenditures. In 1881, he imposed a poll tax, but like the other taxes dumped on the groaning citizenry, it was not nearly enough.

Walkem's sudden departure for the Supreme Court in 1882 catapulted Beaven into the premiership. He was appointed June 13, seven days after Walkem stepped down, but the change did little to strengthen the government. Gamely, Beaven called an election for July 24. He handily won re-election in his own riding, but was saddled with a minority government. He adroitly sidestepped this minor inconvenience by not calling a session of the legislature during the rest of the year.

Part of the reason was the impending visit in September of the new Governor General of Canada, The Marquis of Lorne, and his wife, Princess Louise, who was a daughter of Queen Victoria. The capital city became quite giddy over the vice-regal couple, and the projected two-

Princess Louise was a daughter of Queen Victoria and wife of the fourth Governor General.

week stay stretched into three months. While Lord Lorne beetled about the province, the princess stayed in Victoria and charmed the local folk. According to some reports, Beaven became vaporous himself toward the end of the visit, proposing that Princess Louise become queen of an independent Vancouver Island.

The premier's gaucherie aside, Lord Lorne's presence did much to dampen thoughts of separation. He was able to announce the exact route of the railway through B.C. and a firm completion date. In addition, he said that Robert Dunsmuir, the coal baron, would undertake construction of the Esquimalt & Nanaimo Railway, bringing to fruition Finance Minister Beaven's posting of De Cosmos to London a year earlier. Oh yes, and responsibility for completing the Esquimalt drydock would be assumed by Ottawa, thereby lifting another load from Beaven's shoulder.

Alas, all this positive spin helped Beaven not a bit. His smallness of vision and carping, critical demeanour made few friends. The Beaven ministry lasted less than a week after the legislature opened January 25, 1883. William Smithe, employing that sword which had struck down so many B.C. governments in the nineteenth century, introduced a motion of non-confidence. It was sustained, 16 to 8, and Beaven resigned as premier January 29.

About this time, he received a curious letter from a cousin, Samuel, in Brazil. Sam enclosed a sample "Headless Screwnail" he had invented and asked if Beaven, "as Prime Minister of the colony of British Columbia," could estimate whether they were likely to sell regularly at a higher price than ordinary nails. It is doubtful Beaven replied. By the time the letter arrived, he had been replaced as "prime minister."

Beaven was out of the premier's office, but not politics. For another decade, he remained an effective opposition leader, besting the government on many occasions. His debating points persuaded Premier John Robson to amend a school trustees bill, among others. He also made sharp practice of Finance Minister John Turner's budgets in the Nineties. Debating a loan transaction in 1892, Beaven noted that "it did not take a man with a very long head" to wonder about some aspects of the loan, and supposed that "some may have gone into the pockets of the finance minister."

He also made no secret of his anti-Asian bias. On more than one occasion he proposed discriminatory licences and special taxes against Chinese businessmen, and he even joined in the chorus of xenophobes who wanted Orientals excluded from B.C. altogether.

When Beaven finally lost his seat in 1894, it ended a string of 23 years as an MLA. He also dabbled in municipal politics, serving as mayor of Victoria for three separate terms. The Point Ellice bridge disaster of 1896, which occurred on Beaven's watch, was a factor in his final political defeat in 1897.

The following year, after dumping Turner as premier, Lt.-Gov. Thomas McInnes turned to Beaven. "Knowing your thorough knowledge of the special needs and requirements of the province, and having in view your long and honourable experience throughout a quarter of a century," McInnes wrote Beaven, then asked him to form a ministry. This bizarre request of someone no longer in provincial politics availed the erratic McInnes nothing. Four days later, after failing to muster any support, Beaven asked "His Honour to relieve him of any further duty in this matter."

Beaven spent the last nineteen years of his life as a prominent figure in Victoria's business and social spheres, living comfortably on an income augmented by some canny real estate investments on what is now the Lower Mainland. Predeceased by his wife and one son, Robert Beaven died September 17, 1920, at the ripe age of 84.

William Smithe

(January 29, 1883– March 28, 1887)

I n one of those serendipitous alignments that make politics so unpredictable, William Smithe assumed the premiership of British Columbia just in time to reap the benefits of his predecessors' labours. When he was appointed premier by Lt.-Gov. Clement Cornwall the day Robert Beaven resigned, B.C. was on the verge of a prosperous cycle that included satisfactory conclusions to many of the nagging issues brought on by Confederation.

It didn't hurt that Smithe was a popular, independent MLA and an effective opposition leader. He carried none of the acrimonious baggage that had saddled previous administrations, and as premier commanded a substantial majority of supporters who would help bring a measure of stability to B.C. The member from Cowichan, it seemed, was the right leader at the right time.

William Smithe was born June 30, 1842, in Matfen, Northumberland, England, to Frederick and Ellen Johnson Smithe. In 1862, after a short stint in the merchant trade in Newcastle, he emigrated to Vancouver Island. Barely into his twenties, Smithe began farming at Somenos, north of Duncan. Except for the occasional temporary absence, he would call this quiet community home until his untimely death. For a brief period, Smithe divided his time between Somenos and the Cariboo, where he worked a gold claim, but gave this up in 1864. In 1865, he was appointed road commissioner for the Cowichan district.

It was young Smithe's first public office. A few years later, however, he wandered off to San Francisco, where he was a reporter for the *Chronicle* for several months. By 1871, Smithe was back in Somenos, just in time to run in the province's first general election. Tall, handsome, well-mannered and hard-working, this honest young farmer was easily elected one of the two MLAs for Cowichan. At the age of 29, Smithe had embarked upon his political career.

His marriage July 3, 1873, to Martha Kier, daughter of a prominent Methodist, cemented Smithe's standing in the district and he was easily re-elected in 1875. Although he had refused to align himself with any of the shifting power groups in the factional legislature, Smithe campaigned against the government in that election because of George Walkem's failure to build a promised road to Cowichan. When Walkem stepped aside, Smithe was initially ignored as cabinet material by Premier Andrew Elliott. However, Elliott soon found room for him as finance and agriculture minister after firing the contrary Thomas Humphreys.

While just as dedicated as anyone of his era to the Empire and British Columbia's role in it, Smithe was prescient enough to realize it might not last. In an 1877 letter to Colonel J.C. Colomb of the Royal Marine Artillery regarding war and the colonies, he wrote: "Without doubt the time is at hand when disintegration of the Empire must inevitably ensue." The young cabinet minister was a trifle premature with the obituary, but it did indicate the global range of his thinking.

When Elliott lost his job and his seat in the 1878 election, Smithe became the opposition leader during Walkem's second run at the premiership. Although Walkem was safely settled on the Supreme Court bench by the time Smithe became premier, that former first minister's dogged pursuit of the railway question was about to pay off with a period of happy prosperity for B.C. Problems there were aplenty, but the speech by Governor General Lorne in Victoria the previous October had hinted that these good times were just around the corner.

The key issues were, of course, the transcontinental railway, the Esquimalt & Nanaimo Railway and the graving dock. William Smithe was just the premier to jolly the feds into cleaning up the whole mess once and for all. Inclined to stammer occasionally, Smithe nevertheless had a fine command of the language—both spoken and written—which helped measurably in the delicate business of repairing the strained relations with Ottawa.

In February 1883, a legislative report on the graving dock painted a gloomy picture of sloppy bookkeeping and cost overruns. However, several more months would pass before federal relief finally arrived. In a telegram to Sir Alexander Campbell, the federal justice minister, in September, Smithe gently urged a faster pace. "Important that amount of Dry Dock expenditure represented by vouchers forwarded to Ottawa months ago be paid to the province by Dominion Govt as was promised by you...on your return to the east," he wired.

"Dissatisfaction exists here that no steps have been taken to renew work on the Graving Dock [and] that the opening of the mainland Railway Lands to actual settlers is still delayed..."

Campbell had visited B.C. that summer, mainly to negotiate terms with the Dunsmuir consortium for construction of the E&N. By December, the legislative wheels were grinding nicely. The House passed an act ratifying the deal: capitalization at $3 million, a $750,000 cash infusion from Ottawa, and a land grant to Dunsmuir and his pals. The following March, Sir John A. Macdonald's government passed the necessary federal legislation. Included in the legislative package was the transfer of the Peace River Block—a huge tract of land in northeastern B.C.—to Ottawa as part of the CPR deal.

When Victoria's legislative session ended in mid-February 1884, Smithe went east to confer with Macdonald's cabinet about some other provincial concerns. These included the exact location of B.C.'s eastern boundary (referred to London for settlement), extension of the CPR from Port Moody to what is now Vancouver, and Chinese immigration. Smithe kept notes during his meetings and later wrote a letter politely reminding Sir John about what had transpired.

In the years since the early B.C. governments first struggled with legislation aimed at controlling Oriental immigrants, numerous attempts were made to shield the province from the "Yellow Peril." By the 1880s, the physical presence of thousands of Chinese, hired by Andrew Onderdonk to work on B.C. sections of the CPR, made the menace seem more real. By this time, the governing clique perched in the Birdcages was overwhelmingly composed of solid, successful citizens. In contrast to the formative years, there were precious few visionaries among the MLAs. These were men of a certain social elevation and they had to protect their turf. They also hearkened to the grumbling of the voters, who resented unemployed Chinese labourers loitering on every corner.

Tolerance was not a common virtue in the nineteenth century. The actual white man's burden, so far as Mother Empire was concerned, was the weight of the subjugated classes around the world threatening their way of life. In a constitutional democracy such as Canada, however, simple fiat couldn't keep the aliens (and this included the Native people) in their place. There had to be an acceptable legal framework.

Accordingly, the Smithe government was no different than the others in its attempt to control racial matters. In 1883, a House motion urged the premier to adopt "every constitutional method" consistent with restricting further immigration. By 1885, the legislature had passed several acts regulating the Chinese population. These included the imposition of an annual $10 licence fee on all Chinese aged fifteen and over, an act prohibiting the acquisition of

Chinese labourers, building a railway in a land far from their home,
pause to gaze at the white man's camera, ca. 1884.

Crown lands and one barring immigration altogether. The Macdonald
government struck down this last act.

During his Ottawa visit, Smithe sought a similar federal act that would at
least restrict immigration. What he got (passed in 1885) was a $50 head tax on
all Asian arrivals. In 1885, a House cabinet committee struck to ponder the
plight of the jobless Chinese concluded that "the Dominion Government
insisting that the exigencies of the Canadian Pacific Railway rendered the presence
of these Mongolian hordes indispensable, the duty of providing relief for these
starving people now fairly devolves upon that Government through whose
intervention the unhappy necessity has arisen."

One chip Smithe threw into the pot during his friendly poker game with
Ottawa was a grant of 6,000 acres to the CPR. This land was on Burrard Inlet
close to Coal Harbour, and the offer ended Port Moody's dreams of being the
Pacific terminus of the railway. It also signalled the end of Victoria's commercial
dominance, as B.C.'s centre of gravity began shifting to Vancouver. The premier's
largesse with various chunks of the province did not go unnoticed. He was, in
fact, establishing a precedent: expansion of the economy by spending physical
resources rather than capital. This seemingly inexhaustible asset helped pay for
reclamation schemes as well as the construction of wagon roads and railways.

The voters approved. In the July 1886 election, they took note of the good
times, the construction of the E&N, the cordial relations with Ottawa and the
anti-Oriental initiatives, and returned Smithe and his supporters with an 18 to
9 margin in the slightly expanded House. By this time, the long-awaited steel
link with the East had been forged. On November 7, 1885, Donald A. Smith
drove home the last spike at Craigellachie in the Monashee Mountains. (In
August, Canada's newest Governor General, the Marquis of Lansdowne, rode

Donald A. Smith drives the last spike, completing the trans-Canada railway.

the track to a point near Revelstoke, then switched to horseback for 47 miles to reach a train from the west. After a thirteen-day visit to Victoria, New Westminster and Nanaimo, he returned the same way. The gap by then was only 28 miles.)

Smithe was not at Craigellachie, nor was any other politician. But he was at Port Moody on July 4, 1886, when the first passenger train arrived from Montreal. There were some 1,000 British Columbians on hand to hear his speech of welcome. They had made a Sunday excursion out of the event, arriving by boat from as far away as Nanaimo and Victoria.

On May 23, 1887, the first transcontinental train pulled into Vancouver. Sadly, Premier Smithe would not be there to note the occasion, nor the arrival of HMS *Cormorant*, the first vessel to use the completed Esquimalt graving dock in July. The affable, popular premier had suddenly "drifted out upon that unknown sea that sails around all the world" earlier in the year.

Smithe's final months were marked by private and public concerns. Although in deteriorating health from nephritis, he nevertheless commissioned the construction of a new house on Michigan Street in Victoria early in 1887. He also illustrated the wide gap between the whites and the Indians by deflecting a Native delegation's request for a treaty with the government. The Naas River Indians (Nisga'a) met Smithe and other government officials at the premier's official residence on February 3 after arriving in Victoria by steamer (modern

The first passenger train from the East arrives at Port Moody, July 4, 1886.

A Royal Navy man-o-war, HMS *Cormorant*, is the first vessel
to use Esquimalt's new graving dock in 1887.

historical revisionism has them paddling 1,000 kilometres down the coast in the dead of winter). A lengthy dialogue established that the band's primary need was an expansion of its reserve. "You know," one of the delegation told Smithe, "if they catch a little bird, they put it in a cage. Probably that cage will be very fine, but still the bird will not be free." Despite the Indians' eloquence, however, the Smithe cabinet promised only that it would consult with the Dominion government about appointing a committee to look into the Naas band's concerns.

William Smithe, aged 44, succumbed to the fatal kidney disease March 28, 1887. The province was surprised and stunned. Smithe had been premier for the longest uninterrupted period up to that time, and it seemed he had been around forever. Indeed he had, having been an MLA since November 1871. Everyone joined in the grief of his widow and three children. After lying in state for two days at John Robson's home, the former premier was given a splendid formal funeral. His remains were buried in the Methodist cemetery at Somenos. Mrs. Smithe never lived in the new house on Michigan. She returned to the Cowichan district and died there in 1923.

Smithe left an estate of $1,300.37. In April, the legislature pledged to give his widow $3,000, "being equal to one year's salary."

Alexander Edmund Batson Davie

(April 1, 1887–
August 1, 1889)

"Go down to the house and get a black flag."

These words can be found scribbled inside a bound volume of the B.C. legislature's Sessional Papers for 1887, which are now part of the Special Collections department at the Burnaby central library. According to the flowery signature on the flyleaf, the book once belonged to Theodore Davie.

It does not take even a modest stretch of the imagination to conclude that the younger Davie had written this poignant note to himself about mourning arrangements following the tragic loss of his brother, Premier Alexander E.B. Davie. Like Alexander, Theodore was an MLA; it would not be inconsistent for him to have a book containing official House business close at hand.

The premier's life ended in 1889, barely four decades after it began. A.E.B. Davie was a Somerset lad who soon bade farewell to the pleasant countryside of southwest England. Born November 24, 1847, in the parish of St. Cuthbert to Dr. John Chapman and Anne Collard Waldron Davie, Alexander was shipped off to Silcoate's School, away up in the West Yorkshire town of Wakefield, as soon as he reached the age for studies. When the young scholar was fourteen, Dr. Davie decided to emigrate to Vancouver Island in far-off British Columbia. He departed in 1862, taking four of his five sons with him. Left behind in

England were Mrs. Davie (who was in poor health), a daughter and Alexander's youngest brother, Theodore (another future premier).

The Davies settled in the Cowichan Valley in 1863 and were farming neighbours of William Smithe, who had arrived in Somenos a year earlier. Two of the brothers took up farming on their own, but Alexander began studying law. Meanwhile, Dr. Davie died in 1869, only a year after being elected to the colonial legislative council. Mrs. Davie had predeceased him in 1866, so the Davie clan was orphaned at a relatively early age.

Alexander Davie was called to the bar in February 1873, becoming the first lawyer to receive his complete legal education on Vancouver Island. From 1872 to 1874, Davie was law clerk to the legislative assembly. On December 3, 1874, the budding barrister took a break from dry legalities to marry Constance Langford Skinner. It was a fruitful union, producing three sons and four daughters.

As law clerk, Davie warmed to the bustle of the legislative corridors and decided to enter politics himself. In 1875, he was elected MLA for the Cariboo, where he had established a small law practice concurrent with his duties in Victoria. A co-member in the three-seat riding was George Walkem. With support from Walkem, Davie gained election despite opposition from the local press. Just before polling day, the *Cariboo Sentinel* sniffed that the miners would reject him "on the grounds that that gentleman has no claim on the constituency and has only a very temporary interest in their welfare."

When Walkem lost support of the House in 1876 and resigned, Davie sided with Andrew Elliott, the new premier. Although shifting allegiances were par for the course in those unstructured years, this switch did not sit well with Walkem. He felt he had been betrayed, and when Elliott chose Davie as his provincial secretary, Walkem extracted his revenge. Until the practice was shelved in 1929, cabinet appointees were required to win a byelection confirming their elevation to the executive council. Walkem, the lord of the Cariboo, made sure Davie wouldn't get that confirmation by throwing the support of his political machine behind Davie's byelection opponent, the forgettable George Cowan. Davie lost by 58 votes and was out of politics. It was one of the rare times a cabinet appointee was defeated in the mandatory byelection.

A private citizen again, Davie concentrated on his law practice. He was an active bencher in the Law Society and devoted a goodly portion of his time to this organization. On October 2, 1883, Davie was named a Queen's Counsel and was required to pay $13 for the privilege. He passed on the 1878 election (a good thing, probably, because the Elliott faction got wiped out), but ran in '82. This time he chose the Lillooet riding, safely removed from Walkem's clutches, and was elected in the July vote.

Tidal flats necessitate a raised boardwalk at the
Indian village of Metlakatlah during the 1880s.

When his Cowichan neighbour, William Smithe, became premier in 1883, he made Davie the attorney-general. This time there was no problem with the byelection, won by acclamation. As A-G, Davie took his duties seriously. One of his targets was the federal government and its Canada Temperance Act. He argued successfully before the Supreme Court of Canada that the provinces had the right to control their own liquor sales. He also initiated a consolidation of B.C.'s legal framework.

In late 1884, Davie headed an inquiry into alleged disturbances among the Tsimshian Indians at Metlakatlah on the northwest coast. Charged to determine whether "a feeling of discontent is manifestly spreading amongst our Indian liege subjects," Davie's commission concluded that the natives' behaviour was influenced to some extent by interference from missionaries. Its report, tabled December 9, recommended, among other remedies, the use of force if necessary to uphold the Indian Act. It also urged that responsibility for Indian affairs be transferred to the province from Ottawa.

Davie was returned in the election of July 1886. During the session of 1887, he assumed much of the province's direction because of Smithe's ill health. When a delegation of Naas River Indians met Premier Smithe at his home in February 1887, Davie was present in his capacity as attorney-general. He asked several searching questions and represented the government a few days later when the Indians visited the legislature to repeat their request for an alteration of their reserve status (Smithe was too ill to attend).

Also in February, he introduced a bill to deal with anti-Chinese rioting in Vancouver. Passed into law during the afternoon of February 28, it authorized use of special constables "because there was reason to fear that the municipal authorities were in sympathy with the agitation." This response followed the burning of a Chinese immigrants' camp by an angry mob a few days earlier.

Davie himself was not in top physical condition when he became premier April 1, 1887, following Smithe's death. He was already feeling the effects of phthisis, a consumptive disease. Although saddled with the additional responsibilities of being premier, Davie retained the attorney-general's portfolio. This added to the strain. When the 1887 legislature prorogued, a holiday in the Cariboo helped only a little, so in October Davie decided to soak his tired bones in the warm climate of California and the U.S. Southwest.

Provincial Secretary John Robson ran the government in Davie's absence, notwithstanding a steady stream of correspondence from the recuperating premier. As well as discussing House and political affairs, Davie wrote several letters on such subjects as acquiring a free pass on the Southern Pacific Railway, precious metals, Crown grants and judicial appointments. When Robson made Theodore Davie the acting attorney-general without cabinet pay, the premier was initially upset at the promotion of his younger brother without his knowledge. He demanded details, but was eventually mollified.

Although doggedly optimistic, Davie was not in shape to make a quick return to Victoria. Despite his physician's advice, he wrote Robson on November 23, "I am going to do my level best to have my own way" about attending the next legislative session. Reality finally intruded, and Davie asked the legislature— through Robson—in January 1888 to formally excuse him from the upcoming session. Without the House's permission, the premier would have lost his seat by missing the entire sitting. On March 7, he wrote from Tucson that "it looks very much as if I should have to quit Victoria, its winter coldness and dampness."

Nevertheless, Davie returned to Victoria later in the year. He continued to function as premier, but every decision and every speech was an effort. Like many other politicians obsessed with opening up the hinterland to settlement and exploitation (up to and including W.A.C. Bennett), Davie fussed with schemes to develop the Okanagan and Kootenay districts via railway and ferry construction. Much of this did not come to pass until the 1890s, and it eventually formed part of the CPR's rail and lake steamer network in southeastern B.C.

When the House rose from its 1889 session in April, the end was near. Alexander Edmund Batson Davie, aged 41, died August 1, 1889, in Victoria after receiving the last rites of the Roman Catholic Church. He was buried in Ross Bay Cemetery two days later. Davie reportedly left an estate of $15,500.

John Robson

(August 2, 1889–
June 29, 1892)

M ore often than not, the wheels of government developed an irritating squeak when John Robson was around. He was a muckraking editor, a hectoring MLA and—ultimately—a churlish premier. Like Amor De Cosmos, Robson's journalistic exploits have distorted perceptions of his worth as a politician and leader. That said, he did indeed cut a colourful swath through late-nineteenth-century B.C.

John Robson was born March 14, 1824, in Perth County, Upper Canada. He was the fifth of sixteen children of John and Euphemia Richardson Robson. The elder Robson had been a shepherd in Scotland before emigrating to North America a few years earlier. After attending school, the younger Robson went into merchandising in Upper Canada and Montreal. In Goderich in 1854 he married Susan Longworth, whose father was a captain under Wellington at the battle of Waterloo. In due course they had two sons and one daughter.

Although outwardly a typical, God-fearing pillar of society, the young father eventually succumbed to the restless spirit lurking beneath his façade of respectability. Leaving family behind, he followed a younger brother, Ebenezer, to B.C. Robson arrived in Victoria in June 1859 and immediately headed for the gold diggings. After several months' toil and no fortune, he moved down the Fraser River to New Westminster.

There, he was clearing land when he took a swing at his foot with an axe. While recuperating, Robson was offered the editorship of a new newspaper, the

The settlement of New Westminster, viewed from across the
Fraser River in the 1860s, has a raw, unfinished look.

British Columbian. Its first issue was February 13, 1861, and after a year, Robson was sole proprietor. The type of man to enter wholeheartedly into anything that caught his attention, Robson became consumed by his paper and its role in public affairs.

In his first editorial he laid out his platform. "The cardinal measures that we shall advocate are a resident Governor, and responsible Government, or in other words, representative institutions similar to those at present existing in the eastern British North American provinces and Australia," Robson wrote.

The new editor immediately went after Colonial Governor James Douglas and Judge Matthew Begbie. Much of the animosity toward Douglas stemmed from the power Victoria had over New Westminster. Robson, and a goodly number of Royal City merchants, resented the preoccupation with class privilege that was prevalent on Vancouver Island, and which effectively relegated the mainland colonists to second-class status.

In keeping with its quest for responsible government, the *British Columbian* repeatedly heaped scorn on Douglas. Robson attacked the governor for his "high-handed and oppressive mandates" and once accused him of misappropriating funds he "had screwed out of" the public. However, Robson reserved much of his vitriol for Begbie. This was partly because Begbie was an extension of Douglas's colonial mindset, but mostly as a consequence of Robson's constant attendance in court as a reporter. He developed a longstanding dislike for the judge and his methods.

In 1866, while commenting on Begbie's handling of a mining case, Robson penned one of the most vicious attacks ever to appear in print against a public figure. Here is just one purple sentence:

When the bench is usurped by men of mediocre talents and strong passions, when the fountain of justice becomes contaminated and the ermine ceases to be emblematical of purity, when party passion and personal bias unseat that serene and inexorable justice which should ever preside on the Bench, when a Judge steps forward to sacrifice a proscribed victim, when he will not scruple to prostitute his dignity, and betray the sanctity of his office, whenever an arbitrary point is to be carried for a particular purpose, or the resentment of the court is to be gratified, it is then that the whole machinery of Justice becomes odious and contemptible in the eyes of the people.

Judge Matthew Baillie Begbie came to British Columbia in 1858 from England and was the province's first chief justice after it entered Confederation in 1871.

The pair had locked horns four years earlier when Robson ran an anonymous letter accusing the judge of accepting a bribe from a land speculator in return for a favourable ruling. An incensed Begbie cited Robson for contempt of court and threw him into the New Westminster jail in December of 1862.

As angry citizens paraded in the streets, Robson wrote his next editorial from his cell. Entitled "A Voice From The Dungeon!" it portrayed a press martyr "enslaved" by "the absolute will of one man" and forced to write amidst "the wild shrieks of a dying maniac on the one hand and the clanking of the murderer's chain on the other." (Robson had actually offered a satisfactory apology and was released before the editorial saw print on December 6.)

In 1864, the firebrand editor was joined by his family and took his first political steps by getting elected to New Westminster city council. He also became a member of the House Guards Volunteer Rifle Company, but resigned his lieutenant's commission in March 1869. As a councillor, Robson fought against union of the two colonies. He called it "un mariage de convenance," which would never be consummated with mutual satisfaction. Robson was right. The coupling in 1866 was not a happy one, with the animosity between Vancouver Island and the mainland continuing even after Confederation.

That same year, Robson was elected to the legislative council of the combined colony of British Columbia and began his ardent pursuit of union with Canada. He moved his family and his paper to Victoria in 1869. But it was tough going against the *British Colonist*, and after a few months David W. Higgins bought him out. Higgins, who had taken over the *Colonist* from De Cosmos in 1866,

David Williams Higgins worked for and then bought Amor De Cosmos's *Colonist*, later merging it with John Robson's *British Columbian*. In 1886 he left the papers behind and entered politics, becoming Speaker of B.C.'s legislature in the 1890s.

also supported responsible government and Confederation. He kept Robson on as an editorial writer.

When De Cosmos and other reformists founded the Confederation League in 1868, Robson was there, too. Unfortunately, as the great debate about the terms of union began, he was out of the loop, having lost a re-election bid in Nanaimo. This was probably one reason he was not chosen to go east as part of the negotiating team. Another and more compelling one for Governor Anthony Musgrave was that Robson, like De Cosmos, was too unpredictable and prickly for such a delicate mission.

At any rate, union was achieved and Robson got himself elected to the legislature as the MLA for Nanaimo. When he strode into the Birdcages for B.C.'s first session in 1872, John Robson was in his late 40s and an arresting sight. Surviving photographs provide an image of mutton chop whiskers and a bushy but neatly trimmed moustache, elegant dark trousers, jacket and waistcoat, and the ubiquitous silk hat. Completing the ensemble was his cape—an added touch that emphasized Robson's background as an eccentric journalist.

Snubbed as an Ottawa delegate, he was once again overlooked when it came time to choose the province's first premier. John McCreight got the nod, and Robson lurked on the opposition benches, convinced that McCreight was not progressive enough to put B.C. on the road to true self-determination. When De Cosmos wandered back to Victoria in late 1872 after his stint in Ottawa as an MP, the two enemies laid aside their ink-tipped lances for a brief liaison that would topple the government.

Robson never was much of an admirer of De Cosmos during the latter's time as publisher of the *Colonist*. He called the paper's arguments "vaporings" and sneered that "it is somewhat amusing to witness with what self-complacency *The Colonist* blows its own trumpet." He also observed that the editorials bore "a striking resemblance to the bray of an ass."

After the non-confidence vote of December 1872, Robson still found himself

Nanaimo, one of Vancouver Island's oldest cities, crowds
against its harbour. The historic Bastion is in the distance.

on the wrong side of the cabinet fence. Chosen to succeed McCreight, De
Cosmos obviously settled some old scores by leaving Robson off his short list
for the executive council. George Walkem did likewise when he formed his
cabinet in 1874. Increasingly restive and hostile, Robson was in just the right
frame of mind to seize upon an article written by his boss, Higgins, that parroted
allegations of impropriety against De Cosmos and Walkem with regard to Texada
Island mineral deposits.

On February 20, 1874, Robson rose in the legislature to claim there were
"proceedings of a questionable character" involving the present premier and his
predecessor. In short order, a royal commission conducted hearings. Robson
demanded that a long list of witnesses be subpoenaed, and he became increasingly
agitated by the lack of co-operation from most of them. He even persuaded the
inquiry to send Prime Minister John A. Macdonald some written
"interrogatives." Sir John's answers to the questions were, effectively, "No, no,
no and no."

Although the Texada commissioners did not find any of the principals'
actions "prejudicial," Robson was unconvinced that nothing happened. "I believe
the charges to be true, or in part, however unsuccessful I may have been in
getting the truth out in court," he told the hearing. A year later, Robson left

John Robson is appropriately attired to project the image of a no-nonsense journalist.

politics to accept a job with the CPR. He also gave up his newspaper post and served as paymaster and purveyor for the railway's surveying crews in B.C. from April 1875 to early 1879.

Robson's CPR position was essentially a payoff for his support of Prime Minister Alexander Mackenzie during a period of heavy Ottawa-bashing in Victoria. After Macdonald regained power, the government abolished Robson's position and he returned to the newspaper business. Along with another brother, David, he purchased the *Dominion Pacific Herald* in New Westminster, renaming it the *British Columbian* in 1882—the same year he re-entered politics as an MLA for the Royal City. When William Smithe assumed the premiership in 1883, he took Robson into his cabinet as provincial secretary and minister of finance and agriculture. Robson immediately turned the *Columbian* over to David.

A cabinet member at last, Robson was to bury two successive premiers. Following Smithe's demise, A.E.B. Davie kept the aging warrior in his cabinet. During Davie's long absence from Victoria, Robson functioned as acting premier. Finally, on August 2, 1889, following Davie's death a day earlier, Lt.-Gov. Hugh Nelson chose John Robson as first minister.

Robson was 65 when he became premier. He was not well. Twenty years after the battle for Confederation, crankiness had replaced the zest and energy. Also, the radical who had once thundered his defiance from a jail cell was now a wealthy gentleman. He had profited nicely from his land holdings in Granville, which became Vancouver after the CPR relocated its western terminus.

With the fire of reform banked so low it barely glowed, B.C.'s eighth premier presided over a legislature that was consumed more by acrimony than progress. This despite Robson's "well-drilled battalions" that provided a healthy majority.

John Robson's residence on Government Street was built in 1885, before he became premier. The house is about fifteen years old in this photo.

By 1892, the opposition, the press and his own cabinet had felt the lash of Robson's bile.

In 1891, when Robert Beaven attempted to amend a bill so that Chinese could not be employed, Robson jeered that "the leader of the opposition appeared determined to put John Chinaman wrong-end foremost into the House." Later that year, he clashed with his own attorney-general, Theodore Davie, over the merits of the premier's bill regarding Sunday closing of saloons. The newspapers expected one of them to resign, but neither did.

But it was his attack on freedom of the press that showed how much Robson had changed. In March 1892, the House was in an uproar over an editorial in the *Columbian* attacking the "crookedness" of the private bills committee. Although cries of "cowardice" came from the slim opposition, Robson introduced a motion ordering James and Robert Kennedy to appear before the bar of the House "to answer for the said scandalous libel and for the contempt aforesaid."

The Kennedys (who had taken over the paper from David Robson in 1885) ignored the summons. Discovering that there was no law compelling them to appear, the government rushed through a retroactive bill giving it the power to try offences committed against it. A special committee recommended that the Kennedys be summonsed again. Once more they refused, and the sergeant-at-arms was dispatched to get them. Brought before the House on April 21, the

Kennedys protested their arrest and maintained that the passage in question was in the public interest. Refusing to apologize, they were held in custody until the session ended a few days later.

The entire, inexcusable affair forms a blot on Robson's record. In addition, it diverted attention from some positive aspects of his administration. Redistribution in 1890 increased the number of MLAs to 33 from 27—although it did not quiet concerns about the preponderance of Island seats. Following the election that year (in which his government was handsomely returned), Robson took aim at rampant "landlordism" (speculative ownership of property) in the province by amending the land and mineral acts. Land grants to railways no longer included mineral rights, and coal and water resources were vested in the Crown. Awarding of concessions to railway promoters was curtailed, while the sale of timberland and other property was tightened considerably.

The government also passed legislation establishing a provincial university, but because of several factors the university did not appear for another 25 years. In keeping with the improved diplomatic relations with the Dominion government, Robson endured trips to Ottawa both as premier and as cabinet minister. In 1888, discussions included placement of a warship on the northwest coast, immigration and Indian affairs, insane convicts, the railway lands and the Alaska boundary. In 1891, in response to a "My Dear Robson" letter from Sir John, he went east to discuss similar matters.

Increasingly burdened by the weight of political affairs, Robson began manoeuvring in 1892 to replace Hugh Nelson as lieutenant-governor. He sought support in both political and business circles, as well as in the press, and called in a few favours. Before any decision was made, however, the premier left for London to finalize a crofter immigration scheme. Crofters are by definition peasants; Robson's plan was to resettle 1,250 destitute families of Scottish crofter fishermen on the B.C. coast. To this end, he winkled a £150,000 loan out of the Imperial government to finance the plan.

On June 20, Robson boarded a hansom cab for a trip to the treasury building and crushed the little finger of his right hand in the cab's gate. The injury seemed to be minor, but blood poisoning set in. On June 29, 1892, John Robson, aged 68, died in the Metropole Hotel in London. The remains were transported to Victoria "in a casket of solid English oak" (lined with lead), and he was quietly laid to rest in Ross Bay Cemetery on July 28. A large crowd of mourners attended.

Theodore Davie

(July 2, 1892–March 2, 1895)

A s the second half of British Columbia's only ministerial brother act, Theodore Davie marched a few steps behind his elder sibling for much of his life. Up to a point, the parallels between Alexander and Theodore are notable. Both were educated at Silcoate's School in Yorkshire; both became lawyers after receiving all their legal training in B.C.; both became MLAs and attorneys-general; both assumed the premiership upon the death of the incumbent; and both died before they were 50.

There were some deviations. Theodore Davie, who was born March 22, 1852, in Brixton, south London, stayed behind with his mother and sister when his father and four other brothers emigrated to B.C. in 1862. Finding life at Silcoate's confining, Theodore ran away to sea. One voyage was enough, however, and he returned to school. In 1867, the year following their mother's death, he and his sister joined the rest of the clan in the Cowichan Valley.

Davie was already a widower when admitted to the bar in 1877 at the age of 25. On June 28, 1874, he had married fourteen-year-old Blanche Baker in Saanich (causing quite a stir). The happy couple moved into a home in James Bay, but their domestic bliss ended on April 21, 1876, when Blanche died. According to the *Colonist*, she was buried in Ross Bay Cemetery, with "a large number of friends following the hearse from James Bay." After his call to the bar the next year, the heartbroken Davie practised for a year in Nanaimo before returning to the capital.

The intense young lawyer quickly gained a reputation as a formidable opponent in criminal cases, whether as a defence counsel or acting for the Crown. In August 1879 he balked at prosecuting a larceny case involving a Chinese man until his fee of $500 was paid. It was. Even after his election as an MLA in 1882, Davie kept active in court. In 1886, his clever defence of murderer Robert Sproule hinted at the determination and energy that would propel his career in the legislature.

Sproule was a miner who had shot another in the back on the shore of Kootenay Lake. Davie, his lawyer, picked a fine legal nit by contending that Judge Matthew Begbie had erred by ordering the case tried in Victoria. His point, one of "infinitesimal dimensions," centred on the method by which the change of venue was made. Davie ultimately lost the argument, but not before raising Begbie's blood pressure and precipitating a clash between the B.C. court and the Supreme Court of Canada. Eventually, Sproule was hanged.

After his election as a member for Victoria, Davie supported the Smithe government, which included his brother. Re-elected in 1886, he worked hard for Alexander, who became premier upon Smithe's death in 1887. He took his support beyond the call of duty by acting as unpaid attorney-general during Alexander's long and fatal illness. His position was formalized when John Robson became premier following Alexander's death in 1889.

Theodore Davie had now lost both parents, a wife and one brother. The memories of "dear Blanche" faded eventually, and in January 1884 he converted to the Roman Catholic faith and married Mary Alice Yorke in Victoria. They had four sons and three daughters.

As attorney-general and, later, premier, Davie had to deal with a host of issues: smallpox scares, restless tribes in the Kootenays, a "whiskey sloop" trading with the Indians near Cape Mudge, highwaymen robbing stages on the Cariboo Road, and a long and rambling letter from the "decaying little mining community" of Barkerville seeking a hospital for a certain W. Reinhard.

In 1888, B.C. dinged the CPR $62,925 in taxes, based on the assessed value of $12.8 million for its property in the province. The CPR appealed, but the court of revision upheld Attorney-General Davie. Then on March 11, 1891, he ordered J.B. Plante of the Provincial Police to read the Riot Act to striking miners at Wellington on Vancouver Island. They dispersed quietly.

As attorney-general, Davie has to bear some of the opprobrium for the Kennedy affair. At one point he even suggested the proprietors of the *Columbian* be prosecuted for their alleged contempt whether they apologized or not. In May 1892, Davie again looked foolish when a jury awarded him $1 in damages in a libel suit against the *Colonist*. He had asked for $5,000, so this was the court's way of saying he shouldn't have sued in the first place.

Waiting to be lifted into place, blocks of granite clutter the slope next to the new Legislative Buildings, under construction in 1894.

When Davie became premier July 2, 1892, and laid John Robson to rest, B.C. was edging toward a depression. This was not yet apparent to the politicians, however (it seldom is), and Davie went ahead with plans to build a new set of parliament buildings overlooking the Inner Harbour. On June 16, 1892, public notices had invited architects to submit competitive plans and estimates for construction of four buildings. The cost ceiling was set at "$500,000, within 10 per cent."

In October, five finalists (all with noms de plume) were selected out of 65 entries. They were required to submit a second set of detailed designs, and the maximum cost was raised to $600,000. In early 1893, the winner was chosen. It was Francis M. Rattenbury of Vancouver, who used the nom de plume "B.C. Architect." The bill authorizing construction was passed on April 12.

Even though B.C. was still toying with prosperity, the cost of the project and the fact that the money was borrowed kicked up a considerable tempest. There was also vigorous criticism from the mainland that Davie had "anchored" the capital in Victoria at a time when the city was declining in importance.

Later in '93, the Vancouver boom collapsed. A financial crisis in the U.S. dried up capital investment. Orders for lumber and canned salmon were cancelled. Real estate values hit the dumpster. The Vancouver streetcar monopoly, which had overextended itself with capital expenditures, discontinued service on two lines. Many small B.C. merchants went into bankruptcy, and soup kitchens were set up when the cold weather arrived.

That winter was the most severe on record, and in May the great flood of 1894 laid waste the Fraser Valley. Meanwhile, Davie and his government were enduring a torrent of abuse from the opposition (now led by Charles Semlin) about rising debt and spending priorities. The premier defused another contentious issue by getting an equitable redistribution bill passed during the spring session. Although the number of seats remained at 33, they were shuffled so that the mainland had 19 and the Island, 14.

Davie also posted a satisfying political victory, just before the province went to the polls. In May, he easily survived a challenge by the opposition that he had profited from an act guaranteeing aid to the Nakusp & Slocan Railway. Chief Justice Begbie, after a short inquiry, determined that charges Davie had "been working for the company and not the province" were unfounded. (It was Begbie's last official act. On June 11, he died from the cancer that had eaten away at his stomach and liver for several months. Davie ordered a full state funeral for the man he once battled in court.)

In the House, Davie denounced the allegations as "pre-election claptrap" from "political humbugs." When the election was held July 7, his government was returned with a majority of nine MLAs, 21 to 12. Although this was a decline of three, it enabled Davie to survive comfortably while the depression continued to sap the province's strength. In the late autumn of the year, he

Chilliwack was one of the Fraser Valley towns stricken by the flood of 1894.

played host to Lord Aberdeen, the Governor General.

One Davie method of fighting the depression was familiar: subsidizing more railway lines. Among the beneficiaries was James J. Hill, one of the great robber barons of the nineteenth century. The largesse of the Davie cabinet (and of subsequent administrations) allowed Hill's Great Northern Railway to extend its tentacles into several areas of southern B.C. Even today, the GNR (now part of the Burlington Northern Santa Fe) has trackage through White Rock and into Vancouver.

James J. Hill, a Canadian, became one of the greatest rail barons of the United States.

By 1895, the premier was running out of gas. Through the years, Davie had insisted on juggling a heavy caseload as an attorney along with his cabinet duties. He also had heart problems. He resigned as premier March 2 and was appointed chief justice of B.C. nine days later.[1] Chosen to succeed Davie was John H. Turner, who had been finance minister since 1887.

Davie's tenure on the bench would be as short as his stay in the premier's office. Once again he was alone, his second wife Mary having passed away in 1896, and this no doubt contributed to Davie's decline. On March 7, 1898, one week after completing a consolidation of the statutes of B.C. and two weeks before his 46th birthday, Theodore Davie died of heart disease in St. Joseph's Hospital and was buried in Ross Bay Cemetery.

John Herbert Turner

(March 4, 1895–August 8, 1898)

T he long arm of the sovereign, stretching from London to the shores of the Inner Harbour, is personified by the lieutenant-governor of British Columbia. Although the British North America Act does not spell it out precisely, convention dictates that one of the prime vice-regal duties is to ensure that the province always has a first minister.

From Joseph Trutch to Edgar Dewdney, the occupants of Government House during B.C.'s first three decades selected a premier without any formal party apparatus to help make the choice easier. The lieutenant-governors had to rely on intangibles, private advice and the occasional nudge from the senior government in Ottawa—and then hope the choice was a good one.

But as the nineteenth century entered its final throes, no lieutenant-governor had ever dared to simply fire a premier. The BNA Act is delightfully vague on this point, so when Thomas R. McInnes and John H. Turner went into their intricate constitutional dance in 1898, they opened a Pandora's box of political tumult that would take five full years to abate.

For John Herbert Turner, the first premier in the history of the province to be fired, life began simply enough. He was born May 7, 1834, in Claydon, near Ipswich, to Henry and Martha Turner. John Herbert was educated in local schools and at Whitstable, near Canterbury, before leaving England for Halifax in 1856. Two years later, he moved to Charlottetown and became one of the leading businessmen on Prince Edward Island. Returning to England in 1860, he married Elizabeth Eilbeck of Whitehaven, Cumberland. They would have one son.

The Turners had just returned to Charlottetown when John was selected as a member of the committee greeting the Prince of Wales (the future King Edward VII) upon his visit to the colony. Turner was also active in the colonial militia, helping to organize a local volunteer rifle corps.

However, the sleepy community of Charlottetown was not dynamic enough for the ambitious young businessman. Leaving his wife behind, Turner arrived in Victoria aboard the steamer *Oregon* on July 2, 1862. As a biographical sketch written in 1890 observes, he was among a small band of adventurous young men "of that combative quality and that indomitable energy and perseverance so necessary in the citizens of a young state [who] settled in Victoria, and stuck to her through good and evil report..."

Turner went into the produce business and was joined by his family in 1863. He again became involved with the volunteer rifle organization and was a member of the corps formed in 1865 to guard against an "invasion" by the Fenian group of Irish revolutionaries, who hoped to free their homeland from the Imperialist yoke via the dubious tactic of conquering British North America. (Turner rose through the ranks and retired in 1882 as a lieutenant-colonel in the Canadian militia.)

By the time B.C. joined Confederation, Turner had prospered as a wholesale merchant and become part of Victoria's business elite. He was urged to run as a candidate in the 1871 provincial election, but declined, citing pressure of business. When he did turn to politics, Turner was elected a Victoria alderman in 1877 and 1878, and then mayor from 1879 to 1881. After a long holiday with his wife and son in England during 1882, Turner ignored politics until 1886, when he was

John Turner's wholesale emporium, "London House," was a familiar building on Victoria's Fort Street in the 1860s.

persuaded to seek one of the four legislative seats in the Victoria City riding. He was elected, along with Robert Beaven, Theodore Davie and E.G. Prior. (This riding might be termed the heavyweight division of provincial politics. All these men were premiers at one time or another.)

As a prominent and respectable businessman, Turner would seem to be a natural for the post of finance minister, but Premier A.E.B. Davie didn't get around to offering him the portfolio (along with the agriculture ministry) until 1887. When John Robson replaced Davie in 1889, Turner remained finance minister. As such, he supported the short-sighted government policy of providing generous railway grants to help open up the Interior.

After replacing Theodore Davie as premier on March 4, 1895, Turner began targeting the more prosperous English classes with brochures about the joys of B.C. The CPR joined in, and both the Kootenay and Okanagan regions were touted as desirable destinations. What showed up first, though, were American miners and U.S. and British capital as the mining districts began booming following a sharp rise in the value of silver.

With all this activity, one might assume that B.C.'s bottom line would be solidly in the black. Instead, during Turner's years as finance minister, the province sank steadily into the red. In 1887, the overdraft at the Bank of British Columbia was $213,737.81. By January 1898, B.C. was in the hole to the tune of $1,143,086 (which included the cost of the new legislature, now up to $857,000 and counting). Immediately after taking office, Turner scurried to London in an attempt to raise money. In what became known as "Turnerism," the economy was burdened with extravagant expenditures, poor administration, runaway indebtedness and rising taxes.

Turner did have time to ponder lesser issues. In 1897, he got into a spat with Prime Minister Wilfrid Laurier and the Imperial government over the use of "honourable" for MLAs. B.C. thought the honorific should be for the "life of parliament," which was usually four years, while London suggested members remain "Honourable" for ten years. (The debate expired quietly; only federal and provincial cabinet ministers now earn the title "Honourable.")

On February 10, 1898, Turner preened before a gaping crowd at the official opening of the new Legislative Buildings. Described as a "marble palace," this "magnificent structure which now adorns the southern bank" of the Inner Harbour wasn't exactly cheap. Its final cost of $981,359 was about 40 percent higher than the official budget of $686,425.

In April, Turner took issue with J.C. McLagan, proprietor of the *World* in Vancouver, over McLagan's attempt to introduce party affiliations into B.C. Turner described as "totally without foundation" McLagan's assertions in public that the premier had agreed to add Liberal party "leaders" to his cabinet. This

The legislature convenes in the old colonial assembly hall in 1897 (top). On February 10, 1898, Lt.-Gov. Thomas McInnes mounts the wide granite steps to open B.C.'s new Legislative Buildings with a golden key (bottom).

There were four premiers during Thomas Robert McInnes's four years as lieutenant-governor, from 1897 to 1900.

was a big mistake, as we shall see in a moment, because one of the names mentioned was W.W.B. McInnes, son of the lieutenant-governor.

"I think still that provincial politics ought to be kept entirely free from the introduction of Dominion politics," Turner wrote to McLagan. The newspaperman replied that he must have misunderstood Turner's interest, and that the *World* would still support his government, although he had faint hopes for its success in the next election.

McLagan got that right. With the depression still hobbling the economy, and facing a number of defections by government supporters, Turner went to the polls on July 9, 1898. Earlier that year, the House had increased the number of seats to 38—mostly on the mainland. With all districts but one reporting (the election in the two-seat Cassiar riding was delayed), the government could only muster 18 MLAs. Because of the deferred Cassiar results, which were expected to favour the government, and a large number of protests, Turner decided against resigning. He also did not feel he had to meet the House until final decisions were made on the protest petitions.

In any event, only one protest was upheld (actually resulting in the loss of a government seat), but it became moot, along with the Cassiar outcome, because Lt.-Gov. Thomas McInnes abruptly inserted himself into the equation.

Thomas Robert McInnes was a physician from New Westminster who was once medical superintendent of the provincial insane asylum. Elected to parliament in 1878 as an independent, he favoured Macdonald's Conservative government until the CPR moved its terminus to Coal Harbour. McInnes had invested in land around Port Moody and lost heavily when the real estate boom collapsed. After sixteen years in the Senate, he was appointed lieutenant-governor in 1897 on the recommendation of Laurier.

Until the summer of 1898, McInnes's most visible public act was to preside at the official opening of the new Legislative Buildings. Observing the collection of frock coats, beards and silk hats gathered on the legislature's steps that February day, nobody in the crowd could suspect that this impressive new seat of government would, in short order, ring with cries of dismay and dissent.

On August 8, exactly 30 days after the fateful election, Turner metamorphosed from premier to victim when McInnes dropped the hammer on him. In retrospect, Turner should have seen it coming. McInnes, in the preceding weeks, had refused to sign cabinet orders-in-council dealing with the issuance of treasury warrants. Obviously, he had made up his mind. In the letter of dismissal, McInnes told Turner that, "convinced that yourself and your colleagues are no longer endorsed by the electorate, and have not the confidence of the Legislative Assembly, I have decided to no longer delay in calling for other advisors."

"...I shall not put the Province to the delay, or to the expense, of a special Session of the Legislature, merely for the purpose of formally demonstrating what has been already sufficiently demonstrated to me by the General Elections," he continued.

Turner was incensed. The next day, he wrote a long letter to Government House detailing the accomplishments of his administration and stating his confidence that he could muster enough support. Turner also complained, "...the course you propose is without precedence in constitutional government."

In an equally long letter six days later, McInnes replied that he had "little or no confidence in some of your colleagues." He defended the constitutionality of his actions and had this to say about Turner's plea to reconsider: "Such a request, emanating from you after what has transpired...betrays such lack of knowledge and propriety on your part, or such readiness to advise me to a venal course of action, as to finally demonstrate your unfitness to act as chief advisor to the representative of the Crown."

There had to be something personal in that response. McInnes was probably annoyed at Turner's earlier rejection of his son as cabinet material or at the premier's lack of enthusiasm for the Liberal party. The lieutenant-governor had even sent another son (and personal secretary) T.R.E. McInnes to Turner to discuss W.W.B. McInnes's assistance in securing a House majority. Turner apparently did not reject this scenario out of hand, but wasn't given the chance to pursue it or any other option.

With Turner sidelined, McInnes became even more creative with his interpretation of the constitution. He called on Robert Beaven, a former premier who didn't even have a seat, to form a government. Beaven couldn't, of course, and McInnes finally handed the job to the inoffensive Charles Semlin, the opposition leader. (The wooing of Beaven by McInnes has a certain ironic quality, because Beaven himself had lost an election in 1882 but was not required to resign until he met the legislature six months later.)

Turner, grumbling, retreated to the opposition benches. He resigned in January 1899 because of conflict of interest regarding sales to the government by one of his business outlets. He was quickly returned in a byelection, and was invited in June 1900, by James Dunsmuir—the fourth premier within 31 months—to rejoin the cabinet as finance minister. This didn't last long. In September 1901, Turner was appointed British Columbia's agent-general in London. He was a natural for the job. Good looks, good grooming, good manners and a charming personality—all the things that didn't help Premier Turner when B.C. was sinking into the red—made him an excellent choice. He became a tireless promoter of B.C. as a suitable haven for English settlers.

Turner retired in 1915 and was succeeded by Sir Richard McBride. The legislature voted him an annual pension of $6,000, but then McBride died and Turner had to return to London in 1917 for another year. Retiring for good in 1918, he lost his wife in November of that year and moved into his son's home in Richmond, Surrey. On December 9, 1923, John Herbert Turner passed away, aged 89.

Charles Augustus Semlin

(August 15, 1898–February 27, 1900)

The *fin de siecle* angst accompanying the passage of 1899 owed as much to the raw politics of B.C. as to the completion of 100 turbulent years. The province had been part of Canada for fewer than 30 of those years, but in that short span the populace had viewed the soap opera staged by its elected representatives with growing agitation.

On New Year's Eve, 1899, British Columbians were discarding an old century and preparing to embrace a new one. The *Colonist* reported that "perfect bedlam" was in evidence during those final hours. Victoria's streets were more crowded than usual and the Inner Harbour rang "with the booming of guns, tooting of steam whistles [and] blaring of horns." Some celebrants surely spared a moment to glance at the spanking new Legislative Buildings gracing the south side of the harbour. During the 23 months that had elapsed since the new seat of government had opened, its corridors rang with political drama more raucous than usual. Surely, many hoped, the new century, with Premier Charles Semlin at the helm, would see smoother sailing. Fat chance.

For Semlin, who would rather be reading about history than making it, 1899 was definitely not a tranquil year. Nor was the latter half of 1898. Plucked from the opposition benches to form a government on August 15, a week after Lt.-Gov. Thomas McInnes had fired the incumbent, John Turner, Premier Semlin

Travellers arrive at Bonaparte House, Charles
Semlin's hotel in Cache Creek, ca. 1867.

quickly found he was playing against a stacked deck. The number of supporters
he could muster (eight) was roughly half those in Turner's corner. The premier's
office at the turn of the century was not the place for Semlin. He would much
rather be back on his ranch in the Cache Creek Valley.

Charles Augustus Semlin was born in October 1836, in Barrie, Upper
Canada, to David and Susannah Stafford Semlin. After completing his education,
he taught school for a few years. But the lure of gold beckoned him, as it had
many others in those times, and young Charles came to B.C. in 1862. After
having scant success as a prospector, he settled in Cache Creek, becoming its
first postmaster and later acquiring an interest in a hotel. In 1870, Semlin bought
the 12,000-acre Dominion Ranch, which he would call home until he died.

Semlin began his legislative career by getting his name literally pulled out
of a hat. Deciding to seek election in the three-member Yale riding in 1871, he
tied with a candidate named Coxon for the third and final seat. In those days
there was no secret ballot, and the voting was open and oral. The names of
Semlin and Coxon were put into a hat, and the returning officer pulled out
Semlin's.

The lucky MLA's biggest contribution to the first provincial parliament
was to introduce a bill that ended the practice by B.C. politicians of holding
seats in both the legislature and the Commons. He also helped establish a
government-sponsored boarding school in Cache Creek to which children from

Francis Carter-Cotton was yet another newspaperman in B.C. politics during the late 1800s.

small communities could be sent. Semlin, always interested in education, was proud of the contribution he had made to his own community.

There were no lucky hats in evidence in 1875 and 1878, when Semlin failed to get elected. He concentrated on his cattle and horses at his Cache Creek spread, becoming a prosperous and respected rancher in the process. In the 1882 election, Semlin was finally returned to the House, where he remained until 1900.

The next several years of subsidized growth under the Smithe-Davie-Robson-Davie administrations found Semlin on the wrong side of the assembly floor. He became opposition leader just in time to chide Turner about the parlous state of the books. When Turner was dumped, Semlin became McInnes's second choice for premier after the Robert Beaven fiasco. McInnes had no other option. He couldn't recall Turner, and although Semlin was at odds with factions led by Joseph Martin and Francis Carter-Cotton, he was the official opposition leader and therefore the logical choice.

Trying to knit all the disparate elements into a whole, Premier Semlin chose Martin for attorney-general and Carter-Cotton for finance minister. The two disliked each other intensely and were on opposite sides of political ideology— Martin had Liberal connections from other jurisdictions, and Carter-Cotton supported the federal Conservatives. A newcomer to B.C., Martin was headstrong, combative and brusque, by all accounts a nasty man to cross. Carter-Cotton, editor of the *News-Advertiser* in Vancouver, was steady, deliberate and somewhat secretive. Putting the pair in the same cabinet was a particularly acute case of trying to mix oil with water.

This shaky coalition, however, managed to get a few things done before the split hit the fan. Reformist in nature, it ended the granting of land bonuses for railway developers and brought in legislation limiting miners' hours to eight per shift. A statute regulating water use was made law. The crofter resettlement advocated by John Robson was officially shelved. "The decision of the government is that nothing can be done in the matter of resuscitating the Crofter scheme at present," Semlin wrote to Alexander Begg, one of its backers.

Efforts to limit or control the Asian presence were shot down by Ottawa. B.C.'s Alien Exclusion Act was so broad that it also prevented other foreigners from owning placer-mining claims. The Americans protested successfully to the Laurier government, and the Imperial cabinet—fearful about damage to the Empire's relationship with Japan during a period of tense international affairs—took issue with the attempt to forbid employment of Asians.

These quibbles troubled Semlin only slightly. "The effect of the disallowance is by no means so sweeping as seems to be thought in some quarters," he wrote to an Interior MLA, pointing out that charters granted to companies in 1898-99 already contained anti-Asian clauses.

Stuck in the middle between two opposing forces, Semlin still had links with the peace and quiet of the Cariboo. A lifelong bachelor, he had adopted a young girl named Mary. In 1899, the premier of British Columbia received a letter from his lonely adopted daughter, who missed her "Dear Papa" so terribly. Although Semlin would return to his ranch before long, the "political situation" was much on his mind in 1899. His diary contains several cryptic references to meetings and letters about these "matters."

The simmering bomb that was Joe Martin finally ignited during the summer. After frequently attacking Carter-Cotton in cabinet, Martin went public and accused the finance minister and the rest of the government of inefficiency and neglect. Forced to make a choice between Carter-Cotton and Martin, Semlin fired the blustering attorney-general. It was a mistake, Semlin admitted in later years, because Martin became a bitter enemy.

Once more, McInnes inserted his finger into the situation, demanding that Semlin either reconvene the legislature for a fall session or call an election. Semlin refused. He sought and received support from R.W. Scott, the federal secretary of state, who told McInnes that "your Ministers are the proper judges of the time to summon the Assembly—keeping, of course, within the year's limit." Scott had also informed McInnes in a confidential letter that his dismissal of the Turner government "was a little more drastic" than usual, and advised against a repeat of "so dashing a method of changing your advisers."

When the legislature sat for its normal session in January 1900, Semlin's fragile administration didn't last long. On February 23, with Martin casting a vindictive "nay," the government lost by one vote a crucial division on its redistribution bill. Still, Semlin wouldn't quit, asking for time to stitch together a new alliance. The lieutenant-governor appeared to go along with this, but then abruptly dismissed him.

Having resigned as ordered on February 27, Semlin rose in the House that afternoon to launch an unprecedented attack on the representative of the sovereign. He declared that McInnes's actions were unconstitutional and proposed a resolution that read, in part: "That this House...begs hereby to express its regret that His Honour has seen fit to dismiss his advisers as in the present crisis they have efficient control of the House." After a long and spirited debate, the motion was adopted, 22 to 15. The legislature had, in effect, censured the Queen.

But Semlin stayed fired. In a long letter justifying his action, McInnes claimed several aggravations, including the lack of a full cabinet. He also cited an alleged precedent for his intervention going back to the Duke of Wellington. Semlin's reply included the telling point that the House had supported him, 22 to 15, over his vice-regal adversary.

Martin was named premier, and the rancher-politician returned to the opposition benches until the June 9 general election. In it, Semlin was defeated and out of politics for the first time in eighteen years. This was the last full election fought by individual candidates, and Semlin subsequently (but reluctantly) embraced party politics. He returned to the House after winning a byelection in January 1903, but did not stand again in another election later that year.

Retiring to his beloved ranch, Semlin devoted his time to reading, historical research and local matters. "Charlie," as he was known around Cache Creek, would live another 24 years. One of Mary's daughters, Gladys, became a nurse and cared for her grandfather in his declining years. Charles Augustus Semlin died November 3, 1927, at the age of 91.

Joseph Martin

(February 28, 1900– June 14, 1900)

Fighting Joe Martin was a carpetbagger. From Winnipeg to Ottawa to Victoria to the Mother of Parliaments at Westminster, this prickly, sour-faced political corsair trailed the bitter debris of antagonism in his wake wherever he went.

It is not certain when newspapers and historians started labelling the itinerant politician "Fighting Joe." Perhaps when he took on the CPR in Manitoba, or scuffled with Richard McBride over a chair in the B.C. legislature, or alienated his own prime minister in Ottawa. At any rate, an unsettled family background may provide some clues as to why he turned into such an unpleasant man.

Joseph Martin was born September 24, 1852, in Milton, Ontario. He was one of four sons and one daughter in the family of Edward and Mary Anne Fleming Martin. The senior Martin was a millworker of simple, solid stock. He decided to emigrate with his family to Michigan, where he soon died. Taken out of school, along with his brothers, to go to work, Joseph became a telegrapher, then a railway dispatcher. Because of the uncertainty of a railway career in the 1870s, Martin returned to Canada. He resumed his education in Toronto and qualified as a teacher. Young and quarrelsome, he accused the school board that employed him in Ottawa of being undemocratic.

Quarrels, Martin didn't mind. A future largely devoid of power and prestige, he did. So he switched from education to the law and studied privately before moving to Portage La Prairie. In 1882, Martin was admitted to the Manitoba bar. The same year, he married Eliza Riley.

It didn't take long for Fighting Joe to plunge into provincial politics. Running as a Liberal in the election of 1882, he won his seat but withdrew after his opponent alleged fraud. Martin won the subsequent byelection and quickly got into trouble with the Speaker by accusing that honourable gentleman of partisanship.

Martin was re-elected in 1886 and appointed attorney-general and minister of education in the Liberal government of 1888. He also became railway commissioner, duly granting a contract for a north-south rail line. Unfortunately, the proposed roadbed crossed a CPR branch line, and Canadian Pacific obtained a court order prohibiting construction. Although obliged to back down originally, Martin was eventually vindicated. A lawsuit established in 1889 that the provincial charter was legal and thus had the right to cross the CPR line.

Martin then decided to straighten out Manitoba's separate school system, which was divided into French-Catholic and English-Protestant segments. As education minister, he supported the cabinet's plans to abolish sectarian schools, but took matters a big step further by publicly vowing to also end official use of the French language. This came as a big surprise to Premier Thomas Greenway, who had not contemplated such a drastic measure. Nevertheless, Martin personally guided the relevant legislation through the House.

Although generally supported by the public, Martin's display of one-man power drew the wrath of the *Manitoba Free Press*. In an editorial on April 1, 1890, commenting on passage of the language bill, the newspaper growled that the most conspicuous feature of the legislative session "was the complete control and management over all the proceedings exercised by Mr. Joseph Martin, and this notwithstanding that he was well known by every member of the House to be a most dishonest, unscrupulous and self-seeking individual." Martin, it continued, was the "most reckless and unprincipled politician who ever came to the front of any Canadian Legislature..."

Realizing that his future in the Manitoba Liberal party was now limited, Martin resigned his seat after the session ended and returned to his law practice. In 1891, he was defeated as a candidate for the Commons, but in 1893 became Winnipeg's first Liberal MP. In Ottawa, Martin couldn't stop talking, making speech after speech on all manner of subjects. When Prime Minister Wilfrid Laurier toured the West in 1894, Martin tagged along as a self-appointed western expert. Getting no sympathy from Laurier after losing his seat in 1896, Martin discarded federal politics and headed for Vancouver.

A political maverick who flaunted his independence, Martin was used to functioning under the nominally restrictive label of a formal party. So when he surveyed the scrimmages that British Columbians called politics, he must have rubbed his hands in glee. First, the transplanted Manitoban arranged to be called to the bar and set up a law practice. Then he plunged into the 1898 election campaign. Although running in Vancouver City, he spent a lot of time upcountry. Preceded by his reputation ("For God's sake, keep Martin and send in your blizzard," Kootenay newspaperman John Houston told his Manitoba colleagues), Martin used his special blend of vituperative oratory to gather support from various independent candidates.

When the ballots were counted, Martin's seat was one of several challenged during that election. In his case, the petitioners did not proceed, and Martin became attorney-general in the shaky government of Charles Semlin.

Fighting Joe vigorously prosecuted his duties, sponsoring amendments to mining legislation as well as the Alien Exclusion Act, all of which aroused opponents ranging from the smelter interests of the Interior to the American White House. Delivering a dull speech in Rossland, he responded to the audience's truculent attitude by shouting, "I will not be silenced by hoboes in evening dress!" When the taunting continued, Martin threatened to cancel a $35,000 grant for a new courthouse.

Later in 1899, he locked horns with a fellow cabinet member, Francis Carter-Cotton, who was finance minister. Editor of the *News-Advertiser*, Carter-Cotton was a very private man, exhibiting the British reserve inherent in his background, while Martin was loud and brash. The pair loathed each other. Finally, Martin went public with his venom by accusing Carter-Cotton and the cabinet of financial irresponsibility.

Semlin ended the bickering by unloading Martin, but the surgery was probably worse than the disease, because Joe immediately turned into an implacable opponent. When the session began on January 4, 1900, Semlin's weakened administration, which had only a tenuous hold on matters at the best of times, limped from one crisis to another. Finally, with Martin casting a decisive vote, it was defeated on a redistribution bill. Semlin asked for time to form another coalition, but Lt.-Gov. Thomas McInnes dismissed him.

This was the second time in eighteen months that McInnes had tinkered with parliamentary democracy. His sacking of John Turner in the summer of 1898 had precipitated the present messy state of affairs. After his first adventure in constitutional revisionism, McInnes had been warned by the Dominion government not to try it again. However, "the governor was not a man who cared to be dictated to by eastern capitalists concerning western political situations." Refusing to let Semlin sort the situation out by himself, McInnes looked into the barrel for the next premier. Reaching close to the bottom, he came up with Joseph Martin.

Martin's term in office was nasty, brutish and short. The House had already censured McInnes for his interference on February 27. When Martin became premier the following day, the opposition to his appointment was almost total. At the final sitting, March 1, the situation intensified.

In "the most dramatic, sensational and significant scene possibly in the whole history of British constitutional government," as the *Colonist* reported the next day, a question of privilege was moved: "This House has no confidence in the honourable third member for Vancouver City, who has been called upon to form a government."

It passed, 30 to 1 (two members abstained; under the rules, their votes were counted as "ayes"). But the MLAs were still not through. When McInnes entered the House to prorogue the session, all members except the livid premier and the Speaker left. "As His Honour took his seat on the throne, the last coattail attached to a member of British Columbia's legislature disappeared through the lobby door, and the cheers merged into hisses, laughter and catcalls as the Governor essayed to speak," wrote the *Colonist*. The boos continued to rain down from the public gallery as McInnes stumbled through his speech.

Premier Martin wasn't a quitter. Failing to coax any sitting member into his cabinet, he rounded up various political stragglers from outside the House. He attempted to cobble together a voter-friendly platform, based on his reformist, anti-business stance, knowing that an election was inevitable. Governing in the poisonous atmosphere of 1900 was a tough slog. Martin couldn't even get the newspapers he wanted. After requesting back copies of the *Fernie Free Press*, he was advised that none would be forthcoming until the government paid the $5.40 it owed the paper.

His provincial secretary, "an untutored farmer of Agassiz," quit in May. Days later, on June 9, the election was held. Martin tried to assemble a province-wide Liberal party, but was rebuffed. Battling with all his considerable political skills, Martin retained his seat, but the rest of the legislature remained riven along factional lines, and he could only muster perhaps a dozen supporters or "leaners." Without the confidence of the House, Fighting Joe was sunk. He resigned June 14 after a term of 106 days—the shortest of any premier.

The next day, Lt.-Gov. McInnes, who would soon be without a job along with Martin, found a reluctant James Dunsmuir at the bottom of the barrel and made him premier. Now in opposition, Martin carried on, even reaching a rapport of sorts with Dunsmuir. This mini-coalition unsettled Richard McBride, who quit as mining minister. When the 1902 session opened, McBride was formally elected opposition leader in place of Martin. Despite his erratic support of the government from time to time, Martin still considered that the position belonged to him and was determined to oust the "upstart" McBride.

He was prepared to get physical to retain his official seat at the front of the opposition benches. On opening day, backers of both Martin and McBride shuffled the chairs "like snails carrying their houses on their backs." As the House prayed, Martin slipped into the leader's chair behind McBride. When McBride found himself perched in his rival's lap, a brief struggle ensued between supporters of each principal.

Martin, who had managed to become leader of an unruly Liberal organization in 1901, went on the attack against Dunsmuir's successor, E.G. Prior. He accused Prior's government, which was as sickly as any of its immediate predecessors, of resisting the trend toward party affiliations. He had a point. Away from Victoria, sentiments were hardening along federal party lines—Liberal or Conservative.

When Prior got himself canned for conflict of interest in 1903, the ensuing election saw Martin lose his seat. Ironically, the man who touted party loyalty had earlier been forced to resign as Liberal leader.

Martin practised law for a few years, then ran unsuccessfully in the 1908 federal election. Abruptly, he moved to England and within nine months was a candidate in a byelection for the House of Commons. Martin lost, but in 1910 was elected as the member for East St. Pancras. Unawed by the august precincts of Westminster, Martin promptly attacked his prime minister, Lord Asquith, demanded the abolition of the House of Lords and rudely criticized Earl Grey, the Governor General of Canada.

The British press was unamused. "Really, the Liberal party requires to be saved from its friends," harrumphed the *Edinburgh Evening News*. "There is the Hon. J. Martin, who has sat for six weeks for East St. Pancras. He is straight from the Wild West—British Columbia—and he cannot put up with this slow-going old country and wants to show it things...Why on earth do not men like the Hon. J. Martin remain where they are most appreciated?"

Despite his acerbic manner, Martin was a hard-working MP until 1914, when financial concerns brought him back to B.C. He stayed in Vancouver during the early years of the Great War, twice attempting to get elected mayor. Martin returned to England in 1916, then began flitting between London and Vancouver. During this time, he dabbled in journalism, mining and, of course, politics.

Settling in Vancouver for good, Martin resumed his legal career, but by 1920 his intellectual processes were failing. Once corpulent, he became a shrivelled, pathetic gnome. At the end, his mind wandered. Predeceased by his wife in 1913, and with no children, Joseph Martin died alone on March 2, 1923.

James Dunsmuir

*(June 15, 1900–
November 21, 1902)*

Т he very wealthy do not necessarily live happily ever after. For James Dunsmuir, scion of the coal dynasty nurtured by his father, there was probably a *frisson* of disquiet for almost every dollar in his considerable bank account. In the beginning, however, growing up was normal for this poor little rich kid.

James Dunsmuir was born July 8, 1851, at Fort Vancouver on the Columbia River, to Robert and Joan White Dunsmuir. The family was en route to Vancouver Island from Ayrshire in Scotland. Robert, who came from a long line of miners, eventually settled in the Nanaimo area, where he stumbled across a rich coal deposit near Wellington in 1869. This mine became the basis of the family millions.

After being educated in local schools, James went to work for his father at the age of sixteen. He became a trained machinist and then went east to study mining engineering in Virginia. There, he met Laura Miller Surles, daughter of a North Carolina farmer. They were married July 5, 1876, and would have twelve children (two of whom died at an early age).[1]

Shortly after returning to B.C., James became his father's right-hand man. When the senior Dunsmuir joined the legislature in the 1880s, James took almost complete control of the collieries. By this time, Alexander, his younger brother, was in charge of the San Francisco office and the two worked closely together.

The death of family patriarch Robert Dunsmuir (centre) brought dissension
to his family, especially after his younger son, Alexander (right), died and
Robert's widow, Joan (left), sued her surviving son, James, over estate issues.

Old man Dunsmuir was B.C.'s very first predatory capitalist. When he
died April 12, 1889, his fortune of $15 million had made him the province's
richest man. Four days later, 12,000 people lined the route of the funeral
procession. Robert Dunsmuir had left everything to his wife, Joan, with the
proviso that she would decide when the boys could take control. Between 1896
and 1899, the brothers finally persuaded her to sign over the bulk of the
widespread Dunsmuir assets. An innocuous clause involving Alex's future estate,
however, would soon cause long-lasting dissension within the family.

Devoted as he was to business, James soon found politics intruding upon
his fiefdom. Anti-Chinese legislation passed in 1898 threatened to have an
adverse impact on his hiring practices. As his father and other captains of industry
had done before him, Dunsmuir decided that he'd be better served inside the
legislature than outside it. It was a reluctant decision. The privileged life of a
wealthy capitalist appealed to him more than the unseemly skirmishes of a
political career.

Dunsmuir ran in the Comox district (home of one of his collieries) in the
July election and won easily. This was the inconclusive election that left Premier
John Turner without a majority. Dunsmuir remained relatively quiet on the
backbenches during the Turner and Semlin crises, becoming distracted in part
by a family tragedy.

Alexander Dunsmuir, who was an alcoholic, died January 31, 1900, leaving
behind a wife who would also die within eighteen months, and a host of legal

problems. Alex had made James his sole heir, contradicting the agreement the brothers signed in 1896 stipulating that half the company would revert to their mother should either of them predecease her. In November 1901, while he was preoccupied with the premier's job, Joan sued James. She was joined by several of his sisters (Robert had sired ten children). Further complicating matters, Edna Wallace Hopper, Alexander's wife's daughter by a previous marriage, also sued.

It would take years to unravel the tangled legal web, but that was still over the horizon when Dunsmuir got his name in the papers the day Joseph Martin was repudiated. When the roll call began March 1, 1900, on a motion of non-confidence in Premier Martin, W.R. Robertson and Dunsmuir abstained. "How is the honourable member from Comox voting?" asked the Speaker. "I, too, refuse to vote," replied Dunsmuir, who was apparently endorsing Robertson's sentiment that another election should decide Martin's worth. Despite ducking the Martin issue, Dunsmuir then led 31 members into the corridor the instant Lt.-Gov. Thomas McInnes entered the chamber to read his prorogation speech.

"The crowded galleries instantly caught the significance of the general desertion, and round after round of cheers for the elected representatives of the people rang through the chamber," the *Colonist* reported. Dunsmuir later insisted that the walkout was planned, and the image of his spontaneous leadership was a coincidence. McInnes apparently held no grudge, for he would ask Dunsmuir to form a government a few months hence. (Or perhaps he had run out of alternatives.)

When the June election was called, Dunsmuir switched ridings from Comox to South Nanaimo. This was the home of another of his mines and of the new company town Oyster Harbour, which he had renamed Ladysmith to honour the relief of its namesake during the South African War. One of the promises Dunsmuir made to the miners was that he would replace all Chinese labour with white men as soon as he could. In doing so, Dunsmuir was protecting his own interests by employing the not-unfamiliar tactic of instituting reform before the government did. It was a promise he would find hard to keep.

Dunsmuir did not particularly want to be premier. As with his decision to become an MLA, however, he was motivated by self-interest. The Dunsmuir millions had to be protected. McInnes's appointment of Dunsmuir on June 15 was the governor's last official act. Three days later, Dunsmuir and his supporters met in Vancouver and drafted a resolution condemning McInnes for actions "contrary to the principles, usages and customs of constitutional government," and wired it to Wilfrid Laurier. The prime minister needed little convincing because his cabinet had already warned McInnes about tinkering with democracy.

On July 20, Laurier canned McInnes and replaced him as lieutenant-governor with Sir Henri Joly de Lotbiniere. In a letter to Dunsmuir, Laurier said he was sending him "a gentleman who has had a long experience and is well known for his fairness of mind, ability and other admirable qualities."

Rather than drifting through the rest of 1900 and 1901, the Dunsmuir government ricocheted from crisis to crisis. The province was still in the midst of a depression, out of which would come consolidation of key industries (the names of some companies formed at that time are still recognizable 100 years later: B.C. Electric Co. [1897], B.C. Packers [1902], B.C. Tel [1904], Cominco [1906]). But labour unrest was escalating, and in the mining sector, the bosses were just as mad as the workers were at Dunsmuir, the biggest mining boss of all. They were hit by new taxes on output, a federal law that recognized some of labour's concerns and the fallout from the eight-hour shift legislation of the Semlin regime.

The railway hustlers had their hands out, as usual, and sometimes the government shoved a concession at them. One was the money to build a bridge over the Fraser River at New Westminster.

Dunsmuir also had to deal with the minutiae of office. On July 12, 1900, he was notified by New Westminster that the cost of the great fire of 1898 was $134,397.37. The following month, the Japanese consul in Vancouver complained that his countrymen were barred from voting in the municipal elections.

A fishermen's strike prompted a flurry of telegrams. On July 21, 1900, the Vancouver Board of Trade requested immediate steps be taken to curb the "state of lawlessness" on the Fraser. The canners' association on the same day asked for "armed and uniformed men" to patrol at Steveston. The militia was sent to calm matters, and a settlement was reached July 30.

B.C.'s relationship with Ottawa, relatively cordial since the arrival of the CPR, cooled again. In March 1899, the *Colonist* had grumbled about B.C.'s place in Confederation. The province collected $2.2 million in customs duties, it pointed out, which was more than the three Maritime provinces combined. Yet the Maritimes had three cabinet ministers and B.C., none.

This signalled a return to the "Better Terms" demands of the olden days. In January 1901, Dunsmuir was in Ottawa for a conference with Laurier, at which he presented a long list of grievances. Among them were inequitable railway freight subsidies, Oriental immigration and the Chinese head tax (Ottawa and the lieutenant-governor had a distressing habit of disallowing anti-Asian legislation), Indian reserves, revenue sharing, fisheries and lumber tariffs.

Laurier was pleasant but unbending on most points. Another delegation tried again in 1902, with as little success. Richard McBride, when he became premier later in the decade, would also tilt at the "Better Terms" windmill.

Meanwhile, Dunsmuir kept an iron grip on his business. As promised, he fired "every last Chinaman," but then couldn't fill the vacant positions. There were not enough qualified white coal miners. An attempt to recruit some Scottish workers was an expensive failure. After this embarrassment, Dunsmuir hardened his attitude toward organized labour. The difficulty in replacing the Chinese, he reasoned, effectively demolished any union argument that they were depriving white miners of jobs.

On the social side, the Duke of Cornwall and York (the future King George V) and his consort visited B.C. in September 1901, and Dunsmuir was in constant attendance. In the summer of 1902, Dunsmuir again preened in the presence of royalty. He, Laura and two of their daughters attended the coronation of Edward VII.

When Dunsmuir returned to B.C., he was ready to leave politics, and no wonder. Already uncomfortable in the premier's office, he nevertheless had to

Turner, Dunsmuir, Bryden, (all together).

Good Morning, Mr. Miner, I suppose we can count on YOUR vote for the Turner Govt.

MINER (aside)—You talk about your Smyth Govt., and your Robson Govt., and your Davie Govt., and your Turner Govt., but the only Govt., WE know is the Dunsmuir-Chinese Govt., but thank God the opposition have got the ballot act passed, and we dont care a d— for all the Dunsmuirs.

This is the Government the "Citizen's" Ticket Supports.

Hatley Park, James Dunsmuir's huge stone residence overlooking the
Strait of Juan de Fuca, was designed to resemble a medieval castle.

deal with a variety of mundane matters. Among the files that landed on his desk
were reports of plum rot, a government agent's request for a horse and buggy,
specifications for damming of "certain sloughs," protests over removal of a wharf
on Hornby Island and a letter from the editor of *The Cascade Report* ("Liberal if
not hidebound") seeking clarification of his railway policy.

Nothing much had happened on the legislation front during the spring
session of 1902—apart from McBride's celebrated confrontation with Martin
over the opposition leader's chair. The most notable bill was one increasing the
number of MLAs to 42 from 38. For the first time, the distribution of seats
truly reflected the population patterns of the province.

Dunsmuir resigned on November 21. He was replaced by E.G. Prior, who
had been in the cabinet less than a year.

By December 1903, the case brought against him by his mother and Edna
Hopper had been dragging on for two years. It would last another 30 months,
with the ex-premier enduring a spell in the witness box at one point. Joan
Dunsmuir had combined her suit with Edna's early in 1903, seeking the return
of 4,998 shares in the firm of R. Dunsmuir's Sons. Edna was attempting to
prove that Alexander was so stricken with alcoholic dementia that he was
incapable of drawing up a rational will.

On February 6, 1904, Mr. Justice Drake ruled in favour of James. The
decision was appealed all the way to the Privy Council in Great Britain, which

reached the same conclusion on July 20, 1906. By this time, Dunsmuir was lieutenant-governor of B.C. As with his previous job, it appealed more to his wife than to him. Laura Dunsmuir always pretended to be more than she was: a farmer's daughter. She intimated that her father was an aristocratic planter with hundreds of slaves, and flaunted her husband's wealth and position at every opportunity.

Dunsmuir's stay at Government House was almost as brief as his premiership. He stepped down in June 1909 after a term marked by controversy surrounding the passage of an anti-Oriental bill (Dunsmuir was criticized for attempting to import Japanese miners in 1907 after blocking the legislation).

Laura Dunsmuir, wife of the premier, poses with youngest daughter Dola in 1908. The Dunsmuirs had twelve children.

But Dunsmuir had already made plans for a full retirement. In 1908, he completed construction of Hatley Castle on the Strait of Juan de Fuca (it became Royal Roads Military College and is now a private university). There, he and Laura adopted a stately lifestyle of social engagements, yachting and world cruises. In 1912, Dunsmuir shed his collieries. In selling them to William Mackenzie (of Canadian Northern Railway infamy), he also ended his bitter struggle against unionism, which often escalated into strikes, lockouts and violence.

A final tragedy would rock the family. The youngest son, James (Boy) Dunsmuir, was lost aboard the *Lusitania* when it was torpedoed in 1915. After the Great War, Dunsmuir sold his beloved yacht and never went to sea again. He acquired a cabin on the Cowichan River and spent more and more time there, alone. On June 6, 1920, James Dunsmuir passed away after suffering a massive stroke. He was buried a few days later in the family plot at Ross Bay Cemetery. The Dunsmuir estate was valued at $3,332,000—much less than British Columbians would have assumed. Like his father, he left it all to his wife.

Edward Gawler Prior

*(November 21, 1902–
June 1, 1903)*

If one common denominator could be chosen to define the first fourteen governments of British Columbia, it would be railways. The siren call of the Iron Horse, it seemed, consumed the attention of each cabinet and legislature to a far greater extent than any other issue.

It began with the terms of union. Without that rail link to the East, B.C. was prepared to kiss off Canada. After the CPR finally reached tidewater in 1885, the politicians' in-baskets began overflowing with railway proposals, mostly for the Kootenays. From 1890 until the early years of the new century, charters were granted to such outfits as the Columbia & Kootenay, Kaslo & Slocan, Nakusp & Slocan, Nelson & Fort Sheppard, B.C. Southern, Red Mountain, Kettle River, Midway & Vernon, and the Vancouver, Victoria & Eastern.

The motive behind most of these proposals was the efficient movement of ore, but there was also the need to connect the Coast with the southern Interior. In any event, the CPR and the Great Northern eventually gobbled up most of the charters.

On Vancouver Island, the Esquimalt & Nanaimo had a history of its own. A contentious issue between Victoria and the mainland following Confederation, it generated almost as much political posturing and invective as the CPR. When a consortium led by Robert Dunsmuir agreed to build the E&N in 1882 in exchange for a huge land grant, the opposition was not impressed. Nor was it several years later, when Premier James Dunsmuir tried to peddle the railway and some of its land grants to promoters of the Canadian Northern.

In many cases, land giveaways as well as outright subsidies and bond guarantees accompanied the government charters. The B.C. Southern, for instance, received a total of 3,775,773 acres. The charters for both the Columbia & Kootenay and the Kaslo & Slocan stipulated that they would receive 10,240 acres for each mile of completed railway.[1]

When E.G. Prior ran for the legislature in a 1902 byelection so that he could join the Dunsmuir cabinet, the Canadian Northern was a prime issue. Prior campaigned on the government's railway policy, which was to provide cash subsidies only if the proposed charters brought real benefits to B.C. They would be limited to $5,000 per mile and only if matched by Ottawa. Grants would be repaid out of the railway's profits. It seemed a sensible policy, and Prior won by 55 votes.

Described as a "professional and practical mining man," Prior took over the mines portfolio vacated by Richard McBride. But he was also, it appeared, a railway man. "The only reason I entered your government was to assist you in putting through a contract with Mackenzie and Mann to build the Canadian Northern Railway from Yellowhead Pass," he wrote to Dunsmuir early in 1902. "I pledged my word to the electorate for this, and this only." At any rate, the anointing of the Canadian Northern did not occur. Donald Mann and William Mackenzie would have to wait a few more years to get their precious charter.

The Prior who parachuted into the middle of the railway debate was not a stranger to B.C. politics. He had been there before, after making the long journey to the shores of the Pacific. Edward Gawler Prior was born May 21, 1853, in the Yorkshire hamlet of Dallaghgill to Henry and Hannah Mouncey Kendell Prior. His father was a clergyman, and young Edward had a genteel upbringing until he finished grammar school. Qualifying as a mining engineer, he left England in 1873 for a job in the colonies. After a journey across America (including a stop in Salt Lake City, where he was introduced to Brigham Young), Prior reached Vancouver Island on December 9. His job was assistant manager of a coal firm in Nanaimo, and he stayed there until he was appointed inspector of mines in 1877.

Marriage followed, on January 31, 1878, to Suzette Work. They would have four children, but one wonders when Edward had time for conjugal bliss. In short order he became Nanaimo's super civil servant. By August 1878, he was sheriff; government agent; assistant commissioner of lands; registrar of births, marriages and deaths; collector of votes; land registry collector and assessor.

In 1880, Prior went into the hardware business in Victoria. In due course, E.G. Prior & Co. became the leading hardware and machinery business in

E.G. Prior & Co. occupies a busy Victoria corner in the 1880s. The premier's hardware business would eventually lead to his resignation.

B.C., with connections in New York and London. He ran for the House in 1886 and became one of the four members for Victoria City. That same year, however, a vacancy arose in the House of Commons and Prior was elected by acclamation as the member for Victoria. He represented the riding until 1900, becoming at one point a cabinet member in the Mackenzie Bowell government. Prior's re-election in 1900 was voided because of irregularities; thus he was available when Dunsmuir asked him to run as an MLA.

Prior had barely settled into his cabinet seat when Dunsmuir resigned. Lt.-Gov. Henri Joly de Lotbiniere gave the barrel a good shake, but could only come up with the ex-MP and hardware merchant from Victoria. Prior was named premier on November 21, 1902. When the legislature met the following April, he had a slim majority of two seats.

Within weeks, his cabinet fell apart. Dennis Murphy, the provincial secretary, resigned after three days on the job. Party politics, which could no longer be ignored in B.C., was the apparent reason. Then Prior was forced to fire his attorney-general, D.M. Eberts, and lands and works commissioner, W.C. Wells. The reason, the opposition claimed, was a little railway dodge involving the Columbia & Western and an improper land grant. Eberts and Wells were accused of being agents of the CPR, which owned the narrow-gauge line near Rossland.

Finally, W.W.B. McInnes (son of the departed Lt.-Gov. Thomas McInnes) quit as president of the executive council.

The tottering Prior government crumbled completely when it was disclosed that the premier's own company had been awarded a contract to supply some hardware for the Chimney Creek bridge, south of Williams Lake. When tenders were called, Prior, who was also public works commissioner, asked why his firm was not notified. In short order, it was, and E.G. Prior & Co. underbid everybody and won a contract to supply wire cable.

Asked about this by a committee of the House, Prior frankly admitted his part and claimed he was acting in the best interests of the province. He was, he said, no more at fault than "a member who is a lawyer or who is attorney-general, and his partner takes charge of looking after a private bill and lobbying it through the House."

Sir Henri Joly thought differently. Taking into account evidence that the premier himself had seen the bids submitted by other companies, Lotbiniere dismissed Prior on June 1, 1903, for violating "the true principles of parliamentary independence of members and, above all, of ministers of the Crown."

Prior, whose term was the second shortest in B.C.'s history, hadn't been around long enough to get to know all the members' names. He declined to run in the election held later that year. In 1904, he stood unsuccessfully for a Commons seat, then dropped out of politics. A wealthy man, Prior kept active with business affairs and travelled extensively. His first wife died in 1897, and Prior married Genevieve Kennedy the following year. In 1908, the Priors were received by King Edward VII.

Prior was involved with the military for much of his adult life. He helped found the Nanaimo Rifles in 1874 and joined a garrison artillery regiment when he moved to Victoria. He eventually reached the rank of full colonel in the militia, a title by which he was known for most of his public career. Because of his age (61), the former politician was not called to active service in the Great War.

Prior's short stint as premier was a disastrous one. After watching his cabinet evaporate, he found himself dismissed because Lotbiniere was "unable to continue feeling...confidence in [his] judgment." Nevertheless, Prior himself was appointed lieutenant-governor of B.C. in December 1919, on the advice of Prime Minister Sir Robert Borden, replacing Francis Barnard. The appointment was a popular one in Victoria, despite the spot of trouble he had in 1903. After just a year in Government House, Edward Gawler Prior died December 12, 1920, at the age of 67. He was buried in Ross Bay Cemetery.

Richard Mcbride

(June 1, 1903–
December 15, 1915)

T he twentieth century had only just begun, and already it was threatening to turn into a disaster for B.C. Sure, signs of prosperity were cropping up here and there, ending a depression that stretched back to the early 1890s, but over at the new Legislative Buildings, the political situation was as ugly as ever.

Queen Victoria, whose connection to B.C. was strong (the capital city honoured her name, and she christened the province), had died in 1901 and her loss was still deeply felt. British Columbian lads had fought in their first foreign war, in South Africa, and many did not come home. At Cumberland, on Vancouver Island, and Coal Creek, near Fernie, mine disasters emphasized the dangers lurking in every underground shaft.

On June 1, 1903, another premier—E.G. Prior—had been dismissed, albeit for entirely justifiable reasons this time. He was the fourth occupant of the corner office to be replaced in the first three years of the century. But when Lt.-Gov. Henri Joly de Lotbiniere called on Richard McBride to form a government on the same day he discarded Prior, history would record that, for once, someone had got something right.

Dick McBride had a lot of things going for him. He was young—at 32, the youngest premier in B.C.'s history—and personable, with many useful connections. Also, he was a local boy, being the first premier born in the province.

That occasion is recorded as December 15, 1870. Richard McBride was born in New Westminster to Arthur Hill and Mary D'Arcy McBride. Both the McBrides and D'Arcys were of Irish extraction, which no doubt accounts for the gentle brand of blarney dispensed by Richard during his political career. He also had some of the resolve of his father, who rose from police ranks to become warden of the federal penitentiary at New Westminster (only to leave under a cloud following an investigation into mismanagement).

Richard's early years followed a familiar pattern. He was educated in local schools, then studied law at Dalhousie University in Halifax. Returning home, McBride passed his bar examination on July 25, 1892. The young barrister practised for a while in the northern community of Atlin, where he became versed in mining law. Still in his twenties, McBride was already immersing himself in the convoluted world of political organization. He ran as a Conservative candidate in the federal election of 1896, but lost. That same year, on September 23, he married Margaret McGillivray, a New Westminster girl to whom he was devoted. Her wedding ring was fashioned from B.C. gold. They would have six daughters.

That diversion aside, McBride plunged into provincial politics. He was elected the member for Dewdney in 1898 as a backer of the doomed John Turner. Re-elected in 1900, he waved goodbye to Joe Martin along with the rest of the assembly, then found himself in James Dunsmuir's cabinet as mines minister. McBride was a popular addition, especially to the social scene. The bonny McBrides were a couple much sought after in the capital's drawing rooms. They were a particular favourite of Laura Dunsmuir, the premier's wife.

The McBride-Dunsmuir admiration society soon disbanded. In an effort to defuse the explosive Martin, who was rattling around the opposition like a live grenade, Dunsmuir made a deal. A Martin supporter, J.C. Brown, was admitted to cabinet in return for Fighting Joe's support. This was too much for McBride, who quit his cabinet portfolio. "Resign everything but your honour," his father had advised him, so McBride did, and switched from the government side to the opposite benches.

McBride's scuffle with Martin over the leader's chair added a touch of slapstick to the 1903 legislative session. But the Prior cabinet disintegrated so quickly that McBride, solidly in place as leader of the opposition, had little to do but criticize and wait.

During Dunsmuir's term, federal political parties were preparing to introduce their own labels to the provincial scene. This was good news as far as Sir Henri was concerned. He felt the system of constitutional government could collapse without proper party organization. Because of the B.C. House's chaotic individualism, he wrote his son, "there are a good many thorns in the stuffing of the gubernatorial throne."

McBride was already onside. The day after he became premier, he notified the legislature by letter that things were changing. "After most careful consideration, and in view of the anticipated dissolution of Parliament, I have fully decided that the interests of the country would be best served by a division on party lines," he wrote. "The Government to be formed will be Conservative in character, and after dissolution it is the intention to make an appeal to the country at the earliest possible moment." The session ended June 6, and the politicians spent the summer preparing for an election on October 3.

McBride campaigned on the need for strong government, industrial growth, stability and fiscal responsibility. The message was not entirely successful, for the premier and his Conservatives managed only 22 of 42 seats, with 17 for the Liberals. With one of his members destined to be Speaker, McBride would have to woo the two Socialist MLAs in order to survive.

Shortly after the election, B.C.'s growing sense of alienation was fuelled by the Alaska Panhandle decision on October 20. Earlier in 1903, an international tribunal of "six impartial jurists of repute" was assigned to settle the boundary dispute between Canada and the United States. Both countries had laid claim to Skagway and other areas along the remote northern coast. When Lord Alverstone, Britain's chief justice and a panel member, sided with the U.S., British Columbians exploded into bitterness. "Led Like A Lamb To The Slaughterhouse," mourned a headline in the *Province*, while the *Colonist* wrote that "Lord Alverstone...deliberately proceeded to sign away from Canada the most valuable portion of the territory claimed in order to placate the United States." McBride, although more diplomatic, also condemned the award and filed it away as more evidence that B.C. was getting shafted.

There were more pressing concerns, however. Although the depression was no longer in full spate, the financial outlook was bleak. The treasury was empty and there was a mountain of debt. The deficit in 1903 was almost $1.5 million, and interest charges on the government debt were $500,000. B.C.'s credit rating was almost non-existent. So what did McBride do? He borrowed another $1 million to jump-start the economy (although the bank warned him he must balance the budget forthwith).

During its first session, which opened November 26, 1903, the government brought in a host of taxation measures. Everything from the income and poll taxes to prospectors' licence fees were increased. Happily, McBride had chosen Robert Tatlow as his finance minister. A man of good sense and solid integrity, Tatlow knew how to cut costs and raise revenues. To everyone's surprise (except his own), he announced a slight budget surplus for 1905.

Providentially, the fishing and forestry sectors had consolidated their scattered economies and began experiencing a boom. (The proliferation of timber licences and leases was so rapid and unrestrained that the government was forced to institute an inquiry before the decade was out.) Underground, the formation of the Consolidated Mining & Smelting Co. in 1906 brought stability to the province's other primary resource.

Although more lucky than prescient, "Glad-Hand Dick" took credit for it all. He began travelling around B.C., winning admirers everywhere with a blend of easy affability and Irish smarm. He even charmed the locals at Lac la Hache by dancing with poet Pauline Johnson at a barn dance. Back in Victoria, his social life was hectic, and the premier was in great demand at parties.

The serious side of government did not escape McBride, however. In fact, one incident threatened to cost him his job. In 1904, through a convoluted (some critics said "shady") financial transaction, Lands Commissioner R.F. Green had quietly arranged the sale of 10,000 acres on Kaien Island to the Grand Trunk Pacific Railway for its Prince Rupert terminus. At the urging of a suspicious opposition, a special committee investigated the deal.

Splitting on party lines, the majority report of March 7, 1906, cleared the government of any wrongdoing. It held that the sale "was a deal pre-eminently to the public advantage," and that nobody connected with the government "received any direct or indirect emolument or reward." Because the Grand Trunk was favoured by Laurier's Liberal government, the shadowy Kaien arrangement severely strained relations between McBride and his federal cohorts. Even though he jettisoned Green as the obligatory sacrificial goat, at least one leading Conservative was not happy. "I firmly believe our party will do well to spew the McBride govt. out of its mouth," former prime minister Sir Charles Hibbert Tupper wrote a fellow Tory.

A less controversial rail event was the opening of the New Westminster bridge across the Fraser River on July 23, 1904. Premier McBride, along with Lt.-Gov. Lotbiniere and other dignitaries, rode a special train across the combined wagon and railway span. The *Columbian*, covering the affair, estimated the cost of construction at $1 million.

By this time, McBride had also tapped into the "Fight Ottawa" sentiment revived by Dunsmuir. In 1903, the federal subsidy to B.C. was slightly in excess of $300,000, and McBride began writing to Laurier complaining that it was too low. His campaign had three main arguments: B.C.'s share was unfair when compared with its contribution to the federal treasury; the vertical geography of the province made the cost of running it higher than elsewhere; and freight costs were punitive because of the long distances.

Crammed with dignitaries and celebrants, a train crosses the new Fraser River bridge at New Westminster on opening day, July 23, 1904.

McBride went to Ottawa in 1905, but made little progress with the smooth Laurier. In 1906, however, he made such a strong case at an interprovincial conference that grants and subsidies to B.C. were substantially increased. The cheering crowds that greeted him on his return prompted McBride to call an election for early 1907. Two of his campaign issues were "Better Terms" and "Fight Ottawa."

Because the 1903 election was so close, the *Vancouver World* later mused that party politics were perhaps not such a good idea. "It was argued by many that the population was too scattered, the interests too diverse and the issues that divided men at the East into two camps were not understood here," wrote one editorialist. "Results have shown that these misgivings were well grounded."

After the vote totals were tallied the night of February 2, 1907, however, all such doubts evaporated. McBride's anti-Ottawa rhetoric, plus Tatlow's budget surpluses, labour peace and the signs of a booming economy, brought his Conservatives 26 of the 42 seats in the House.

With the new mandate safely tucked away in his suitcase, McBride went to London in April as a "special agent and delegate" in an attempt to get the BNA Act altered in B.C.'s favour. He made a good impression on Winston Churchill, under-secretary of state for the colonies, but did not readily get what he was after—removal of a clause limiting increases in subsidies. The premier proved to be a potent ambassador for B.C., however. His "agreeable exterior" elicited a cordial reception wherever he went.

During the federal election of 1908, McBride helped the Tories campaign, charging that the Liberal government was allowing B.C. to be overrun by aliens. Ottawa had given the province too many Orientals and not enough revenue, he said in one speech—neatly playing both the racial and "Better Terms" cards at once. The premier's stance arose from frustration as well as ideology. For several years, all B.C. legislation aimed at curbing Asian immigration had been rejected either by the Dominion government or the lieutenant-governor. These were generally known as Natal Acts, from Natal in South Africa, which required immigrants to pass an educational test.

McBride was openly in favour of exclusion. "Living as we do here among thousands of these yellow men and knowing them so well as we have come to know them, makes me feel that if some of our friends in the Old Land might have enjoyed the same experience things would have been different," he once wrote Earl Grey, the Governor General. The racial tension of 1907 and the Imperial government's relationship with Japan obviously fuelled that sentiment.

That summer, a short-lived recession, which idled a number of workers, was exacerbated by a heavy influx of Japanese and Chinese immigrants. On September 7, a group of disgruntled whites called the Asian Exclusion League staged a parade in downtown Vancouver that ended with a mob looting and wrecking property in Chinatown. Then they turned on nearby Japtown. The Japanese, unlike the Chinese, fought back, so the damage was not as extensive.

The shock in higher circles was palpable. London, because of an Anglo-Japan treaty, growled. Laurier's government apologized to the Japanese and dispatched W.L. Mackenzie King, a deputy labour minister, to assess the damage claims made by both Asian countries. The Chinese eventually received $20,458 and the Japanese, $9,175. Of more interest, however, was that King uncovered evidence of a conspiracy to import cheap Asian labour. One of the miscreants was Lt.-Gov. James Dunsmuir, the coal baron.

With boom times returning and the federal election of 1908 out of the way, McBride and his ministers toured the province, dropping promises here and there of a provincial university, more railways and good fortune for everyone. Everywhere, from the fruit orchards of the Okanagan and the land boom up north to the industrial growth of Vancouver, prosperity beckoned.

In McBride's view, these good times could only be made better by the laying down of even more steel rails. On October 18, 1909, he persuaded Dunsmuir to dissolve the legislature and then called a quickie election for November 25. The people, he said, could ratify a deal he had been working on all year.

It was, as his cabinet found out for the first time, an agreement with William Mackenzie and Donald Mann to bring a third transcontinental railway into B.C., the Canadian Northern Pacific. Included was a guarantee of the railway's bonds at 4 percent interest on $35,000 per mile. The line would run from the Yellowhead Pass on the Alberta border south to Vancouver, and no Asiatics would be employed on the labour force. McBride's plan to lavish more money on yet another railway adventure split the cabinet. Tatlow, his trusted financial wizard, quit, along with F.J. Fulton, the minister of lands.

With a campaign to fight and a cabinet squabble to paper over, McBride was stricken by a personal tragedy. His son, Richard, died October 29, five days after being born. Heartbroken, McBride nevertheless plunged into the election he had just called. The campaign was a stormy one because of McBride's handling of the Canadian Northern issue, but he could point to a buoyant economy and a strong legislative record. He and Attorney-General William Bowser went on a 2,000-mile campaign jaunt, visiting 25 towns in two weeks, ranging from Ladner to Revelstoke. They topped it off with two huge rallies in Vancouver.

John Oliver, the new Liberal leader, didn't have a chance. "The People's Dick" rode his railroad promises to a landslide victory with 38 out of 42 seats. It was, the *News-Advertiser* observed, "a decisive triumph for the Railway Policy." As the first decade of the new century neared its end, it seemed McBride could do no wrong. By this time the province's longest-serving premier, he was now certainly its most popular.

In 1910, B.C. boasted a cash surplus of $5.9 million. The 1911 census pegged the population at 392,480, more than double the 178,657 of 1901. Names, both big and small, poured into the province. Among the more recognizable were Rockefeller and Weyerhaeuser, who grabbed sizeable chunks of timber. (A Forest Act passed in 1912 finally put B.C.'s most important resource under regulatory control.)

Some of that surplus went to the Songhees Indian tribe. After years of negotiations, the B.C. and Dominion governments paid the tribe $421,552.60 for its reserve on the northwest shore of Victoria's Inner Harbour. "We feel that the interests of all have now been amply protected, and that the settlement arrived at has been reached upon fair, honourable and reasonable terms," McBride told the tribe in 1911. The reserve was relocated on Esquimalt Harbour. (Two years later, an embarrassing scandal surfaced when it was disclosed that McBride had arranged a payment of $75,000 to Sam Matson, proprietor of the *Colonist*, for services rendered during negotiations.)

In 1911, and again in 1912, McBride was back in London. He and Margaret attended the coronation of King George V and were later presented to his majesty. Prematurely grey and getting a little paunchy from the good life, the "silver-

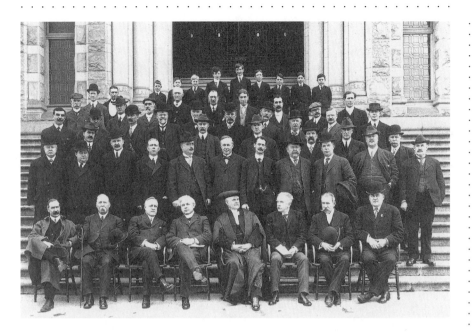

Members of the 1912 legislature gather on the steps of the Legislative Buildings.
Premier Richard McBride is fourth from the left, seated in the front row.

haired gentleman from B.C." basked in the limelight. The following year, McBride had a five-hour audience with the King, the upshot of which was a knighthood. Sir Richard McBride was the only B.C. premier to be so honoured.

During the 1912 trip, McBride renewed his friendship with Churchill, who was now First Lord of the Admiralty. Stopping in Ottawa on the way home, the premier passed on some thoughts from Churchill about Canada's future role in the Empire's naval defence. Two years later, McBride's interest in the navy would take a bizarre turn.

The boom that seemed so indestructible in 1910 began fraying by the end of 1912. Despite another huge election victory in March (39 seats), McBride and Bowser were soon on the receiving end of some disenchanted mutterings about corrupt machine politicians. Gloom replaced euphoria as British capital dried up.

In 1913, while Sir Richard was back in London trying to attract investment, labour unrest exploded into violence. The Big Strike in Vancouver Island's coal mines, which began in 1912, turned ugly when Nanaimo rioters raged out of control. Bowser had to send in the militia.

Undeterred by criticism of his Canadian Northern bargain, and ignoring early signs of a sputtering economic engine, McBride had pushed through another big railway deal in 1912. The Pacific Great Eastern was chartered to

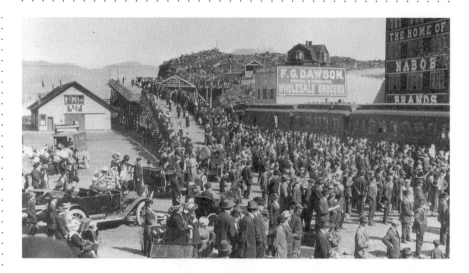

A huge crowd in Prince Rupert greets the arrival of the first Grand Trunk Pacific
train from Winnipeg in 1914.

Curious residents flock to hear Premier Richard McBride
(in lower right of photo) speak in Port Alberni, June 12, 1914.

run from North Vancouver to Fort (later Prince) George, with the government supplying guarantees similar to those for the CN. The PGE would not be McBride's finest hour, but for the time being it was obscured by the clouds over Europe.

Just before the Great War began in August 1914, the London financial markets, which controlled the world's credit system, collapsed under the weight of the crisis. It became almost impossible to borrow money or trade in stocks and bonds. British Columbia, so dependent on foreign investment, sank to its knees. During most of the war, the province was a basket case.

The cabinet kept spending, but revenues were falling. Construction of both the Canadian Northern and the PGE fell far behind schedule. The feds eventually took control of Mackenzie and Mann's dream, but McBride couldn't unload the "Prince George Eventually" and was stuck with it.

For a provincial leader, Sir Richard had a strong international outlook. One of his pet platforms was naval policy; McBride favoured a strong Royal Navy rather than establishment of a Canadian one. His friendship with Churchill prompted him to support a Canadian contribution to England's battleship fleet. The plan came to naught, but naval matters were much on McBride's mind in the summer of 1914. That is when his thinking switched from dreadnoughts to submarines.

The last week in July, with war in the air, J.V. Paterson, the owner of a Seattle shipbuilding firm, let it be known that he had two submarines for sale because a deal with Chile had fallen through. Paterson was in Victoria's Union Club at the time, and in short order news of his remarks reached McBride. The premier was as concerned as anyone in B.C. about the possibility of German raiders savaging the West Coast, so he asked for more details.

The price for the subs was $575,000 each, take it or leave it, Paterson told a McBride emissary on the phone. B.C.'s first thought was to get Ottawa and the British Admiralty interested, but the naval commander at Esquimalt could not get a firm commitment. Time was of the essence, because U.S. President Woodrow Wilson was about to sign a neutrality declaration, which would quarantine the subs.

On his own initiative, McBride closed the sale with Paterson. "Have advanced to-night one million and fifty thousand dollars...for purchase two modern submarines lying Seattle harbour and built for Chile," he wired Prime Minister Robert Borden on August 4 (the erroneous figure relayed to Borden would later cause McBride some grief). Late that evening, with Paterson and the Canadian representative, W.H. Logan, aboard, the submarines slipped out of Seattle without clearance.

They were met by a Royal Canadian Navy vessel the next day, just outside Canadian waters five miles south of Trial Island. After a four-hour inspection, a cheque for $1.15 million, drawn by the Province of British Columbia on the Canadian Bank of Commerce and endorsed by Richard McBride, was handed to Paterson, and B.C. briefly had its own navy.

Later in the day, Ottawa ordered the Esquimalt base to buy the two craft. "Have purchased submarines," came the terse reply. The Dominion government assumed responsibility on August 7 and the subs, named CC1 and CC2, remained on the West Coast for three years.

McBride's decisiveness on the submarines was his last grand gesture. In 1915, he lost his grip on the cabinet by pushing for a $7 million loan to the troubled PGE. He even called an election for that spring, but recanted under pressure from Attorney-General Bowser and others. It was painfully obvious that "Glad-Hand Dick" had outstayed his welcome. The caucus, led by Bowser, simmered while the premier travelled to Ottawa and London. When he returned in August after a three-month absence, the spring was gone from his step. His obvious ill health, the unruly cabinet and criticism of the submarine purchase did not make life in the corner office any easier.

McBride was forced to endure a royal commission inquiry into the acquisition of CC1 and CC2. The unfortunate clerical error in McBride's 1914 wire to Borden, which seemed to indicate $100,000 was missing, was pounced on by a malicious Liberal MP and McBride's enemies, of which there were a growing number. In any event, Sir Charles Davidson, the commissioner, fully cleared McBride with the observation that the deal was, "throughout, of blameless character."

On his 45th birthday, McBride submitted his resignation to Lt.-Gov. Francis Barnard. On that same day, December 15, 1915, Barnard asked Bowser to form a government; three weeks later, McBride was given a boisterous, heartfelt farewell as he and his family left for England. McBride assumed the agent-general's post relinquished by John Turner, but had to give it up May 19, 1917. Fatally ill with Bright's disease, he desperately wanted to come home to die.

However, just as he was completing arrangements for the voyage, Sir Richard McBride passed away on August 6, 1917. The funeral was held August 8 from the family residence on London's Thurloe Square to the Golder's Green Crematory. The remains were quietly cremated, far from the admiring crowds of his home province, and later returned to Victoria for burial in Ross Bay Cemetery. In 1918, the legislature paid tribute to the premier who had served his native province for so long by voting a $5,000 stipend for Lady McBride and her children.

William John Bowser

*(December 15, 1915–
November 23, 1916)*

Just like his predecessor in the premier's chair, Billy Bowser had a lot of nicknames. None of them were as positive as the labels pasted on Richard McBride, however. Sir Charles Hibbert Tupper, the Conservative elder statesman, called Bowser the "Little Kaiser." He was also dubbed the "Napoleon of British Columbia" and a few other epithets synonymous with "tyrant."

A lot of this was politically motivated, because Bowser was single-minded in his pursuit of the Tory party agenda. At not much more than five feet in height, he was B.C.'s shortest premier, but Bowser compensated for his lack of physical stature by being cold and ruthless throughout his political career. He ran the Conservative machine in Vancouver for 21 years, much of the time as McBride's dark paladin.

The pair had known each other since university days, although McBride had a much longer journey to Dalhousie in Halifax. William John Bowser was born March 3, 1867, in Rexton, New Brunswick, to William and Margaret Gordon Bowser. After completing schooling in his home province, young William enrolled as an arts major at Dalhousie. Two years later he switched to law and was called to the New Brunswick bar in 1890. A year later, perhaps at the urging of Dickie McBride, his college friend, Bowser was in Vancouver. He was called to the B.C. bar in June 1891.

Lawyering was okay and Bowser was good at it, but he quickly became attracted to politics. Part of the lure was his faculty for manipulating people, which compensated for his temperamental infirmities. The voters were less than impressed by the public Bowser the first couple of times he sought office, however. In 1896, he ran in the federal election but lost badly. The same year, he found someone who was impressed by him: Lorinda Doherty of Vancouver. They were married and adopted a daughter.

In 1898, Bowser sought a Vancouver seat in the B.C. election. He ran on a "citizen's ticket friendly to the government," but finished second to last. Skipping the 1900 race, Bowser slid behind the scenes and became a powerful force in the Conservative party. In 1903, Bill Bowser and Dick McBride found themselves part of the government of British Columbia.

Even though Bowser had known McBride ever since college and recognized the premier's appeal to the masses, he was not wholly committed to the man in the corner office. The Kaien Island affair, he thought, was poorly handled. According to one source, Bowser decided to straighten McBride out on what was needed to stay in power. In a remarkable article in *Collier's Weekly* in 1913, Britton Cook describes a conversation (almost certainly apocryphal) between the two sometime before the 1907 election. First, Bowser speaks:

> "You can't maintain a government here for another year before there'll be trouble. You've got to get the party whipped into shape. The country needs a stable government and you can't get it if you take chances on the whim of the voters. You've got to be sure how your next election's going to go before you take the oath."
>
> "Yes," replied McBride, "but how?"
>
> "Listen." And Bowser explained the game of politics to his leader.

That game, as practised by the master, involved heavy-handed control of provincial affairs from the street level upward. Patronage, bribery and the occasional threat were the tools he used.

Bowser's Vancouver apparatus had increased in importance after the redistribution of 1902, when the city gained the number of seats commensurate with its growth. In the 1907 campaign, the Little Kaiser's machine helped deliver a majority that solidified the Conservative party's hold on the province. Bowser was admitted to the cabinet as attorney-general. In 1909, he also became finance minister for a year, replacing Robert Tatlow, who had quit over McBride's deal with the Canadian Northern Pacific Railway.

Bowser stuck by the premier during that cabinet crisis. When McBride called an election in 1909, the pair toured the province, defending the railway policy. While McBride charmed the locals, Bowser made sure the party's wheels were turning smoothly. During the campaign, he easily deflected an accusation he was the solicitor for an importer of Japanese labour named Gotoh at the same time he was sponsoring anti-Oriental legislation in the House.

After the Conservative landslide of 38 seats, Bowser turned to the serious business of running the province. During the next six years, with McBride constantly on the CPR shuttle to Ottawa and London, Bowser's office was the place to go if you wanted anything done in B.C. As well as standing in for McBride, he ran the attorney-general's department with one firm hand while fine-tuning his Vancouver machine with the other.

It was said that Bowser's control of the booze trade was so tight that saloon keepers would lose their licences if they couldn't deliver Conservative voters. He also controlled the local police and politicians in Vancouver and Victoria, and dispensed patronage in the boonies so as to influence rural public officials.

Bowser made sure his legal firm had lots of work, though he denied it profited from the purchase of the Kitsilano Indian reserve in 1913. "We have…got the Indians off the reserve and it has not cost the province a cent," he told a legislative committee inquiring into the transaction in 1916. Normally, "a bit of greasing sometimes had to be done, but not in this case," he added.

The labour peace that distinguished the early years of the Conservative mandate evaporated in 1912. That was the year the Big Strike started at the Vancouver Island collieries. In August 1913, violence spread like deadly fire damp through the mining towns. As attorney-general, Bowser ordered the militia into Nanaimo after the Provincial Police were overwhelmed. Mass arrests— some conducted at the point of a bayonet—soon brought matters under control. Most units were withdrawn by the end of the month, but there was a militia presence in Nanaimo until 1914.

In May 1915, Bowser took decisive action to quell anti-German rioting in Victoria. Again the military was sent in, and the Riot Act was read to a mob of 500 protesting the torpedoing of the liner *Lusitania*.

The spring of 1915 was not a good season for the government. McBride had announced an election in March, then cancelled it and left town again. By this time, his close relationship with Bowser had deteriorated to coolness. Their first-name camaraderie was gone, and Bowser started manoeuvring against the premier. The press reported that the attorney-general had persuaded a majority of the caucus to take his side over McBride's. "A state of war exists in the Conservative party," crowed the *Vancouver Sun*, which was a Liberal newspaper. Not quite war, perhaps, but a skirmish serious enough that the party's fortunes would soon change.

When McBride resigned December 15, Bowser was sworn in as premier. His first priority was to mould a cabinet in his own image. That done, he presented a vigorous program to the House during the 1916 session that somehow promised both progress and restraint. Financial tidbits were dangled before farmers, returning soldiers and workers. He even promised plebiscites

Armed militiamen escort Ladysmith strikers off to jail during
the Big Strike of Vancouver Island miners in 1913.

The bar at the Kaiserhof Hotel in Victoria, one of the targets of anti-German
rioters following the torpedoing of the *Lusitania* in May 1915.

on prohibition and female suffrage—two undertakings that curiously aroused more enmity from entrenched interests than support from those affected.

In contrast to McBride's breezy populism, Bowser's dour exterior and abrupt manner endeared him to nobody, including elements of his own party. Stuck with the dirty laundry of the administration, the summer of 1916 was not an easy one for the "little czar." He called an election for September 14, and despite his vaunted machine, could not prevent the total defeat of the Conservative party. Liberal leader Harlan Brewster, said the *Victoria Times*, scored a notable victory over "Bowserism, the party machine and the patronage system." Repudiated by the people (with only 9 seats compared to 36 for the Liberals), Bowser nonetheless hung on to the premiership until November 23.

Leading the rump of his party across the aisle (where he started collecting $1,500 per session as official opposition leader, a role formalized by the legislature in 1915), Bowser clawed at successive Liberal governments for eight years. He was, according to noted newspaperman James Morton, the party's best debater. Commenting on Bowser's resemblance to Napoleon, Morton wrote: "If the secret of his prototype's success was that his hand lay always close to his brain, Bowser's tongue performed the same function. There was no impediment between his mind and his speech...and the rush of his arguments bore down his opponents like a flood."

But the flow of rhetoric inside and outside the House subsided to a trickle. In the election of June 20, 1924, the man who once held his thumb on the political windpipe of the province lost the Vancouver seat he had held for 21 years. Bowser clung to the party leadership until 1926. At a pivotal Tory convention in Kamloops during the month of November, he suddenly withdrew from a bitter contest. "The voluntary retirement of Mr. Bowser...is the crowning act of a career that has at least been useful," damned the *Sun* with faint praise. "This withdrawal is Mr. Bowser at his intelligent, fearless and generous best."

The Bowsers moved to Victoria, where they lived a quiet life together until Lorinda died in 1928. Alone after more than three decades of married life, the doughty warrior started thinking about politics again. In 1933, he was persuaded by dissident Conservatives to run as a non-partisan candidate in the November election.

The ex-premier was contesting seats in both Vancouver and Victoria (a practice disallowed in 1940), and was campaigning on the Lower Mainland when he died of a heart attack on October 25, 1933. "This is my last contest," he had told a rally the night before. William John Bowser's body lay in state in Vancouver before the remains were cremated.

Harlan Carey Brewster

(November 23, 1916–
March 1, 1918)

T
he newspaper as an unblushing advocate of a political party is a
phenomenon rarely seen at this point in our history. In the early
years of the twentieth century, however, the daily press was not shy
about whom it supported. There was no pretence of separating
opinion and editorials from the news columns.

One newspaper, the *Vancouver Sun*, was founded in 1912 for the express
purpose of nurturing the Liberals and counteracting the Conservative viewpoint
of the *News-Advertiser*. The other Vancouver dailies, the *World* and the *Province*,
also blended their news coverage with their political agenda. On the Island, the
Colonist was true-blue Conservative while the *Victoria Times* was Liberal.

In 1916, four years after the *Sun* pompously claimed that "the necessity
for a paper to consistently advocate the principles of Liberalism had been
making itself felt for some time," the morning broadsheet did its very best to
influence the provincial election. During the run-up to the September 14
polling day, it managed to prominently display pictures and fawning
descriptions of Liberal leader Harlan Brewster and his fellow candidates.
Premier William Bowser and his Conservative buddies were virtually ignored
in the news columns. This is not to say that the *Sun*, or such other Liberal
newspapers as the *Times*, influenced the election greatly. British Columbia's
honeymoon with Sir Richard McBride had long since dissipated, and
"Bowserism" was the accepted epithet of the day.

For the premier-to-be, a friendly press made up for a lot of bumpy spots on his way to the corner office. Politics had not been as productive as other aspects of his life. Harlan Carey Brewster was born November 10, 1870, in Harvey, New Brunswick, to Gilbert and Amelia Wells Brewster. The elder Brewster was in the shipbuilding business, and Harlan divided his time between school and his dad's shipyard. His enthusiasm for nautical matters led to a deep-sea mate's ticket, but Brewster spent little time afloat. He drifted into the printing field for a few years, but gave it up because of poor eyesight. In 1892, Harlan Brewster married Annie Downie and the pair struck out for B.C. Brewster worked for coastal shipping firms and merchants and became proficient as an auditor. In November 1899, while keeping books for a Clayoquot firm, he and several others rescued the crew and passengers of an American steamer adrift and on fire off the stormy west coast of Vancouver Island. For his part in the rescue, Brewster was awarded medals by the U.S. Congress and the Royal Humane Society.

In due course, Brewster got into the salmon canning business. He was instrumental in introducing machine-made cans to the packing houses, thereby making himself a wealthy man. The new cans were more reliable than the handmade version and, not incidentally, reduced the labour force (mostly Asians) considerably. By 1907, Brewster was a respected businessman. He decided to enter politics, ran for Alberni in the provincial election and topped the poll. Two years later, in McBride's quickie election, he was re-elected as one of two Liberals in the legislature.

The election of 1912 was a disaster for the Liberals, the anti-Tory press and Brewster personally. Switching to the four-seat Victoria riding—where McBride was one of the MLAs—Brewster lost by a few dozen votes. Although without a single seat in the House after that election, the Liberal party quietly started rebuilding itself. Brewster was elected party leader at its Revelstoke convention in 1913. He then toured the province, giving the voters a glimpse at the Liberal platform of free land for settlers, aid for farmers and orchardists, prohibition and female suffrage.

On April 28, 1915, Brewster's denunciations of wanton Tory excesses were given a boost by a pamphlet called "The Crisis in British Columbia." Published under the auspices of a Lower Mainland union of clergymen, it attacked the McBride government for its systematic fraud and evasions, especially in regard to land transactions. The pamphlet caused a sensation in the Liberal press, although the Conservative-leaning *Province* buried the story inside. It did report, however, that one speaker at a mass rally claimed that "this is the morning after a wild carouse."

With the pamphlet's shrill invective still in the voters' minds the following March, Brewster got his chance to return to the legislature. There were three

During a visit to the Peace River country in September 1917, Premier Harlan Brewster travels on horseback near Giscome Portage.

byelections in the spring of 1916, and the Liberals took two of them. Brewster ran in Victoria for the seat vacated by McBride when he resigned as premier, and won.

The leader of the two-man opposition wasted no time attacking the government's failings. In June, after Bowser extended the sitting of the House past its prorogation date, Brewster brought an action in the B.C. Supreme Court seeking to halt the "unlawful" use of public money in building the PGE. The suit claimed a "misapplication" of $7 million through "secret orders in council." The judge wisely allowed the matter to await the course of events.

After Bowser finally set the date for the general election, Brewster returned to his Alberni riding and won by 38 votes. It was among the 36 seats out of 47 taken by the Liberals in one of those quirky reversals of political fortune that dot B.C.'s electoral landscape. From zero representation in the 1912 election, Brewster's party had dealt the Conservatives a crushing defeat. It was victory over "Bowserism, the party machine and the patronage system," burbled the *Times*.

Bowser didn't get around to resigning until November 23. The same day, Lt.-Gov. Francis Barnard appointed Brewster the premier. By this time, at the age of 46, Brewster had the mien of a conscientious and honest bookkeeper. With his rimless glasses and balding pate reinforcing the image, he wasted no time in assembling a strong executive council. Within a short span, four future

Cartoons such as this helped bring prohibition to B.C., if only for a brief period.
In 1921 the province restored a "wet" economy and began a decade
of rum-running into "dry" Washington and Alaska.

premiers of B.C.—John Oliver, John MacLean, Thomas Dufferin Pattullo and John Hart—were helping direct the province's affairs from the cabinet table.

The 1917 legislative session, which opened March 1, was as animated as it was long. Special committees and commissions of inquiry, struck to rake through the ashes of B.C.'s first party government, shared the headlines with a flood of reformist legislation. British Columbia's mood during the third year of the Great War was not a cheery one. Returning soldiers bore the scars of the awful conflict in France and Belgium, and the casualty lists grew longer and gloomier. Added to this sombre mood was the spectacle of the people's representatives squabbling over election returns and financial misconduct.

One of the inquiries had an immediate impact on the Brewster government. A special commission probing charges that the new attorney-general, M.A. Macdonald, had accepted $25,000 in personal campaign funds from the Canadian Northern, resulted in his resignation. Brewster asked Macdonald to step down so as to quash "the slightest suggestion that there is any corporate interest, railway or otherwise, controlling this government."

The drive for female suffrage is the occasion for some gentle propaganda.

Another investigation involved the soldiers' vote during the prohibition referendum, which was held at the same time as the general election. Although a reasonable majority (39,893 to 30,839) approved the banning of strong spirits, the vote from the overseas soldiers overturned the result. The inquiring committee determined that "gross frauds and irregularities were committed" overseas, and its report was accepted. The prohibition bill was passed into law during an August session of the legislature.

A third high-profile committee picked at the scabs of McBride's PGE agreement. During its deliberations, R.D. Thomas, the railway's secretary-treasurer, refused to answer questions about campaign contributions to the Conservatives. He was ordered into custody April 18 for contempt of the House and held until May 19, the day the session adjourned. There was some talk of incarcerating Thomas until August, when another session was expected, but the members decided that the dignity of the House had been maintained and voted to let him go. Thomas was the first "prisoner de luxe," as one MLA put it, since the Kennedy brothers from the *Columbian* were held in 1892.

When not rushing off to committee hearings and tribunals, the Brewster government passed some significant legislation. This included the creation of a treasury board to help bring the province's financial affairs under control, a new department of labour, an amusement tax and the passage of bills dealing with a taxation board, public accounts, workmen's compensation and war veterans. There was an amendment authorizing "collection of a tax on persons."

A civil service commission was also established to regulate government jobs. When the opposition complained about Conservative appointees being replaced by Liberal hacks, Railways Minister Oliver said he intended to hire party supporters until "a reasonable balance was struck."

Female suffrage, which was also approved by a solid majority during the 1916 election, resulted in an act giving women the right to vote and to run for the legislature.

Combined with all this legislation was a retrenchment in government expenditures. Profligacy was out. Positions were eliminated. This came despite the Liberal faithful grumbling about not getting their share of political plums. Starved for years, they had assumed they would be taking long draughts from the patronage tap. But Brewster was reluctant to follow in Bowser's footsteps. "He had many obstacles to meet but he did not yield to the machine," a newspaper later commented.

The premier also attended to business outside the House. In August, he attended the national party convention in Winnipeg and moved a resolution calling for the return of the railway lands in the Peace River district. Although the resolution was carried unanimously, Brewster was more than a decade ahead of his time on that one. The Peace River Block, transferred to the Dominion government in the previous century, was not returned until 1930 (and under a Conservative administration at that).

Back in B.C., the premier took time to denounce the smeltermen's strike in Trail. He called the strikers "mostly foreigners" and claimed they destroyed material promoting a Victory Loan drive. Brewster may have been reacting to overblown press reports about loan literature being fed to a strikers' bonfire, because Trail officials promptly called the accusations "gross libel." Brewster's remark about foreigners had some basis in fact, however. A large contingent of smelter workers was of Italian descent; at one point a consular official for Italy tried in vain to coax his countrymen back to work.

In February 1918, Prime Minister Robert Borden summoned Brewster and the other premiers to Ottawa for a conference. After several days in the capital, Brewster headed home in late February and was stricken with pneumonia on the train. He was taken to hospital in Calgary and seemed to rally. But at 10:15 p.m. on March 1, 1918, Harlan Carey Brewster succumbed. The *Times*, which had chronicled his every achievement, both large and small, marked Brewster's passing with this huge headline on page one: Premier Brewster Passes Into The Great Beyond, And Closes A Brilliant Life Of Service.

Exhaust rising from autos adds a surreal aspect to a misty March day in 1918 as Premier Harlan Brewster's funeral cortege passes along the causeway in Victoria.

The legislature had been in session in Victoria and immediately adjourned upon hearing the news. The late premier's body arrived in the capital city on March 4, and members of his cabinet carried the casket into the funeral home chapel. After lying in state in the legislature, Brewster was buried in Ross Bay Cemetery the next day after a "great throng" attended his funeral.

William Brewster had been predeceased by his wife, Annie, in 1913. On April 23, the B.C. legislature passed a bill authorizing "payment of certain moneys" to his four orphaned children. The amount was $5,000; the same act also authorized a similar amount to Lady McBride.

John Oliver

(March 6, 1918–
August 17, 1927)

Whose life was work, whose language rife
With rugged maxims hewn from life.

Those lines from Tennyson's "Ode on the Death of The Duke of Wellington" were once suggested by author and veteran newspaperman James Morton to describe the career of Honest John Oliver. Morton was Oliver's biographer as well as his personal secretary, so he may have been somewhat sympathetic in his treatment of the farmer-premier. But the measure of the man comes through even more in his public speeches and his conduct in the legislature.

Simple, honest, often blunt and unyielding, the eighteenth man to assume the premiership of British Columbia lived a life steeped in toil and sweat. His beginnings were hard and his ending was hard. In between, this man of the soil brought a concept of duty that is often missing from politicians' resumes.

John Oliver was born in Hartington, a village in Derbyshire, on July 31, 1856, to Robert and Emma Lomas Oliver. He was one of nine children. Robert was a farm labourer and could provide few advantages for his growing family. John's education, therefore, was brief and crude (he never did master grammar, although he did his sums adequately), but he became an avid reader.

In 1867, at the age of eleven, John went to work in a lead mine with his father. Robert, trying to get ahead, had acquired a lease on the mine, owned by the Duke of Devonshire. After local farmers complained about the elder Oliver stealing their hired hands by offering higher wages, the absentee peer closed the mine for good. A bitter Robert Oliver and his family left England for Canada in 1870. An unexpected inheritance helped with expenses and the purchase of a farm in Ontario. John, fourteen, switched from scrabbling in the mine to the equally physical life of a farmhand.

After seven years, John headed west with $100 in his pocket. He took the train through the United States to San Francisco, then a steamer to Victoria. Oliver arrived May 5, 1877, and soon hired out as an axeman for a CPR survey crew. All summer he blazed a trail inland from Port Moody and hoarded his pay. In the fall, John Oliver, aged 21, pre-empted 160 acres in the Fraser Valley and began clearing the land.

While he struggled to establish his homestead, Oliver took a job as clerk for the raw municipality of Surrey. Part of his duties was to assess property and collect taxes. When, in 1882, Oliver decided to sell his bottom land in the valley and move to new acreage in Delta, he resigned his clerkship. Because Oliver's accounts were not neatly laid out in a proper ledger, certain councillors questioned his honesty as a collector of revenue. An outside auditor was hired to go over Oliver's records. He found that the accounts, although not kept in a traditional manner, were correct and in good order. A chastized Surrey council accepted the auditor's report vindicating Oliver, thus laying the foundation for the "Honest John" persona that would follow him the rest of his life.

Oliver's dirt farm in the estuary of the Fraser brought more unrelenting toil. He raised cattle and hogs and fought the encroachment of the river with dykes and ditches. After a few years alone in Delta, he found himself a wife to share the burden. On July 20, 1886, John Oliver married Elizabeth Woodward, the daughter of a neighbouring farmer. They would have five sons and three daughters—another large Oliver family.

Despite his struggle to make the farm profitable and his new responsibilities as a family man, Oliver still found time for public affairs. He served as school trustee, councillor and reeve of the municipality. Now in his early 40s, the pit-boy from the lead mine of Derbyshire had matured into a bluff, square-hewn, stocky example of British perseverance. In 1900, after contemplating his future for a long time, Oliver sought election to the B.C. legislature. He ran in Dewdney and won by a comfortable margin. Just weeks before his 44th birthday, Oliver began his career in provincial politics at a time in life when many of B.C.'s premiers would be ending theirs.

Although the 1900 election repudiated Premier Joseph Martin, Oliver supported him for reasons that have long remained obscure. While in Ontario, the young Oliver became a fan of George Brown, the Reform party icon who published *The Globe* in Toronto and championed liberalism. Perhaps Oliver was drawn to Martin's fighting nature and his zeal for reform. At any rate, he ran as a Liberal in the Delta riding, with success in the 1903 and 1907 elections. Because Richard McBride and his Conservatives were in the early years of their power trip, the Delta dirt farmer spent the next several years on the opposition benches. As one chronicler of the period remarked, "he became a living interrogation mark," hectoring the government with question after question. Oliver never wavered in his conviction that it was the business of the opposition to oppose.

In 1909, he became Liberal party leader, just in time to participate in a disastrous election campaign. McBride had announced the Canadian Northern deal and made railway development the prime issue. Oliver, while attacking the Tories for handing great chunks of the province to the corporate robber barons, nevertheless felt obliged to offer his own scheme. He produced a hand-drawn map, suitably coloured, showing how railways in B.C. should be developed. It was a logical plan, but "John Oliver's Map" was roundly ridiculed by the McBride forces, who had a legal agreement with the Canadian Northern to wave at the voters.

When all the ballots were counted, only two Liberals were left in the legislature. Oliver was not one of them, having lost out in two ridings—Delta and Victoria. It was the start of many years in the political backwaters for him and the party. "I am out of politics for good," Oliver told the newspapers, and he resigned the party leadership. Two years later, he was back, running in the Dominion election, with the same negative result. When the next B.C. election came in 1912, Oliver ran in the same two ridings that rejected him in 1909 and was spurned once more.

That vote removed the last two Liberals from the House. For four years, Oliver concentrated on his pigs and dabbled briefly in municipal politics. He did not participate in the three byelections in the spring of 1916 that followed the resignation of Premier McBride. But he ran and won in Dewdney in September, when a Liberal landslide deposed Premier William Bowser. Harlan Brewster, the new premier, promptly invited the party's old warhorse, John Oliver, into his cabinet as minister of both railways and agriculture.

The first file Oliver opened as railways minister was the Pacific Great Eastern. This ill-conceived line from nowhere to nowhere had quickly steamed into trouble after being granted a charter in 1912. Undercapitalized and poorly managed by the contracting firm of Foley, Welch and Stewart, the PGE was rapidly draining the money pot guaranteed by the government, and construction of the line from Squamish had halted near Clinton. By 1918, the books were in disarray, the company had relocated to Seattle and one partner, John W. Stewart, was fighting the war in France. A select legislative committee uncovered several instances of corruption and irresponsible handling of trust funds.

After protracted negotiations, the company and the province reached an agreement: The PGE would turn over all its assets to B.C. and pay a penalty of $1.1 million—$500,000 of it immediately. Late on a Saturday night, February 23, 1918, Railways Minister Oliver signed the agreement in Seattle along with a representative of the "Please Go Easy." B.C. now owned a railway of its very own, although Oliver never was enthusiastic about the outcome. Because of the financial drain, however, he settled. "We have been 12 months trying to get service of papers on Brigadier Stewart in France, meanwhile paying out $1 million annual interest charges," he told the *World*. "I think the settlement fully equals the results obtained from a successful lawsuit."[1]

Two weeks later, Oliver was premier. Following the sudden death of Brewster, he was chosen Liberal leader by the party caucus. Oliver was sworn in on March 6, and the legend of "plain John" gathered fresh steam. Sturdy of frame and stout of form, he still sported the tweed clothes and square-toed boots of the country squire. Bowser, his old antagonist, charged that the "Bolsheviki" had made Oliver party leader, and that he would try to be a one-man government. If plain-speaking meant a one-man rule, then Bowser's latter remark was correct.

Soon after moving into the corner office, Oliver confronted 2,500 soldiers and supporters on the front lawn of the legislature. Rejecting their demand for a civil service commissioner to dispense government jobs, he called it "a bill of indictment against the government" and refused to consider actions contrary to his conscience. (Oliver had much sympathy for war veterans. He laboured on plans to resettle soldiers in government-sponsored communities on Vancouver Island and in the East Kootenays and the Bulkley Valley up north, but few took up the offer. Another one of his schemes for their benefit was irrigation of the southern Okanagan. This led to new acreage for orchards and a burgeoning town called Oliver in honour of the premier.)

Oliver was also forthright about the shortcomings of some elected officials. When municipal delegates looked for provincial help, he suggested they "doff your broadcloth and don your overalls." In other words, straighten out their own tangled affairs (which were brought on by a real estate boom cut short by the Great War).

The premier was said to have a battered alarm clock hanging on the wall of his office and to drink tea out of a saucer at social gatherings if he felt like it. In the legislature, he alternated humorous aphorisms with sharp attacks on the Conservative record. Some of Oliver's bluntness was directed at his own party. He reminded the hordes of job-seekers that the Liberals had a non-patronage plank in their election platform and he could not honourably ignore it. He

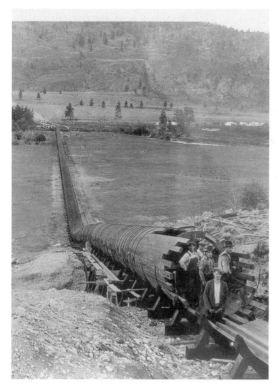

A huge irrigation pipe stretches away
from the site of Oliver in 1920.

would not tolerate, Honest John added, dishonesty and corruption on the part of a patronage appointee. (That Oliver did allow some patronage appointments can be deduced from the 1918 Journal of the Legislative Assembly. It contains dozens of opposition questions about civil service hirings and firings.)

The premier's stand on honest money earned by honest toil was sharply emphasized early in 1920 during a speech to the legislature. "Many a time I have laboured and every morsel of food bore the imprint of my fingers in dirt," he said. "The wearing of the blue denim overall or jumper is just as honourable as the wearing of fur or broadcloth. When I dug ditches, I was just as good as I am today and who is a better man now?"

He called for the end to class legislation favouring one class of person over another, and warned that present politicians must plan far ahead because "we have no right to mortgage the future generations." The present "maniacal idea" that only railways brought prosperity must end, he insisted, and people should abandon the assumption there was something degrading about honest work.

An election was generally expected later in 1920, and Oliver prepared for it by drafting—with the stub of a pencil—a Liberal manifesto detailing the good things the government had done for the people. Included was the array of progressive legislation instituted by himself and his predecessor. One act, providing destitute widows and other women with a monthly allowance for their children, was warmly endorsed by Mary Ellen Smith, B.C.'s first female MLA, and a number of women's groups. After stomping the province from end to end, displaying his homespun enthusiasm, Oliver expected a solid Liberal majority on December 1. As solidity goes, however, it was not as comforting as

Mary Ellen Smith was B.C.'s first female MLA, elected after the death of her husband, Liberal MLA Ralph Smith.

the 1916 result. The Liberal presence in the House was pared to 25 members (including Oliver), with 15 Tories and 7 independents.

The presence of such a large number of fringe-party MLAs was the first symptom of a malaise that would cause grave problems for the government in the next election. But that was four years down the road, and Premier Oliver would have a busy, controversial term before he next went to the electorate.

Before 1921 was half over, British Columbians could again enjoy a legal pick-me-up. Oliver's government had committed itself to a new referendum on prohibition. On October 20, 1920, the people spoke and overwhelmingly decided to have another drink. On June 15, 1921, the new policy was officially launched "on a sea of foaming liquor." The cunningly worded referendum question had given the masses the chance to vote for moderation—through government control of sales. Thus was born the B.C. Liquor Control Board, or as some wags put it, "John Oliver's drug stores."

A lot of people needed a snort in 1921. A brief recession had set in, leading to falling land values and a rise in unemployment. Oliver was beset by many delegations urging that he do something. The self-made premier was of the opinion that a man should raise himself up by his own bootstraps, so he offered little solace. There was also dissension within his own party, leading to a few cabinet resignations (including that of Mrs. Smith, who had been the first female minister in the British Empire).

Oliver's leadership was the problem. He had self-confidence and a ready wit, but his pugnacious exterior alienated more than one British Columbian. One of Honest John's failings was that he tried to do too much. He was punctilious about trifles and disturbed others at their work. Any lack of efficiency made him impatient. Although the tender feelings were eventually soothed, Oliver had the first inkling that others in the party were finding fault with his style.

One of the dissidents' concerns was the growing cost of the PGE. The cabinet had approved an expenditure of $18 million to continue work on the line, and its spiralling debt led to cartoonists' taunts about "John Oliver's white

Premier John Oliver (to the left of the tricorned Speaker) and his
government gather for the formality of a group photograph.
Mary Ellen Smith is recognizable in the second row.

elephant." Oliver went to the federal government for help. Stung by Prime
Minister W.L. Mackenzie King's dilatory response, he embraced the "Fight
Canada" policy that had lain dormant since McBride's years. With Gerry McGeer,
a lawyer and former Liberal MLA, assisting, he concentrated on the Crow's
Nest freight-rate agreement. Complex and bristling with technicalities, the deal
between the federal government and the CPR in 1897 essentially provided for
higher freight rates for westbound commodities than for those going east.

Presenting himself in Ottawa in February 1922, Oliver laid out B.C.'s
position. The immediate outcome was a slight reduction in the mountain
differential, which was an additional impost on B.C. traffic. Oliver's final victory,
after further hectoring in Ottawa, would not come until September 1925, when
rates for grain shipments were equalized between the east and the west. The
decision made Vancouver the Dominion's primary grain export port.

Another rail problem simply would not go away. A new political group, the
Provincial Party, alleged in 1923 that the PGE's operations were riddled with
graft and incompetence. The government was obliged to form a royal commission
to examine the allegations. The inquiry, by Appeal Court Judge William Galliher,
began hearings on February 25, 1924, into charges that "gross waste of public
money" and fraud were committed during construction of 213 miles of track.
On April 22, Galliher ruled that there was nothing in the evidence to support
any imputation of wrongdoing by the government. Earlier, he had dismissed,
for lack of evidence, a related charge that the PGE had paid a $50,000 bribe to
Premier Bowser so as to ensure favourable treatment.

John Oliver's populist appeal was never hurt by his way with
words, including the comment that inspired this cartoon.
*The speculators, with the connivance of the government, sometimes get their
land for a dollar and a drink and sometimes for a drink without the dollar.*

The PGE decision came just two months before the election of June 20.
The positive outcome didn't seem to help. Complicating the campaign was the
presence of the Provincial Party, which was loaded with disaffected Liberals and
Conservatives. They were led by A.D. McRae, a Vancouver millionaire whose
"Hycroft" mansion overlooked the downtown peninsula. Oliver didn't have
much to offer the voters except his honesty and his record.

Newspaper ads implored the voter to ignore "peanut politics" and vote for
Honest John Oliver, the Farmer Premier, who "plows a deep, straight furrow."
But the electorate seemed to be weary of the old-line parties' usual pattern of

sharing the spoils. A vote for the Provincials was a vote of protest—and enough were cast to seriously shake up the system. Only 23 Liberals were returned to the 48-seat House, with 17 Conservatives and 8 others aligned with the Provincials or fringe parties. Oliver, Bowser and McRae were defeated in their personal races.

The premier was soon back in the legislature, thanks to a convenient byelection in Nelson. With the House balkanized for the first time since the pre-McBride years of chaos, Oliver had to manoeuvre his minority government around the obstacles tossed up by a revitalized opposition. He reorganized his cabinet, making John MacLean his finance minister. Then he was off to Ottawa, "a white-haired giant of a man," to thump a few desks and seek further concessions on freight rates. On one of those trips, according to a newspaper report, he discussed the Doukhobor problem with Mackenzie King. "I understand that they are in the habit of parading in *puris naturabilis*," King remarked. "Worse than that," Oliver said. "They go around without a stitch on."

The Doukhobors were members of a devout and stubborn religious sect that did not recognize the right of any outside authority to control their actions. Their nude processions were meant to demonstrate the purity of righteous living. In 1922, the Doukhobors ended their peaceful acceptance of provincial regulations by rejecting the B.C. school system. After they withdrew their children from the classrooms, parents were fined and property seized as punishment. During the next few years, the Sons of Freedom splinter group of zealots burned down nine schools. In 1924, the situation escalated into a major crisis after some harsh remarks from a Nelson magistrate and the murder of the Doukhobor leader, Peter Verigin. Because of the incendiary nature of the situation, Oliver ordered that telegrams from Nelson be sent in code.

The following year, after another wave of arson, Oliver had an angry confrontation with sect activists in Grand Forks. Defending the justice system, but carried away by the tension of the moment, he told one puzzled protestor: "The laws would probably be more right if you are dead, than you are now." Then, in Nelson, he told another group of Doukhobors that they should leave the country if they could not abide by the laws.

On the legislative front, Oliver reduced both taxes and the debt, expanded welfare programs, accelerated road construction and even found money for the new University of B.C. campus at Point Grey. The House also unanimously passed a resolution on December 17, 1924, formally asking Ottawa to renounce trade treaties (especially with Japan) that inhibited B.C.'s anti-Asian initiatives. This came despite federal legislation virtually outlawing Chinese immigration, something B.C. had advocated for scores of years. (During the 1909 election,

Oliver had suggested that the Chinese live up to the white man's standards or get out of the country.) Only a year earlier, the House had passed another resolution asking Ottawa to deny the franchise to "British Indians." "While the number of Indians in Canada is limited, they have a population of between three and four hundred million to draw on and we must not offer them any encouragement," one MLA said.

On his 70th birthday, John Oliver was the oldest first minister in Canada. Bruce Hutchison, the nonpareil political correspondent for the *Victoria Times*, wrote this to describe, in part, the man who had reached such a milestone:

> At seventy, however, this much can be revealed—the Premier is not half as much in love with the office as he was at sixty. He has found out too much about it. Few tears, one imagines, would trickle down his grizzled face if the trail led back to the good old Delta at the next turning. John Oliver is nearing the twilight of his career in the rough and tumble of public life. The Premier has mellowed.
>
> ...On the whole, life has been good to John Oliver, but it has given him a full share of those secret sorrows that lurk in the council chambers of the great and echo but faintly in the market places of democracy. That is why the end of seventy years finds graven deep in his heart the knowledge that a politician's life is not, and never will be, a happy one.

With the premier now assuming the mantle of an elder statesman, it was a good time to recall a few of his terse aphorisms:

"The hog that gets fat first is usually killed first." (Try that one on the ward heelers.)

"Sometimes it requires more courage to stand still than go forward."

"The man on top of the stack has the widest view, but he gets all the wind and flying ants."

"No man is a whit bigger than his soul, whether digging a ditch in overalls or addressing the legislature in a tailored suit. I've done both and I know."

But, as his secretary recalled later, Mount Oliver was no longer in daily eruption. He still started the day at an early hour and finished late, but his sturdy frame was now feeling sharp stabs of discomfort. During the premier's final session, from mid-December 1926 to March 1927, he missed several sittings because of illness. One bill, however, was important enough that Oliver—an old man pleading for the old—arose from his sick bed to pilot it through the House. It was the Old Age Pensions Act, which didn't provide much—$20 a month for people over 70, with a strict means test—but was a landmark bill that was linked to parent legislation in the Commons.

After prorogation, Oliver went to the Mayo Clinic in Rochester, Minnesota, for an exploratory operation. The result was what the old campaigner must have long expected: cancer. In July, old John had to be helped up the steps of

A kilted band leads the way through downtown Victoria as John Oliver, the farmer-premier, is borne away to his last resting place in August 1927.

the Legislative Building to meet his caucus. He offered to resign, but they refused to accept another leader while he was still alive. It was agreed that MacLean would become premier-designate.

John Oliver died August 17, 1927. His body lay in state in the legislative chamber, then was borne down those wide granite steps for the last time. The funeral was held at First United Church and was attended by both the notable and the ordinary. A representative of the Prince of Wales, who had just arrived in B.C., was there, as were Lt.-Gov. R. Randolph Bruce, federal cabinet ministers and other dignitaries. A special steamer was pressed into service to ferry Lower Mainland mourners to Victoria. On August 20, Honest John was buried on a sunny slope in Saanich's Royal Oak Burial Park.

John Duncan MacLean

(August 20, 1927– August 20, 1928)

So far as British Columbians were concerned, the Roaring Twenties were mostly a Yankee phenomenon. While there appeared to be unfettered growth south of the border, B.C. had no such luck until late in the decade. Oh, a few hedonistic by-products of the U.S. boom trickled north: jazz, flappers, the Charleston, bobbed hair, syncopated swing, raccoon coats, the Tin Lizzie.

But until the effects of the 1921-22 depression became just a memory, the only roar emanating from the province was that of powerful speedboats ferrying illegal booze southward. Just as B.C. was ending its experiment with prohibition, the Americans were beginning theirs. By 1927, however, there were legitimate profits to be made from vastly increased grain shipments to Vancouver, an expanding agriculture industry, shipping (aided by the new Ogden Point docks in Victoria) and business growth. The resource industries—forestry, mining and fisheries—were healthier than they had ever been.

All this would have to be regarded as good news for the Liberal party and John MacLean, its new leader. MacLean had taken over in the warm afterglow of Honest John Oliver's popular premiership. But this John had no folksy persona or ready supply of pithy observations, although with his well-rounded background he could boast far more career skills than Oliver.

John Duncan MacLean was born November 8, 1873, in the village of Culloden, Prince Edward Island, to Roderick and Effie Matheson MacLean.

His education included enrolment at Prince of Wales College in Charlottetown, but it was interrupted by a family financial crisis. A big-framed, capable lad, John had to withdraw to help out on his father's farm for several months, teaching school on the side.

Like John Turner, another future premier, MacLean found the tiny province too confining. In 1892, he emigrated to the Prairies and ended up as a rural schoolteacher in what is now Alberta. Moving to B.C. the following year, he continued his teaching career on the Lower Mainland and in the Interior.

By 1898, MacLean was a principal in the Rossland school system. At the age of 28, he quit his steady but low-paying job and went back to university. The young schoolmaster had decided to become a doctor. He enrolled in the McGill medical school and laboured so hard at earning his degree that his health faltered and he had to recuperate in the U.S. Southwest. MacLean returned to Rossland in 1905 and went into partnership with another doctor before moving to Greenwood, which was a thriving mining community, the following year. In 1911, he married Mary Watson, who bore him three sons and three daughters. In the succeeding years, MacLean built up a prosperous practice as surgeon and general practitioner.

The good doctor, popular and well-respected, entered local politics in 1912. He served as an alderman in Greenwood for three years before becoming mayor. On September 14, 1916, Dr. John MacLean also became an MLA. That November, he joined Premier Harlan Brewster's Liberal cabinet as provincial secretary and, later, minister of health and education. Brewster wanted someone safe and solid who had experience in education and public health, and MacLean was that man.

As a member of the executive council, MacLean was thorough and diligent. The former country doctor improved medical treatment in several areas. He took the Tranquille Sanitarium near Kamloops out of private hands and transformed it into a first-class centre for the treatment of tuberculosis. He also established the first hospital dedicated to the long-term care of patients.

On the education front, MacLean reorganized the school system, leading to a noticeable improvement in the quality of schooling. He promoted the establishment of technical schools and urged that delinquent boys be given a proper education. MacLean was also instrumental in getting the University of B.C. physically established on its Point Grey campus, a feat that earned him an honorary Doctor of Laws degree in 1928. He also helped Brewster develop social legislation in the fields of soldiers' aid, adoption and mothers' pensions.

When Oliver took over as premier in 1918, MacLean served his new boss with loyal imperturbability. Although he also had a rural background, MacLean

Tranquille Sanitarium offered a haven for tuberculosis sufferers.

was far better schooled than the rustic Oliver and could offer a more sophisticated take on various subjects. He retained his Greenwood seat in the 1920 election. Oliver gave up his railways ministry in 1922 and passed it on to MacLean, who had become his lieutenant. While Oliver fretted about freight rates, MacLean was saddled with the PGE, which was becoming far more costly and controversial than anyone in government had ever dreamed. During 1923, he undertook a "retrenchment" of the railway, which resulted in a number of layoffs.

When the 1924 election rolled around, MacLean stood in the riding of Yale and was one of the 23 Liberals elected to Oliver's minority government. John Hart, the finance minister, had retired from politics shortly before the election, so Oliver tapped the trusty, loyal MacLean for the post in his new cabinet. MacLean retained his education portfolio. As finance minister, he steered a cautious and steady course. The unpopular personal property tax was abolished and MacLean touted a gross income tax in its stead. His aim was to establish a minimum income tax on businesses. "One object of tax is to get everyone in business paying taxes," said one of his handwritten notes on the subject.

During Oliver's last, feeble months, MacLean ran the province. He did his best to smooth the final path for the old warrior and agreed to accept the "premier-designate" label while removing all burdens of office from Honest John's shoulders. John MacLean was sworn in as premier August 20, immediately following Oliver's funeral.

With a shaky hold in the House, the new premier knew he would have to face the electorate at any time. But first there were a few things to be done. In November, he travelled to a Dominion-provincial conference in Ottawa, carrying B.C.'s concerns with him. In fact, MacLean made "Better Terms" the title of his submission. These now included the return of the railway lands in the north, provincial subsidies and "special considerations arising out of the peculiar physical conditions" of B.C., as well as the standard anti-Asian rhetoric. He was accorded little more than polite interest.

MacLean also kept the PGE on the front burner; he announced that his government intended to extend the line to Prince George and open up the vast hinterland of B.C. to settlement. During the 1928 session, he indicated that new bonds would be issued to help pay for the completion of the railway.

Also during that session, on March 14, the legislature passed the obligatory resolution deploring the federal government's policy on the Asian question. This motion, which was adopted unanimously, was more detailed than usual. It noted, for instance, that there were 46,500 Orientals in British Columbia in 1927 (approximately one in every twelve persons), and that the aggregate value of their land and improved property was more than $10 million.

Furthermore, "the Japanese birth-rate...is 40 per 1,000 as compared with a general birth-rate (not including native Indians) of 18 per 1,000, and in three years the number of Japanese children in the public schools...has increased by 74 percent and now totals approximately 4,000 children," one clause said. Another claimed that "the presence of such large numbers of Orientals and their economic activities constitute a serious menace to the welfare of all classes of other citizens, including those engaged in agriculture, commercial business, professional occupations, and labourers in industry."

One detects the fine, pedantic, schoolteacherish hand of John MacLean in the dry litany of "whereas" clauses. What the legislators were really annoyed at was the impending establishment of diplomatic relations between Canada and Japan. They called for the Dominion government to accept all of B.C.'s proposals for restricting Oriental immigration, and to immediately repatriate all Chinese and Japanese in B.C. "to the countries of their respective origin" until the number of Asians here matched the number of Canadians in China and Japan. B.C.'s recommendations—especially that last one—were carefully filed away and forgotten by the federal politicians.

MacLean called the election for July 18, 1928. During the campaign he dropped the hint that the PGE might be sold to Canadian National Railways (which would greatly reduce the drain on the province's finances). He also proposed a general reduction in taxes and pointed to the Liberal record of major road building—without stressing the fact that the government had just imposed a gasoline tax on vehicles using those roads.

A month before the election, the party lost one of its most distinguished MLAs. Brigadier-General Victor Odlum, proprietor of the *Morning Star* in Vancouver and a much-admired war hero, decided not to run again. In a candid open letter to MacLean's new finance minister, Dugald Donaghy, published in his newspaper June 22, Odlum said he would not seek re-nomination because he perceived a conflict of interest in the two roles. "I feel that I have an obligation to the thousands of *Morning Star* readers, which is greater than any obligation I owe to the Liberal party or to my personal friends," he wrote.

Donaghy had been named finance minister at the last minute to give Vancouver a seat in the cabinet, an oversight that had been a sore point on the Lower Mainland during the Oliver administration. In the end, MacLean's manoeuvring didn't help. While he campaigned on the Liberal record and the need for resource development, Simon Tolmie, the new Conservative leader (and former MP), talked of prosperity and the good things to come. In 1928, the Twenties were finally roaring in B.C., with wages at a record level, so Tolmie's talk about a glistening future resonated with the voters.

The Conservative leader was also helped by his penchant for dispensing folksy metaphors, a la Honest John Oliver. "As a self-maintaining country, we need a more balanced ration of motor cars and milking cows," was one of them. In contrast, MacLean came across as humourless and plodding. He tried to capitalize on the popularity of Oliver, but the coattails of the farmer-premier were long in the ground by then.

Nevertheless, MacLean was optimistic right up to the end. In a telegram to campaign workers just before polling day, he claimed that "reports from all over the province indicate a sweeping victory." It was a wildly inaccurate assessment. In another one of those extreme swings of the electoral pendulum, the Conservatives won 35 seats to 12 for the Liberals. MacLean lost in Yale, as did Donaghy in Vancouver. He resigned as premier on August 20. His stewardship lasted precisely one year, and during that span nothing transpired that would unduly excite the historian or the biographer—or, for that matter, the voter.

The ex-premier still had trust and honour to offer, but he was again rejected when he ran for the Commons seat vacated by Tolmie. The federal party did not forget him, however. He was appointed director of the Farm Loan Board in 1929, a post where his organizational skills became invaluable. MacLean's success as an administrator was such that he was retained by R.B. Bennett's Conservative government of the early Thirties. He was named a Commander of the British Empire in 1946.

John Duncan MacLean died March 28, 1948, in Ottawa, where he had lived since taking up his federal appointment in 1929. He was 74 and had retired only three months earlier. By then, MacLean's brief stint as premier of British Columbia had been largely forgotten and his passing was little noted.

Simon Fraser Tolmie

(August 21, 1928– November 15, 1933)

On January 1, 1929, the city of Vancouver swallowed up the neighbouring municipalities of South Vancouver and Point Grey. Its population instantly rose to 228,193, and every single citizen was enjoying the greatest boom the city had ever known.

Business was good all over. The working stiff could make a comfortable living if he was willing to apply himself. People were spending and acquiring as never before. A small lot on Hornby Street in downtown Vancouver sold for $1,000 per front foot. Credit was available almost for the asking. The stock market became the focus of many lives, with the giddy spiralling of share prices feeding a growing hysteria.

To the discerning observer, there were signs that the end was nigh, but most of the populace paid scant attention. Fatal policy errors by central governments, which led to the erection of trade barriers, helped grease the skids. When world trade started to wither, rising taxes and restrictive monetary policies would squeeze the life out of domestic economies.

For British Columbians, perhaps the last hurrah of the Twenties came in September 1929, when Olympic sprint hero Percy Williams rode through the streets of Vancouver with Premier S.F. Tolmie. For Tolmie, Williams and the excited throngs that lined the parade route, all was well. For the premier especially, the exciting days of 1929 seemed to bear out the "gospel of optimism" that he had been preaching all along.

Within weeks of its election in August 1928, Tolmie's party was producing a slick newsletter called "British Columbia Bulletin." Along with the usual self-serving twaddle, it painted a picture of benign prosperity. The issue for December 1928 crowed that mineral output showed a heartening increase. Wheat-growing acreage in the Peace River country was also expanding rapidly, the publication said, and B.C.'s beekeeping industry was healthy and profitable. In a speech to a Cumberland audience, Tolmie was quoted as saying that "the country was bustling with opportunities; all they wanted was men to take hold of them."

To be frightfully frank, Tolmie didn't have a clue about the financial precipice over which British Columbia was about to plunge. Nor did his finance minister, W.C. Shelly, or other advisers. They seemed as credulous about the frenzy attending the final years of the decade as a bunch of rubes mesmerized by a carny barker. And when the collapse came, Tolmie was not the man to seize a complex problem and sweat the details. He was a farmer and a veterinary surgeon with little practical exposure to high (or low) finance.

Simon Fraser Tolmie was born January 25, 1867, in a farmhouse in Saanich, north of Victoria. He was the last of twelve children of William Fraser and Mary Work Tolmie. W.F. Tolmie was a former Hudson's Bay Company factor who became a noted B.C. politician. Originally a doctor, he is credited with discovering coal on Vancouver Island. The elder Tolmie was a stern father with fixed ideas about idleness and waste. Each day, young Simon arose at 5 a.m. to do his farm chores and study the classics before breakfast. He would then walk to school; upon his return, more chores and studying awaited him before bedtime. His allowance was $5 a year.

Simon was an imposing, raw-boned youth who was seventeen before he saw his first railway carriage or streetcar. But at eighteen he paraded a prize-winning bull before the grandstand at the New Westminster Fair. With a solid education in local schools and a farming background, he decided to enter veterinary medicine. After gaining his degree at Ontario Veterinary College in 1891, Tolmie returned to the Island to practise. He married Annie Harrop in 1894; they would have two sons and two daughters. By 1901, Tolmie was an inspector of livestock for both the Dominion and provincial governments. He became chief veterinary inspector for B.C. in 1904, but resigned in 1906 to accept a similar position with the federal government. He also became B.C.'s representative on the Dominion Livestock Commission. Because of his new responsibilities, Tolmie spent much of his time in Ottawa, but still maintained his Saanich home as a model farming operation.

Although reluctant to leave his civil service niche, Tolmie was drafted by Robert Borden in the 1917 federal election. On December 17, he won the Commons seat for Victoria and sat on the Conservative backbench for eighteen months. In August 1919, he was appointed agriculture minister, was re-elected the following October and retained his portfolio when Arthur Meighen succeeded Borden in 1920. As agriculture minister, Tolmie travelled to London in 1921 to successfully present Canada's case against the United Kingdom's 30-year embargo on imported livestock.

Loyal, affable and tactful, Tolmie avoided controversy in his portfolio, leaving the actual day-to-day routine to his deputy. The portly, effusive minister preferred to glad-hand his way from county fair to county fair. When the Meighen government fell in December 1921, Tolmie managed to get re-elected. An opposition member now, he helped reorganize the Conservative party. This paid off with solid gains in the 1925 election. A Conservative attempt to form a government in 1926, when the minority Liberal administration faltered, was rejected by the voters later in the year. Tolmie had managed to hang on to his Commons seat during all these vicissitudes and was B.C.'s most prominent Tory when the party held its convention in Kamloops that November.

The B.C. wing of the Conservatives was not a happy party in late 1926. Haunted by the ghosts of misdeeds past and essentially rudderless, it gathered in the dry, bracing air of the Interior and hoped for inspiration. William Bowser, the former premier, had clung to the leadership since leading his party into the shadows after the disastrous 1916 election. After losing three straight elections, the delegates were in a mood for change, but infighting among various factions made the process chancy. The problem with the Conservative party was that it had been held together by power, patronage and the popularity of Richard McBride. With McBride gone, the party had no principles to adhere to and no vision of its own goals. Thus, it was easily frustrated.

Bowser suddenly withdrew from the leadership race on November 24. This seemed to muddle things rather than clarify them. Late into the next day the delegates wrangled and voted. Finally, after six ballots and no consensus, there was a surprise nomination: Simon Fraser Tolmie. Sitting in a corner of the hall, reading a telegram, Tolmie suddenly heard his name. Even though the delegates, attracted by the scent of a fresh saviour, endorsed him unanimously, Tolmie refused the nomination. Only after a series of tense meetings did he consent. "Under these circumstances, I could not refuse you longer," he told the convention.

The new Conservative champion promptly left town. He returned to Ottawa and devoted the next eighteen months to his obligations as an MP. When John MacLean called an election for July 18, Tolmie resigned his federal seat and lumbered back to B.C. Carrying no baggage and owing no favours, he was a welcome diversion. A ruddy, honest face bursting with good cheer was what the voters wanted, not the stern visage offered by Premier MacLean.

W.C. Shelly had the unenviable position of finance minister as the Great Depression began.

Tolmie's party manifesto concentrated on industrial development, immigration, labour legislation and an energetic mining policy. It promised prosperity based on government efficiency, lower taxes and economic expansion. Actually, this was little different from the Liberal platform, but Tolmie's had the ring of sincerity. He also used homespun quotes to emphasize his placid nature. "For me to get angry and paw up the ground like a mad bull would not bring the train here one second sooner," he told an interviewer. "A man who loses his temper only hurts himself."

After twelve years in office, the Liberals were rudely cast out by the voters. The Conservatives won 35 seats to 12 for the MacLean forces. MacLean resigned August 20 and Tolmie was sworn in as premier the next day. At well over 300 pounds, he was the biggest man ever to occupy the corner office. And, as heavy men are wont to do, he moved slowly. The next legislative session was several months down the line, so Tolmie drifted through the rest of 1928, making speeches and travelling.

In a speech in Portland, Oregon, the premier revealed that he was an early advocate of conservation. Forests could only be saved through education, he maintained. "We must endeavour to...saturate and permeate public thought and opinion," he said. That December, he conferred with the federal government in Ottawa about the return of the Peace River Block railway lands, among other things.

When the legislature opened January 22, 1929, Tolmie was still blinking contentedly at the world around him. His cabinet, although drawn from all parts of the province, was as clueless as the premier. Seven of the eleven ministers had never been elected before. That the new government was slightly out of touch with reality was illustrated by the first bill introduced in the House. "An Act to Amend the Counties Definition Act" was on the order paper simply to overturn a Liberal decision setting up a new judicial district in Comox. The Throne Speech didn't promise much except "a thorough survey of the provisions of the Taxation Act." Later, the House managed to repeal the longstanding provision calling for confirmatory byelections for cabinet appointees.

Meanwhile, the public accounts were tabled and showed that in the eleven fiscal periods from 1917-18 to 1927-28, only twice did the province record a surplus. By March 31, 1928, B.C. was in the hole to the tune of $13,318,879.

As his cabinet looks on, Premier S.F. Tolmie signs the agreement
that returns the Peace River lands to B.C. in 1930.

Those figures would get worse very rapidly. When the world's economy went into the toilet in October 1929, the Tolmie government was as surprised as anybody. As it tried to cling to the status quo, the timber industry—B.C.'s primary profit engine—led the economic collapse. Suddenly, there were jobless instead of jobs.

The premier was big on talk but short on specifics. Although 1930 was marked by the return of the 12.5 million acres of the Peace River Block, there was little else that could be called positive. The number of unemployed mushroomed, especially in Vancouver. Finance Minister Shelly's take on welfare was that it was "paternalistic legislation" and should be avoided. By the end of the year, the province, in concert with the Dominion government, rushed relief projects into place.

Tolmie shuffled his cabinet. Shelly was replaced by J.W. Jones, who was just as unsympathetic to the poor and unemployed. During the 1931 session, the government imposed a one-percent "supertax" on all incomes. It kicked in at $25 a week earned by married men, and $15 for all others. "One Percent Jones" was roundly castigated for taking "food from the table of humble working people." T.D. Pattullo, the opposition leader, wrote a friend that "governmentally, the whole lot of them are the biggest bunch of boobs one could possibly think of" for imposing the tax.

The visit of the King of Siam in April was a welcome diversion for Tolmie. The year also marked the province's diamond jubilee. Newspapers from San

Francisco to Fife ran special stories and sections calling B.C. the last land of adventure in the Empire. While they quoted Tolmie as saying there had been changes "comparable to the difference between the England of the Middle Ages and the England of today," the jobless infested every street corner. Tolmie spoke of "courage, faith and a little patience" before the province entered its "golden age."

Later in the year, a delegation of business leaders, which included H.R. MacMillan, George Kidd and Austin Taylor, urged Tolmie to establish a committee to consider economic reform. The businessmen were particularly worried about the level of the debt and government expenditures. Tolmie dithered until 1932 before agreeing.

Barely three years into the Depression, municipal relief funds had become a drain on the government. Someone got the bright idea of constructing work camps to house the single unemployed. But the camps cost money. The feds in Ottawa rejected pleas for assistance, and the Bank of Commerce demanded payment of a $9 million overdraft. In July 1932, B.C. had 35,906 men (both single and married) on relief, plus 48,087 women and dependents. It was into this cauldron of despair that the committee dropped its findings.

Tolmie sat on the Kidd Report, as it was called, all summer. When it was released simultaneously to Pattullo and the public on August 30, one could see why. The report called for a drastic revision of the political scene. It said party politics, patronage and self-interest were largely responsible for the mess B.C. was in and concluded that the party system should be abandoned and the legislature cut to 28 seats. Other recommendations included sale of the PGE, closure of the University of B.C., replacement of the Provincial Police with the RCMP, slashing of the civil service payroll and a reduction in public works spending.

Tolmie's first reaction was one of "sympathy" with the spirit of the report; he promised to give it full consideration. Upon due reflection, the government decided not to swallow the bitter Kidd medicine. On September 23, it released, in the form of an appendix to the report, a virtually complete rejection. Clause by clause, the cabinet turned down every proposal of any importance.

The only thing Tolmie seized upon was the abolishment of the party system. He started sending out feelers about a union government. "The time has come for some sort of union in British Columbia," he said at one point. "The public is sick and tired of political backfiring and bickering day after day and what it desires is a combined effort..." His model was the British system of national government. Pattullo and Bowser, who was still a force in the Conservative party, were offered seats in a coalition cabinet. The opposition leader rejected the idea out of hand, while the wooing of Bowser irked several of Tolmie's colleagues.

The government had nothing to offer except routine legislative amendments and platitudes during the 1933 session. With no new policies except coalition and no insights about ending the economic agony, Tolmie's fatal hesitation split the party. Bowser formed his own non-partisan faction and took a chunk of Tolmie's supporters with him.

The desperate premier hung on throughout 1933, knowing that his chances of re-election were nil. Finally, with his five-year mandate rapidly running out, Tolmie called an election for November 2. It was a day Pattullo thought would never come. Even then, he had to wait an extra 25 days before he and his Liberal party knew the extent of their victory. Bowser had died suddenly October 25, necessitating a voting delay in the two ridings in which he was a candidate.

When all the votes were counted, the Liberals were back in the saddle again with 34 out of 47 seats. The party of Richard McBride, William Bowser and S.F. Tolmie did not elect a single member. Some new kids on the block, the Co-operative Commonwealth Federation, formed the official opposition with seven seats, while six others went to fringe groups.

Tolmie, without a seat, without a party and without a future, resigned November 15 before the delayed votes were counted. In ill health and burdened by personal debts, he retired to his Saanich farm and stagnated there until 1936. In June of that year, he won a federal byelection in Victoria and returned to the Commons. But his stay was brief.

Simon Fraser Tolmie died October 13, 1937, on the farm where he was born. The *Vancouver Sun*, which once called the Tolmie government "that dish of political tripe," eulogized the former premier as a man whose "greatness of heart and kindliness of spirit made him a well-beloved figure even in the darkest days of political misfortune."

Premier Pattullo ordered a state funeral, and the body lay in the legislative chamber before being interred in the Royal Oak Burial Park, on land the Tolmie family once owned. Tolmie was laid to rest beside his wife, who had predeceased him by several years.

Thomas Dufferin Pattullo

(November 15, 1933–
December 9, 1941)

Thomas Dufferin Pattullo strode purposefully into the ornate lobby of the Hotel Vancouver on Monday morning, June 20, 1938. As usual, his elegant dark suit, properly knotted tie and stiff white shirt conveyed the crisp, no-nonsense image of the premier of British Columbia. Two blocks to the north, traces of tear gas still lingered in the federal post office building, site of a confrontation the day before between police and jobless squatters.

It was the aftermath of that clash—which became known as the Post Office Riot—that Pattullo was to address this warm, pleasant day. And despite the violence, the damage and the disturbing photographs published in Vancouver's newspapers, the premier was in no mood for compromise or apology. Members of the Relief Camp Workers' Union had taken over the post office, the art gallery and the lobby of the Hotel Georgia exactly one month earlier. A city promise of $500 in instant help induced those men occupying the hotel to leave, but the other groups settled in. Most of them had drifted into the city that spring when winter relief camp projects had closed down. They expected further help, but Pattullo insisted there would be no handouts for those who gravitated to B.C. from outside the province. "They've come from all parts of Canada, then they gang up and act contrary to the law and expect us to feed them," he charged, maintaining that single, able-bodied men "should get out and rustle" for themselves.

The premier who marched into the hotel that June day for a series of meetings with the unemployed, opposition politicians and Protestant clergy had been a politician for 34 years. Before that, he was a newspaperman, a government functionary and a real estate hustler. And always, Duff Pattullo was a Liberal.

Thomas Dufferin Pattullo was born in Woodstock, Ontario, January 19, 1873, to George Robson and Mary Rounds Pattullo. The Pattullos were lowland Scots who had emigrated to Canada in 1820. Young Duff drifted in and out of several brief careers before becoming editor of the tiny *Galt Reformer*. He also grew up in an area of Ontario intensely devoted to politics and the Liberal party.

That connection paid off when the Liberal government decided to establish Canadian sovereignty in the Yukon. Pattullo suddenly found himself the recipient of a patronage appointment on the staff of the new territorial commissioner, James M. Walsh.[1] Pattullo arrived in Dawson City early in 1898 and married Lillian Riedemiester of Toledo, Ohio, in November of 1899. The Pattullos' only child, Linda Doris, was born April 2, 1905. By this time, Pattullo was in real estate. He had also entered politics, winning a seat on the Dawson city council in 1904. Dawson, however, was fading fast as the gold fever abated, and by 1908 the Pattullos were on their way to Prince Rupert.

Established as the western terminus of the Grand Trunk Pacific Railway, Prince Rupert was alive with promise and expectations. Pattullo became involved in various ventures, sure that the arrival of the railroad would transform the city into one of the biggest on the coast. By 1910, he was on city council and in 1913 was elected mayor. But the dreams of a metropolis at the mouth of the Skeena River never did pan out, either for Duff Pattullo or the Grand Trunk Pacific. In March 1915, Pattullo secured the Liberal nomination in the provincial riding of Prince Rupert. He was ready to step onto a bigger stage.

That step was made in the election of September 14, 1916, when the Liberals replaced the Conservative government. In a two-man race, Pattullo defeated his opponent by 116 votes. The newly elected MLA promptly ended his eight-year stay in Prince Rupert. In early 1917, he, Lillian and daughter Linda took up permanent residence in Victoria. For Lillian, the final escape from the relentless climate of Prince Rupert was a blessing. She suffered from a variety of maladies, chief among them arthritis and chronic rheumatism. Lillian's constant illnesses and her husband's single-minded focus on politics strained their relationship throughout their marriage. They were not a happy couple.

Although there were recurring accusations that he neglected the riding which first elected him to the legislature, Pattullo represented Prince Rupert for the entire 29 years he was in the House. He never forgot the north, even though it was a major undertaking to visit his riding and others upcountry.

At this stage of his career, Duff Pattullo would not demur if you called him a professional politician. From the Twenties onward, he grew in expertise in his chosen craft, and by the time he became premier in 1933 he was putting the finishing touches on his image: a sharp dresser and somewhat of a dandy; courteous and polite when the occasion warranted, but hard as a slab of British Columbia granite when he intended to get his own way.

It didn't hurt Pattullo's apprenticeship as a legislator that he was afforded access to the corridors of power right from the beginning of his career. As minister of lands from 1916 through 1927, he remained part of the select circle that was the executive council. So when he became leader of the opposition following the Liberal defeat in the 1928 election, he was well aware of how the government really worked. This made him a particularly effective critic, haranguing the bumbling Simon Tolmie cabinet at every opportunity.

The Great Depression had not yet been formally designated as such when the Tolmie administration entered its death throes. In 1932, as Pattullo glowered across the aisle, Tolmie allowed a group of business leaders to conduct an autopsy of B.C.'s moribund economy. When the Kidd Report on government financing was released, Pattullo scoffed. The businessmen on the committee were as naïve about political reality as they were hard-headed about how a provincial government should be run.

Already upset because he was not consulted during the committee's deliberations, Pattullo became even more angry when Tolmie refused to let him see the report until August 30—the very day it was released to the public. As a result, the overtures that the premier made to Pattullo about a coalition cabinet fell on deaf ears. Pattullo dismissed the commission, its recommendations in general and union government in particular.

"Instead of indulging in all the present blithering, kite-flying and cheap intrigue in a pitiful effort to hang on to their jobs...Tolmie and his cabinet, as men of honour, should hurry off to the lieutenant-governor and resign," he said in a press statement as soon as he read the report. Pattullo was a party man through and through, a true Liberal who would not compromise his ideals for a system whereby "the worst forces of both political parties would concentrate to hold control, with the public the common prey." Besides, it was obvious the Liberals would be running the place as soon as the election was called. Although a number of Liberal faithful were not averse to coalition, Pattullo's strong grip on the party carried the day. During his time in opposition, Duff had accomplished just as much behind the scenes as in the legislature. The party, left in disarray after the 1928 election, had been reorganized and cast in the image of its new leader.

Tolmie refused to accept reality until November 1933, when the election results confirmed the total disappearance of his party. Pattullo took over as premier November 15. His Liberal party had won 34 out of 47 seats.

In 1897, Duff Pattullo had climbed the Chilkoot Pass in a nasty blizzard en route to his new government job in Dawson City. That physical challenge was no more daunting than the political path the new premier embarked upon in 1933. During the next eight years, he would take on Canada, the unemployed, the medical industry, the opposition parties and, finally, his own Liberals. Pattullo had to do battle with two prime ministers with radically different styles and political leanings, but who were both committed to keeping federal money away from the provinces. R.B. Bennett was as stubborn as Pattullo but with a tendency toward dogmatic rudeness. W.L. Mackenzie King, the Great Procrastinator, was a blander, smoother product, but just as adept at foiling B.C.'s wishes.

However, Ottawa's apathy regarding B.C.'s economic crisis seemed to whet Pattullo's appetite. "Better Terms" was the slogan he adopted as he made several lunges at Ottawa's purse strings. In his first foray, Pattullo wanted Bennett to fork out $8 million in aid, but the best he could get was a $750,000 interim increase in the Dominion subsidy, plus some help in funding public works and relief programs.

"Work and Wages" was another of Pattullo's slogans. He used the phrase freely during the 1933 election campaign as a catchy label for his visionary notion of "socialized capitalism." In truth, this slogan was even more sparing of real results than "Better Terms," and it gradually disappeared from Liberal rhetoric.

The new premier and his cabinet started out on a positive note in the first legislative session in 1934. They introduced a number of measures designed to ease the tax burden on wage earners (and exempted the lower paid from the one-percent income tax imposed by Tolmie in 1931). They also established a minimum wage and a 48-hour work week, repealed the meal tax and made several important changes to the Public Schools Act.

This was all very fine, but then Pattullo introduced the Special Powers Act on March 16, 1934. It gave the cabinet sweeping new powers to deal with the economic emergency. In its page one story, the *Vancouver Province* noted that the act "asks for power to control business of all sorts, regulate, co-ordinate or prohibit it, and limit its production. It could also borrow money 'on the sole credit of the province' or lend it to any industry. Finally, it could generally control all matters 'of a merely local or private nature in the province.'"

The D-word surfaced on many a front page. "The old Conservative *Colonist* made the capital's flesh creep this morning with screaming headlines announcing that Premier Pattullo had declared a complete dictatorship," wrote one reporter from Victoria. The *News-Herald* in Vancouver decided it didn't have headline type large enough to describe its outrage and borrowed a bigger font from the *Province*. The opposition went bonkers. Pattullo was unmoved.

"We propose to maintain the integrity of our institutions, see that none of our people are allowed to suffer for want of proper sustenance and leave no excuse for sinister influences to sow seeds of discord in the minds of our people," he told reporters when the bill was introduced. In the House, Pattullo rejected charges of dictatorship but insisted he must have broad powers because he had "no idea what the federal government was going to do about anything."

The SPA was Pattullo's version of Franklin Delano Roosevelt's New Deal in the United States. Roosevelt, who had adopted the phrase as a description of his own approach to state interventionism, had impressed Pattullo with his inaugural address of 1933. The opposition and other critics branded Pattullo a copycat who imported his policies from south of the border. The premier always maintained, however, that the president had got the idea from him.

"I feel I should state that many of the policies which our British Columbia Government have been and are carrying out were enunciated by me when I was leader of the Opposition several years before Mr. Roosevelt became President," he wrote in 1938 to the editor of the *Financial Post*.

The furore over the Special Powers Act died down in due course and it passed into law largely intact (although some provisions were softened by amendments in 1935). The clatter of jackboots was not heard in the land after all, and Pattullo pursued his goals of reform, stability and government activism. However, there was little stability on the labour front and plenty of activism of another kind. As mid-decade approached, few sectors of the provincial economy escaped workers' unrest. Strikes came and went in the mines, forests, orchards and on Vancouver's waterfront.

The relief camp phenomenon, one of the major mismanaged aspects of the Great Depression, fomented unrest almost from the day the first single, unemployed males were shipped from the cities to the outback. As Pattullo began gritting his teeth over the wave of unwanted jobless washing up on B.C.'s relief rolls from the Prairies, the inhabitants of the camps became more and more disenchanted with the harsh conditions they were forced to endure. The Relief Camp Workers' Union was formed, and in 1935 some 1,800 very militant males gravitated to Vancouver. There were meetings, exhortations, marches and scattered vandalism and violence. Canada's top Communist, Tim Buck, was there to egg them on, as was the Co-operative Commonwealth Federation—the newly minted socialist political party. Premier Pattullo blamed Ottawa. The unrest confirmed B.C.'s contention that there must be a wholesale change in federal relief policy, he said from Victoria.

Robert Cromie's *Vancouver Sun*, ostensibly a Liberal mouthpiece, viewed the events of 1934 and 1935 with particular acidity. The paper called Pattullo a "popinjay" and accused him of moving too slowly to combat the economic crisis. Pattullo, not one to offer the other cheek, lashed back at the press, mainly via several radio addresses. He described Cromie, who had long been a party supporter, as a gadabout "given to fads and fancies," who was prone to absorbing neurotic ideas while globetrotting. As for the *Province*, the premier observed that it displayed "a spleen and a venom which a self-respecting newspaper should avoid." At one point, he hinted darkly at the need for press censorship.

All this sniping and petulance was played out before an ominous backdrop displaying some very hard numbers. B.C.'s funded debt in 1935 was $145 million; it owed $18.755 million in treasury bills and had a floating debt of $4.067 million. More than 100,000 men were out of work.

Contrary to the criticism from the press, Pattullo did take several steps toward meeting the emergency. He established an economic council to examine several policy areas. The state of the coal industry was one target. Another was to make state health insurance affordable for all.

In 1936, a health insurance bill was introduced. To provide coverage for employees, costs would be met by a two-percent levy on wages and a one-percent contribution from employers based on payroll. Businesses were firmly opposed because their share of the bill would push up costs at a time when profit margins were thin. The doctors also disliked the plan intensely, not least because it gave the government control of their fees. The bill duly passed, but was not proclaimed, so it never became law.

Premier Pattullo had also decided to build a bridge. It was your classic, high-profile, job-friendly public works project, to be constructed across the Fraser River at New Westminster as a replacement for the wagon-rail span built in 1904. The decision to build upriver was controversial. Vancouverites complained that the Royal City was too far to go just to get to the other side of the Fraser. Several critics called the contract a patronage-laden boondoggle (which it probably was; many government projects are). R.B. Bennett in Ottawa attempted to block the project because he viewed it as another example of B.C.'s extravagance. But the man in the corner office was adamant. Besides, he had vowed to squash a deal made by Tolmie to build the bridge at Ladner.

On November 15, 1937, the premier shivered in an inconvenient sleet storm on the north bank of the Fraser. He gingerly manipulated an acetylene torch to cut away a chain and open the Pattullo Bridge to traffic. This functional, arching structure most deservedly took the name of the visionary politician who conceived it, championed it and fought the federal government to a standstill over it. And Pattullo was right. His bridge was much better situated at New

Once the sole western gateway to the interior of B.C., the arching Pattullo Bridge
spans the Fraser River at New Westminster. It opened in 1937.

Westminster than on the dead-end flatland of the delta. It opened up the Fraser
Valley and eventually made access to the Interior easier.

The completion of the bridge was not the only significant event of 1937. Before
the year was ended, Pattullo also would gain re-election, develop a singular
relationship with a politician he admired very much—Franklin Delano Roosevelt—
and pilot labour legislation through the House that would drastically redefine
employer-employee relationships. As all this was waiting to unfold, however, family
matters gave Pattullo an uncharacteristic mien of despondency. In 1936, his alcoholic
youngest brother, Andrew, killed himself in California after his plans to visit Duff
were rebuffed. Another brother, George, had turned into a vociferous foe of Roosevelt
and his New Deal. In the big house on Beach Drive overlooking the Strait of Juan
de Fuca, Lillian's health continued to deteriorate.

Pattullo called an election for June 1, 1937. After more than 40 months
steering the good ship British Columbia through the treacherous tidal rips of
the Depression, the premier felt it was time to get new sailing directions from
the electorate. On the surface, there were two issues—health insurance and
annexation of the Yukon—but in reality Pattullo campaigned on his government's
record. His election ads trumpeted the claims that B.C. was the only province
not to raise any taxes since 1933 and that the provincial debt had been reduced

by exactly $5,858,662.63. He also claimed an increase of 25,000 jobs in three years. On polling day, the Liberals were easily re-elected, with 31 seats out of 48. The Tories, left for dead in 1933, returned to become the official opposition with eight seats, relegating the CCF to third place with seven.

Things were looking up when FDR came to town at the end of September. The U.S. president was on a tour of the Pacific Northwest when he nipped across to Victoria aboard a destroyer. The two New Dealers hit it off right away and discussed, among other things, an Alaska Highway north from British Columbia. In fact, they were so alike in their thinking that a further meeting was arranged. "We'll see you soon," Eleanor told Pattullo as the Roosevelts sailed away, and within two weeks he was sipping tea at the Roosevelt family estate near Hyde Park, New York. His unofficial visit to the presidential hideaway, without any regard for diplomatic niceties, raised several hackles in Ottawa. It also got the attention of Bruce Hutchison, who at this time was writing for the *Vancouver Sun*.

"Ever since he drank tea with President Roosevelt at Hyde Park, Premier Pattullo has gone about like a man with a great secret locked in his heart," Hutchison reported. "He has spoken mysteriously about things he would like to reveal if he could. He has dropped guarded hints

President Franklin D. Roosevelt salutes the crowd from an open car during a brief visit to Victoria in 1937. He and T.D. Pattullo forged a friendship that went beyond political considerations.

in the legislature of the great developments that are yet to come. He has maintained an unshakeable optimism as if he knew something wonderful hidden from other men." That wonderful secret was, of course, the American plan to finance the building of the Alaskan road, but it took the onset of war to make it finally happen.

During the December legislative session, the Industrial Conciliation and Arbitration Act was introduced, debated and passed into law in three days. Although the act was opposed by labour (originally, strikes were banned during the arbitration process), it gave workers for the first time the right to organize, bargain collectively and demand arbitration of disputes. It remains the cornerstone of labour-management law in the province.

Although Pattullo could deservedly put a positive spin on his efforts to keep B.C. afloat, he was still getting nowhere with Ottawa. Trips back east by himself and John Hart, his savvy finance minister, who had returned to politics in 1933 after a nine-year hiatus, were largely unproductive. Hart, who was closer to Pattullo than anyone else in politics, had even brought in a deficit-free budget that impressed British Columbians but left the feds unmoved. In 1938, Prime Minister King's Royal Commission on Dominion-provincial relations held the first of its hearings in Victoria. In due course, the Rowell-Sirois Commission produced a spate of recommendations that ignored the premier's concept of regionalism. Pattullo extracted his revenge by helping to torpedo the subsequent Dominion-provincial conference in January 1941.

When the commissioners left town in 1938, the cabinet was still grappling with the jobless problem. It reduced loans to municipalities, noting that the numbers on relief had dwindled in 1937 and that there were other positive signs of recovery. The government argued that the unemployed should now be able to support themselves during the summer months and offered a free ride home to 1,800 men from the Prairies who had worked in provincial forestry camps during the winter.

Instead, most of these workers gravitated to Vancouver. On May 10, the labour ministry exacerbated the situation by decreeing that these Prairie transients would not be eligible for aid. On May 20, just before Pattullo left on another trip to Washington, the occupation of the Hotel Georgia, the art gallery and the post office began. The city, which had added to the tension by outlawing begging, essentially bribed those in the hotel to leave. The others squatted until city police and the RCMP—at the suggestion of Pattullo—moved in on June 19.

Pattullo was back in Victoria at the time, content to manage the crisis at arm's length. However, news of the sudden turn of events prompted a quick plane ride and his meetings in the Hotel Vancouver. And when the premier sat down with the first of the groups, there was no mincing of words.

Flushed out by tear gas, the men who occupied the
Vancouver Post Office in 1938 head down Hastings Street.

"You were very ill-advised to do what you did," he barked at the jobless delegates in a confrontation that lasted only twenty minutes. He stuck to the government's position that there would be no food or relief for any person not eligible. "We are not going to guarantee every man will be given a job," he said. "It will destroy initiative." The CCF delegation urged temporary aid and a reopening of the camps, but Pattullo reiterated that the government "has already indicated what it will do. We are not going to change." He then dismissed the opposition politicians with the observation that "obviously you are out to criticize the government."

Pattullo was only slightly less blunt with the clergymen representing the Anglican, Baptist and United faiths. To their suggestion that emergency food rations be provided, he replied: "I think it has come to a time that the church is showing a little too much sympathy."

Thus the ugliest incident of the Depression drew to a close, along with the wasted years themselves. This final year of the Thirties would bring a change in B.C.'s fortunes as dramatic as the one in 1929. It began with hope and renewal as government prodding and the improving economy provided more and more jobs. As 1939 gathered steam, the port of Vancouver hummed with increased grain shipments as the Prairie wheat harvest approached a record. Meanwhile, a king and a queen headed for B.C. while the newspapers started taking note of the war clouds gathering over Europe.

On the eve of war, King George VI and Queen Elizabeth visit Victoria May 30 during a tour of Canada in 1939. Premier Pattullo is in attendance.

King George VI and Queen Elizabeth, accompanied by Mackenzie King, visited Vancouver and Victoria in May, and British Columbians wallowed in patriotism. The Royal visit was particularly tiring for Lillian Pattullo, who was by now suffering constant pain from her arthritis. Photographers covering the Royal arrival at the Legislative Buildings noted how Lillian, clinging to her husband, haltingly navigated the long sweep of steps down from the main entrance.

When war came in September, Pattullo energetically threw himself into the planning of home defence. Despite his enthusiastic support for the Empire's fight against Nazi Germany, however, the premier could not discard his vision of provincial autonomy. It was a message wearing thin with the voters and even within his own cabinet.

The Rowell-Sirois report recommended the central government's control over the provinces be strengthened, not weakened. Pattullo, along with William Aberhart of Alberta and Mitch Hepburn of Ontario, flatly rejected the smug conclusions of the commissioners at the doomed Ottawa conference in 1941. "We do not want to be hogtied and hamstrung, and that is exactly what will happen if this report is implemented," Pattullo told the prime minister as the conference sank into the fog of failure.

Pattullo's stubbornness did little to enhance his popularity back home. He was regarded as a self-centred deal-wrecker at a time of national emergency.

John Hart defended his old colleague's stand with faint conviction, and the whispers about change began to grow louder. "Coalition" was on some lips as well. When the premier called an election for October 21 and watched in dismay as his government was reduced to minority status, "coalition" became a roar.

Not only that, Hart was being touted as the new party leader, premier in a Coalition government of 21 Liberals and 12 Conservatives against a CCF opposition of 14 MLAs. Pattullo went off on another long train trip to Ottawa despite the evidence that his centre was collapsing. When he returned, Hart came out openly for some form of union government. The concept was as hateful to Pattullo in 1941 as it was in 1932 and he fired Hart as finance minister.

When other cabinet ministers echoed Hart's position, he asked for their resignations, too. Finally, at a party convention in early December, delegates approved the principle of coalition by an overwhelming margin. Pattullo tried to carry on, but he was now little more than an irritating reminder of a bygone time, betrayed by his inflexibility. "Goodbye, girls and boys," he told the party in his farewell speech. A few days later, Pattullo made his last formal appearance in the legislature as first minister. Bruce Hutchison captured the moment:

> And now the doors fly open and the Lieutenant-Governor appears with his guard of honour. With him comes the man of the hour, whose hour is now 59 minutes spent—Mr. Pattullo himself, ruddy of face, jaw outthrust, figure immaculate in tail coat, lapel ornamented with two civilian medals.
>
> ...A tired Titan he has been through these last grim days, but he seems now neither tired nor titanic. He is simply Mr. Pattullo as we have always known him—sure of himself, perhaps a little too sure as events have turned out, the very picture of pink dignity.

Duff Pattullo resigned as premier on December 9, 1941 as his countrymen were still digesting the news of Pearl Harbor. He retreated gracefully to the backbench, where he remained until losing his seat in the 1945 election to a CCF candidate. The great Liberal's years of enforced retirement were not happy ones. He hung around the legislative press gallery for a while and wrote some carping articles for the *News-Herald*. At home, years of neglect in his marriage made life with a pain-wracked Lillian even more empty.

Thomas Dufferin Pattullo died March 29, 1956, at the age of 83. Although there were almost 1,000 mourners at his funeral, none ranked higher than the mayor of Victoria. Premier W.A.C. Bennett was away on holidays, and Lt.-Gov. Frank Ross was also out of town. Only the ordinary people of the province attended—the ones whose burdens he shouldered in 1933. Pattullo's remains were later cremated.

John Hart

(December 9, 1941– December 29, 1947)

The surviving image of John Hart is that of a prim, bespectacled, white-haired gent who helped keep the dreaded socialists at bay for much of the Forties. Or perhaps that of a trusted lieutenant undermining his boss, Thomas Dufferin Pattullo, while he was out of town. Of more importance, however, was Hart's grasp of dollars and cents.

For a goodly part of 30 years, he was the shrewd financial manipulator in a string of Liberal governments. Even taking into consideration W.A.C. Bennett's performance in the portfolio over 20 years, Hart may have been the best minister of finance British Columbia ever had.

When Hart retired from politics in 1949, he ended a singular odyssey of 50 years devoted to the orderly arrangement of columns of figures. As early as 1918, he was explaining the sticky subject of taxation and royalties to the mining industry. That he had the heart and soul of a bookkeeper is not strictly true, for Hart was much more than that. He was, to begin with, a farmer's lad who developed a liking for sports as well as numbers. The first push toward a career that would shape the destiny of this province came from his lukewarm approach to farming. The second came from an uncle who had done well on the West Coast of North America and wrote back to the family to tell them all about it.

John Hart was born March 31, 1879, in the village of Mohill, County Leitrim, Ireland. His father, also named John, had tilled the soil around Mohill, not far from the River Shannon, for years. Although young John had an agreeable country upbringing, interspersed with attendance at Ross's School, he did not see himself carrying on the family tradition of farming. Instead, he found arithmetic much more to his liking. Two of his sisters had emigrated to B.C. to keep house for their uncle, Michael, and it was this connection that lured John to the colony.

He arrived in Victoria in 1898, just shy of his twentieth birthday. Although Hart certainly thought about all the gold to be dug up in the Klondike, or perhaps of using his rural background to start a cattle ranch in the Interior, he succumbed instead to his passion for figures.

He applied for a junior clerk's position with the Bank of Montreal. There were none immediately available, so Hart went to work for the financial and import concern of Robert Ward & Co. His starting salary was $10 a month, but Hart was soon earning more than that. After six years, Hart switched to another prominent Victoria business house, R.P. Rithet & Co. In 1909, young Hart was confident enough about his own abilities to go into business for himself as a part of the financial firm of Gillespie, Hart & Co., Ltd. He would keep this partnership throughout his lengthy political career.

Gradually, Hart became part of the sporting and social life of Victoria. He played football, tennis, grass hockey, handball and golf (in later years, Hart would win the Pacific Northwest Seniors Golf Championship three times). He also joined the militia, becoming a member of the B.C. Coast Regiment. At age 29, just before he formed his business partnership, John Hart negotiated another liaison. In 1908, he married Harriet McKay, whose family was part of the old Hudson's Bay Company establishment. They would have no children.

Hart also became a Liberal. During the party's long sojourn in the opposition wilderness, he served (with little effect, apparently) as campaign manager. When the Great War began, Hart went overseas with his regiment, but was released from active duty after stating his intention to run in the 1916 provincial election. The Liberal sweep in that election included Hart, who won his seat in the Victoria constituency.

To the surprise of some, Hart was not included in Premier Harlan Brewster's first cabinet. Ralph Smith, the finance minister, died the following year, however, and Brewster handed the portfolio to Hart. Impeccably (if somewhat severely) dressed and prematurely silver-grey, Hart looked like a finance minister. He was an effective one, too, although the immediate post-war years were not auspicious ones for the government or its finance minister.

Whatever boom the war had generated collapsed, and the province slid into a brief depression. Hart, who was retained in the finance post when John Oliver became premier in 1918, had to allocate large sums of money to the Pacific Great Eastern Railway, which now belonged to the province. The deficit spending was engendering a provincial debt of alarming proportions. By 1922, however, the picture brightened and there was guarded optimism along the Liberal benches. They had been returned to power in the 1920 election (Hart included), so there were four more years in which to turn things around.

Hart's 1922 budget included $18 million for the PGE, because he was convinced the line needed to be put into operation as soon as possible so it could start generating income. The budget, said opposition leader William Bowser, was "a doleful repetition of deficits...and political camouflage," but increasing revenues from motor licences, liquor sales and succession duties helped the bottom line considerably. The finance minister also decided to tinker with the wildly disliked personal property tax, which had been instituted by the Conservatives. Hart's plan was to transfer the tax to municipal jurisdiction, but this generated so much opposition that Oliver had to step in and declare that the tax would stay unchanged for the time being. (It was eventually replaced by John MacLean, Hart's successor in the finance portfolio.)

By 1924, Hart had been planning to leave politics for some time. His partnership, now called Gillespie, Hart & Todd, was losing lots of lucrative government insurance underwriting because of Hart's status, and he had promised to step down. In 1920, the PGE had placed a large insurance policy with the firm, drawing opposition criticism, and Hart's partners wanted him to discard his political baggage. Just before the 1924 vote, Hart resigned as finance minister and did not seek re-election.

His departure was a relief to many in the Liberal caucus as his property-tax crusade had led to grumbling among the foot soldiers. Hart was also regarded by some as a shady financial manipulator who had Oliver in one pocket and a handful of suspect fiscal dealings in the other. This bothered Hart not one whit. He was probably unaware of the unrest. His resignation was simply a business decision. After leaving politics, he settled in Vancouver for nine years and tended to the affairs of his partnership.

Meanwhile, Oliver died, J.D. MacLean suffered through his short, unhappy stint as premier, Simon Fraser Tolmie won the 1929 election and Duff Pattullo became the leader of the Liberals. When Tolmie finally called an election for November 1933, Hart rejoined the fray at the urging of Pattullo. He ran in his old Victoria riding and was elected as part of the Liberal sweep. Premier Pattullo promptly asked Hart to take over the finance ministry once more. Pattullo was no dummy about economics, but he recognized Hart as the expert he was.

Hart and Pattullo's relationship as political benchmates went back to their cabinet days in the Brewster government. This friendship would deepen over the succeeding years as they battled the Great Depression together. Hart was the only man to reach any degree of intimacy with the premier. Pattullo's granite-hard persona was a barrier to many, but Hart could bypass it with ease. There was a "touching friendship and loyalty between the two," one observer noted. To Duff, the finance minister was "Jack" Hart—a diminutive seldom employed by casual acquaintances.

When Hart opened the province's books following the election, he found them in worse shape than the ones left behind by the Tories in 1916. British Columbia was essentially bankrupt. Hart himself had contributed to the red ink by running up deficits during the early Twenties, but the onset of the Depression and the Tolmie cabinet's feckless handling of the crisis put the situation almost out of control. Finance Minister Hart's first budget in 1934 added another $2 million or so to the debt by funding a substantial public-works program. He also reduced or removed some taxes that were especially onerous to those at the lower end of the wage scale. B.C. then asked Ottawa for $8 million to help tide it over. Prime Minister R.B. Bennett, while denying this request with a sneer, also demanded that the deficit be reduced to $1 million before the Dominion would consider any help whatsoever.

Hart made several trips back east in 1934, but Bennett, a tight-fisted Old Loyalist Tory who would rather attack than negotiate, was unbending, apart from a few crumbs tossed B.C.'s way—mostly in respect to the relief programs. The province was essentially on its own. In 1935, Hart borrowed $7 million from New York bankers. Because the Canadian dollar was at a discount, he gambled that it would strengthen by the time the loan needed repaying, thus saving B.C. hundreds of thousands. He was right. (Hart was held in high esteem by U.S. banking interests, who recognized the extent of his financial acumen.)

In 1936, Hart's budget was brought down "without accident and without any notable thud," according to Bruce Hutchison, writing in the *Victoria Times*. In it, Hart announced a current surplus of $1.7 million, with a further surplus projected for the following year. Contributing to this bright package, he said, was increased production in B.C.'s resource sector. It was a cheerful budget, although lacking details, as Hutchison pointed out. Nevertheless, Pattullo leaned on Hart's fiscal management to a large extent when he called an election for June 1937. Increasing revenues, not higher taxes, were helping B.C. climb out of the glue, the Liberal campaign ads stressed. The government won re-election easily, although its margin of seats was trimmed slightly.

The architecture of a provincial budget can be something wondrous to behold. Behind the droning litany of digits and percentages lies an intricate framework that is usually constructed of little more than wishful thinking and wild optimism. This blue-sky material is interspersed with the legitimate accounts, debentures and sinking funds that litter a budget presentation as if it carried equal weight. Some finance ministers coyly overestimate expenses so they can announce a surplus the following year—due, of course, to the government's canny husbanding of the taxpayer's money. Others have simply lied, announcing balanced budgets when they knew their administrations were deeply in the red.

Hart's budgets were more honest than most, although he was occasionally accused of "tossing his statistics about as a juggler tosses rubber balls." The delicate matrix of checks and balances he usually sought, however, was beset by a whole new set of problems brought on by the Second World War. Shortages, rationing, military manpower requirements and the uncertainty surrounding defence expenditures all contributed.

The 1940 budget contained record-breaking disbursements of more than $29 million, along with a sharp rise in revenues. The demand for workers reduced relief costs, he said, and because of the war effort, taxes would not be increased. On the other hand, they wouldn't be decreased, either. The budget, Hart said, was the first truly balanced one since 1925-26. This didn't cut much ice with the press, which generally condemned the expenditures. "Something fundamental must be done to swing provincial authorities away from their placid adherence to the present financial setup," the *Sun* grumbled.

In March of the following year, Hart amended his 1941 budget by announcing a reduction in both income taxes and spending. This "new budget" was widely regarded as a pre-election morsel for the voters. Complicating the picture in 1941 was the growing parochialism of Jack Hart's old friend and colleague, Duff Pattullo. The premier was becoming increasingly obstinate about his "Fight Ottawa" campaign, to the extent that he helped scuttle an important Dominion-provincial conference in 1940 devoted to a new cost-sharing structure. Pattullo's stance was interpreted as a blow to the war effort. As his popularity sank, Hart began to distance himself from his compatriot.

After the election in October, when the Liberals found themselves clinging to power with a minority government, Hart aligned himself with the party faction calling for a coalition with the Conservatives. With the Co-Operative Commonwealth Federation winning fourteen seats and becoming the official opposition, Hart's pragmatic mind could easily deduce the consequences if the two traditional parties did not join together in some fashion.

Pattullo was of the opposite opinion. He regarded Conservatives as the enemy, with a creed so different from Liberalism that the two parties could never be on the same page. At the end of October, he and Hart went to Ottawa to discuss taxation matters with the federal government. Ominously, the two Liberal stalwarts took separate trains, and Hart returned to Victoria a few days before his chief did.

When Pattullo got back on November 8, he recognized that his finance minister was truly in the union camp. "The coalitionists, of which Hart is now

The Coalition government's executive council gets down to work in the cabinet room in 1941. Premier John Hart is at the head of the table. Pat Maitland (inset) was the Conservative leader and attorney-general.

the spearhead, have been doing everything possible to get me out before the House meets," he wrote William Lyon Mackenzie King. "This plotting has been going on for several months...If Hart had been loyal, he would have squelched it himself." On November 17, Hart went public with his coalition sympathies. Pattullo asked for his resignation and got it. He also dismissed other cabinet ministers who held the same views.

Mounting pressure from the caucus led to a convention in Vancouver on December 2. It was a short affair, and by the time the clock struck midnight, John Hart was the new leader of the Liberal party. After a bitter four-hour battle, the delegates endorsed coalition by a vote of 477 to 312, then unanimously chose Hart to replace Pattullo. "[You are] no longer Liberals, you are coalitionists," Pattullo growled as he bowed to the wishes of the party. Presciently, he predicted that coalition would eventually mean suicide for the party.

Hart's acceptance speech was low-key. "I feel this party is in somewhat of a mixup," he said, "especially when you find our good premier and myself separated." Hart claimed he "never aspired" to the office, but "as far as I am concerned, I shall give the best that is in me to rehabilitate and revitalize and rejuvenate the grand old Liberal party." He stressed that the party must be more than "middle of the road" in the future in order to meet changing conditions and needs, particularly regarding social welfare and social security.

Hart's original coalition thrust was to have all three parties represented, but this scenario was scorned by the CCF's Harold Winch. Royal Lethington (Pat) Maitland, the Conservative leader, was amenable but had several conditions. In an exchange of letters with Hart in early December, he stated that coalition "means a division of responsibility," which to him meant equal representation in the cabinet.

"I appreciate the friendly spirit of co-operation evidenced by the meeting of your Conservative caucus," Hart replied, but insisted the split be five to three to reflect the relative strengths of the two parties. "We are starting with a clean sheet," he added, "as rational people..." Hart also emphasized that any B.C. government of the near future must concentrate on prosecuting the war. The early exchanges between Hart and Maitland did not dwell on the need to combat the CCF menace, but that became the prime mission of the Coalition government later on.

Pattullo resigned as premier December 9 and Hart was sworn in the same day by Lt.-Gov. W.C. Woodward. A week later, the new premier named his cabinet. It consisted of five Liberals and three Conservatives. Hart retained his finance portfolio; the attorney-general's post was given to Maitland. A few days later, Hart and Maitland left for Ottawa to discuss new tax-sharing arrangements. This new deal, long opposed by Pattullo, gave B.C. more revenue in return for federal control over income and corporate taxation.

The first legislative session of the Coalition government in January 1942 was, in the words of Bruce Hutchison, "not the old game any more." The jealous guarding of provincial autonomy had been replaced by "sadder and wiser" men whose first priority was to dispense with the business at hand. The assembly quickly endorsed the new tax arrangement. It also created a Post-War Rehabilitation Council, which would lay the groundwork for the future, once the shooting stopped. Another piece of legislation was a controversial bill allowing oil exploration in the Peace River country.

Of more concern to both the legislators and the public, however, was the war in the Pacific. The Hart government had come into being on the same weekend that Pearl Harbor was bombed, and the fall of Hong Kong on Christmas day sent a shock wave up the coast. The traditional anti-Asian sentiment in B.C. was now being fuelled by actual images of Japanese perfidy. Politicians, the press and the guy in the street clamoured for the removal of all "Japs" from the province.

The federal government, after a few feeble attempts at half-measures (Mackenzie King, the Great Ditherer, was prime minister, remember), ordered the evacuation of all Japanese from coastal areas on February 27, 1942. A figure of 23,428 aliens was mentioned. Premier Hart had taken the matter up with King in December, and other B.C. delegations also pressed the Dominion government to do something "about the very disturbing situation in connection with aliens on the Pacific Coast, and more particularly Japanese." Hart found the federal action "gratifying."

Seized Japanese fishboats are tied up near New Westminster in 1942.

The 1943 session of the legislature dealt with 74 bills. Most were of a minor nature. However, important changes strengthening workmen's compensation were passed, as was legislation extending the power and scope of unions as collective bargaining agents. A purchasing commission was established, removing (theoretically) the buying of supplies for government from political influence. Except to note increasing revenues, Hart's budget was unremarkable, as was the one in 1944. In this latter session, several provisions were made to ease the return of veterans. Social security legislation became a priority, with even the Tory dinosaur wing of the Coalition approving (outwardly). The council delving into post-war rehabilitation made its final report, but the lawmakers did little about it, except to set up a bureau.

In February 1945, Hart delivered a major policy speech. In it, he announced a $45 million spending program, most of it for "the immediate post-war period." Details included construction of the Hope-Princeton and Peace River highways, public works, hydro-electric expansion and money for hospitals, universities and schools. Most of this was translated into legislation. One bill established the B.C. Power Commission, which would (with an allocation of $10 million) consolidate several private power systems and generally organize rural electrification of the province.

Hart's performance impressed Bruce Hutchison no end. "You will never get exciting government from John Hart," he wrote in the *Sun*. "He is unexcitable and he is giving us a new brand of quiet, unheroic government which is certainly the most competent and honest we have had within the 25 years of this reporter's intimate experience." Hutch was gratified, as no doubt many were, by the money pouring into B.C.'s current accounts. Wartime spending had boosted the revenue stream considerably, and surpluses became almost commonplace. Although Finance Minister Hart could not take credit for the profits of war, he was canny enough to know what to do with the money and how to manage it properly.

When July rolled around, the premier was ready with some more policy goodies. He presented the Liberal faithful with his re-election formula, which essentially called for his party and the Conservatives to stay out of each other's way. Government candidates would not oppose each other, except in dual ridings, and they would split the task of running against sitting CCF members.

In October, Hart laid out the Coalition manifesto in a pre-election radio speech: reduce taxes, spend $10 million on power development, examine the financial burden on municipalities,

Gordon Wismer's appointment as attorney-general ignited a crisis in the Coalition government.

extend the PGE (he didn't say where), allocate an extra $10 million for roads. On October 25, the Coalition swept the socialists aside, winning 37 of 48 seats. Following the government's re-election, Hart said he would press for completion of the "progressive measures" he had announced in February. "The sweeping victory...can only be interpreted as a complete endorsement of our manifesto," he boasted.

The 1946 session, which opened in February, was a relaxed one. A report on the forest industry, by Chief Justice Gordon Sloan, had been released the previous month. Sloan called for major changes regarding tenure, licensing and administration, but the government did little more than note his recommendations.

On April 4, the outwardly serene façade of the Coalition showed the first signs of distress. Hart appointed Gordon Wismer as attorney-general to replace Maitland, who had died. Because a Liberal was replacing a Conservative in the cabinet, the Tories became upset. They wanted Hart to wait until a convention was held to replace Maitland, but he maintained an A-G was needed immediately because the government couldn't function properly without one. The mood in the House, said observers, was "electric." Hart defused the situation somewhat the following week by surrendering his finance portfolio to Tory Herbert Anscomb.

The 1947 session saw progress made in two key areas. One was in forestry, where legislation was passed adopting the Sloan commission's recommendation about timber management licences. The other was a controversial labour bill mandating (among other provisions) supervised secret ballots before a strike could be called.

Meanwhile, rumours abounded that Hart would renounce more than his finance ministry. Several scenarios were advanced, from an ambassadorship to a seat in the Senate. The premier denied everything until October 2, when he announced that he would be stepping down. "I have been advised to take a much-needed rest and acting upon that counsel, I am therefore recommending that a convention be called early in December so that a leader can be chosen," Hart said.

Three weeks later, the Conservatives held a convention of their own. They unanimously backed Anscomb for the premiership. Anscomb had replaced Maitland as party leader. The Tory initiative was regarded as an ultimatum, moving the Coalition onto even shakier ground.

The Liberals held firm, however. On December 9, Hart said farewell to his party: "I did my level best to do a good job." Byron (Boss) Johnson was chosen leader (and by inference, premier) the next day.

"I shall, before Christmas, take Byron Johnson by the hand and say to the lieutenant-governor, 'Here is the new premier,'" Hart told the delegates. The Tories glowered, but went along with the change in the corner office. On Boxing Day, Johnson called reporters to Anscomb's home to read a joint statement that the Coalition would continue "as it exists at present." Hart resigned December 29 and Johnson was immediately sworn in. He announced that the new administration would be known as the Johnson-Anscomb Coalition Government.

Hart moved to the backbenches. He was asked to become Speaker of the House in 1948 and accepted this honour with grace and pleasure. When the next election came, in 1949, he declined to run, thereby ending his political career. An offer in 1950 to become lieutenant-governor was also turned down because Hart felt he was too old (71) and because his wife was in ill health. He and Harriet spent their remaining years quietly in their home on Gonzales Hill. In 1954, John Hart suffered a stroke, which left him incapacitated. He died April 7, 1957, and was interred in Royal Oak Burial Park.

Byron Ingemar Johnson

(December 29, 1947– August 1, 1952)

The first thing to remember about "Boss" Johnson is that he wasn't really bossy at all. His nickname didn't denote control over a political organization, such as Boss Tweed of Tammany Hall infamy. Rather, it stemmed from a pet name given him by his Icelandic-born parents. The Icelandic "Bjosse" became corrupted to "Boss" by schoolyard chums. Similarly, his given name of Bjorn became anglicized to Byron.

Bjorn Ingemar Johnson was born in Victoria on December 10, 1890, to Oliver and Gudron Finson Johnson, who had emigrated from Reykjavik to B.C. Young Bjosse made his way through the local educational system before entering Victoria High School. There, he prepared himself for a business career by taking a course in commerce. Johnson was also an accomplished athlete. He played several sports, but excelled in lacrosse. Johnson was so proficient in the sport that he turned professional at the age of 22. He was to make $120 a game, but the league folded after only two were played.

In his spare time, Johnson worked in his father's cartage business. During the Great War, he served in the army and the Royal Flying Corps. When peace came, Byron and his brother John bought an old truck in Port Alberni and started their own business. In due course, Johnson Brothers became one of the more successful building supply firms in the province. Byron took time out in 1920 to marry Kate Simpson. They would have one son. In 1934, another company absorbed the Johnson operation and Johnson became a director and general manager of Evans, Coleman and Johnson of New Westminster.

He did not get actively involved in politics until 1933, when he was elected in Victoria City as a Liberal. His presence in the legislature made a favourable impression on the peripatetic Bruce Hutchison, who was back at the *Victoria Times*. He wrote: "Our own 'Boss' is obviously one of the more promising young men heaved up by the last election. Business eagerly appropriates and rapidly advances such young men who could do much in government." In a speech to the House, Johnson stressed the need for a department of trade, which would barter for goods with other nations. "Trade is Mr. Johnson's economic religion," Hutchison suggested.

As Hutchison surmised, Johnson's stay in the legislature was brief. He soon resigned to devote his full attention to his general manager's job. Boss, Kate and Byron Jr. moved to New Westminster. Johnson hopped back to Victoria in 1937 for another run at the legislature, but was defeated. He wouldn't try again until the Second World War was almost over. During that conflict, he contributed to the war effort by supervising the construction of airfields in B.C. Among them was the new base at Patricia Bay, on the Saanich peninsula north of Victoria. The airfields were of particular importance because the RCAF contributed heavily to the British Commonwealth Air Training Plan, which trained recruits from all over the Empire. Johnson was made a Member of the British Empire for his services.

All the while, Boss Johnson was an influential backroom presence in the Liberal party. He played a prominent part from the floor during the 1941 convention that endorsed the coalition movement. In May 1945, he won a byelection in New Westminster occasioned by the death of a Coalition cabinet minister, A. Wellesley Gray. For the next two years, Johnson sat on the backbench, loyally supporting John Hart. On November 17, 1947, he entered the race to succeed the premier.

Although not in the public eye, Johnson had no enemies in the party and was known to be a strong supporter of the Coalition government as well as Liberalism. His opponent, Gordon Wismer, had a high profile as attorney-general and was the favourite to succeed Hart. However, some delegates regarded him as too partisan to work well with the Conservative half of the Coalition. The vote was taken December 10. The next day, a reporter from the *Vancouver Province* described the scene: "There was colour—and there was pathos, too—in the carpeted halls of Hotel Vancouver on Wednesday as the premiership of B.C. was at stake. And when it was over, 'Boss' Johnson, personable, affable, name-remembering businessman, was flushed with excitement as hundreds shook his hand."

Premier Boss Johnson is flanked by Conservative leader
Herbert Anscomb (left) and Highways Minister Ernest Carson
at the opening of the Hope-Princeton Highway on November 2, 1949.

Johnson had won by eight votes, 475 to 467. Kate Johnson admitted later
that she had "butterflies in my knees" as she shook hands with the loser, Wismer.
One of the reasons the delegates took to Johnson was his commitment to keep
the party healthy. "It's time we got down to earth and implemented the things
we have talked about for 25 years," he told the convention. "We have no
organization in B.C. Too long have we turned a deaf ear to young people of the
party." The new premier longed for a Liberal resurrection, but he never really
got it.

For Johnson, Herbert Anscomb and the other members of the Coalition,
1948 was supposed to be another year of business as usual. When the spring
session commenced, the first tiny cloud to appear on the bright horizon was
hardly noticed at the time. This was legislation establishing compulsory hospital
insurance "because of the serious condition of the hospital situation." Despite
getting non-partisan support in the House from the Liberals, Conservatives
and even the CCF, it would become one of the most disliked pieces of legislation
in the history of B.C. And even though it would win another election, the
Coalition crawled into its sick bed the day that bill was passed.

The 1948 session also saw the imposition of B.C.'s first sales tax. Called the
Social Security and Municipal Aid Tax, it slapped a 3 percent levy on a wide
range of goods. Despite several exceptions such as groceries, the *Colonist* grumped
that the tax was so far-reaching it covered "everything from automobiles to
aspirins and from perambulators to penpoints..." Wildly unpopular with the

masses, the tax came into effect July 1. Meanwhile, Health Minister George Pearson was reminding everyone that registration for the hospital insurance scheme was compulsory and the collection of premiums would start in October. The plan would come into effect January 1.

As 1949 would also normally be an election year, Johnson and the boys set out to divert the attention of their disgruntled electorate. At the February legislative session, Johnson announced that the PGE would be extended from Quesnel to Prince George as part of a $90 million, five-year expansion program for the province. Also included was an aluminum plant on the B.C. coast. Some $30 million was allocated to road building, and a highway from Squamish to West Vancouver (where the government owned 3,000 feet of foreshore on Vancouver Harbour) would be built along Howe Sound. (This latter project was delayed for several years.)

The program was "indicative of the tremendous growth taking place in our province," Johnson said. "This growth has been achieved under free enterprise." Six weeks later, legislation was passed empowering the government to make a deal with the Aluminum Company of Canada for the development of a smelter. This was the genesis of Alcan's Kemano project.

The House was then dissolved and an election called for June 15. During the campaign, Tory leader Anscomb delivered an all-out attack on the CCF, linking it directly to the "evil cancer" of communism. When a CCF campaign rally ended with the singing of "The Red Flag," a left-wing marching song, Gordon Wismer said it was evidence of an agreement between the socialists and the ultra-left Labour-Progressive party. The CCF threatened to sue for libel, but didn't.

Meanwhile, Premier Johnson took a higher road. During a radio speech in April he repeated the promises about the PGE and the Squamish highway. He didn't mention hospital insurance, except to promise a "constant review." During a Penticton speech in early June, he observed that "there is a job for anyone who wants to work" in B.C. He said the Liberal-Conservative Coalition made "a swell financial team," and again promised an aluminum plant for B.C.

Once again, it was a resounding victory for the Coalition—39 seats to 7 for the CCF. That the Liberals had elected enough candidates (28) to form a government on their own did not go unnoticed. Anscomb and the Tories began to wonder exactly what end of the Coalition they were attached to. Shortly after, Finance Minister Anscomb, who had embraced the sales tax reluctantly, began dragging those hind feet. He refused suggestions that the tax be increased to help pay for the Hospital Insurance Service plan. That scheme was quickly getting out of control because of increased costs and the reluctance of many citizens to pay their premiums.

In 1950, costs rose even more, until the plan's deficit passed the $6 million mark. Premiums were jacked up, payroll deductions made compulsory and the cabinet given the power to set the rates for hospital care. In a February speech to the legislature, Johnson stressed that "for the first time the hospitals...have been freed from worry and anxiety of whether they can keep their doors open, and...those citizens stricken with illnesses are free from worry and anxiety." Despite the rhetoric, confusion abounded in hospitals as the medical staffs and bureaucrats battled over who was entitled to a bed.

Johnson went to London in the spring of the year in an attempt to drum up more trade. Then in September, he attended a Dominion-provincial conference in Quebec City. At the close of the conference on September 29, Johnson and his wife were driving to Montreal when their vehicle collided head-on with another on the fog-shrouded highway. He suffered a broken hip and other injuries. Mrs. Johnson was also injured. Hospitalized for several weeks in Victoria, Johnson's recovery was slow but satisfactory after returning from Quebec. However, his doctor was compelled to issue a bulletin toward the end of December stating that, contrary to rumours about his deteriorating health, the premier would be leaving hospital shortly.

On January 5, 1951, the premier's office announced a $300 million deal with Alcan for development of the Kemano power and aluminum complex. But when the spring session opened in February, fear and loathing replaced dreams of megaprojects. Insurance premiums were raised even higher, and patients were also required to pay $3.50 a day in "co-insurance" toward their hospital bills. On March 13, Anscomb reported that the hospital plan was $12,750,000 in the hole. Labour unions held strident meetings to denounce the scheme. "Organized labour challenges the government to ask for a vote of confidence from the people in accordance with British parliamentary traditions," one spokesman said.

The press stepped up the pressure with increasingly bitter comments. One editorialist demanded that the cabinet use "some of its huge three-percent sales tax surplus" to meet the funding deficit. After the session ended in April, the *Vancouver Sun* noted that 106 bills were passed, but only a few of them might prove useful. It said the accent throughout the session was on the politicians' negative attitude toward popular feeling, and noted: "When they go out seeking votes, they'll want something better to talk about than higher hospital premiums and co-insurance charges."

The politicians started bailing out. Health Minister Pearson resigned. Backbencher W.A.C. Bennett quit the Coalition to sit as an independent. "I disassociate myself 100 percent from the present cabinet and Coalition government," he told the House. Bennett attacked the cabinet on several fronts

Princess Elizabeth and Prince Philip take leave of the Legislative Buildings in
1951. In attendance are Premier Byron Johnson and a military aide.

but said its tinkering with hospital insurance was the main reason he pulled the
plug.

On April 17, Anscomb called for an end to the Coalition. It was time, he
said, for the party to fight a "free-for-all" election under its own banner.
"Assuming the world is reasonably stable, there will be a straight Conservative
candidate seeking re-election under the transferable vote system in every B.C.
riding," he said in a radio speech.

The transferable vote system was the subject of new legislation bringing in
a new voting method. Provincial Secretary W.T. Straith had opened debate on
the bill a few days earlier by noting that the end of the Coalition government at
the next election was "probable, possible or likely."[1] The change in voting was
touted as insurance against a CCF victory, but like the flawed hospital scheme,
the cure was worse than the disease. Although both Liberals and Conservatives
assumed the exact opposite, their days were numbered.

Anscomb, who never got over the notion that he should have been boss,
became even more arrogant in his attitude toward Johnson. He developed the
habit of taking credit for any gains Johnson had made in negotiations with
Ottawa. The premier seemed unable to curb his finance minister's rudeness. If

he had been a Pattullo or a Bowser or a Hart, the peace-loving premier would have told Anscomb to shut up, but he wasn't that kind of leader. When John Hart and Royal Maitland were in the cabinet, Liberals and Conservatives found it easy to coexist. But Anscomb was no gentleman like Maitland, and Johnson didn't have the icy resolve of Hart. (He even got patronized during a Royal visit in October. When Princess Elizabeth and the Duke of Edinburgh arrived, the "committee of arrangements" gave the premier an almost minute-by-minute guidance schedule so he wouldn't mess up.)

The year 1952 had hardly broken a sweat when a *Sun* headline informed the world at large: "Coalition Government Blows Up." On January 18, Johnson finally demanded Anscomb's resignation because of "a flagrant and arrogant disregard of the procedure of constitutional government." Anscomb's final sin was to announce publicly the details of a tax agreement with Ottawa before discussing it with the cabinet. Johnson told Anscomb to get lost at 10:30 a.m.; by 12:15 p.m., the erstwhile finance minister and three cabinet colleagues quit the Coalition and joined the opposition. They were joined by the seven other Conservatives.

Despite the lack of Conservative support, Johnson still had a province to run. He plugged the cabinet holes with Liberal MLAs and told the House that a fall session was likely because several items of reform legislation were pending. "I feel that the Coalition government...as it is now constituted, has no mandate from the people to carry on since the main partnership has been broken," he declared in February.

In March, Johnson tabled a record-shattering budget that totalled $141,905,433. A surplus of $5 million was expected for the 1951-52 fiscal year, another $32 million was allocated to road building, and there would be no new taxes. In his February speech, Johnson had promised an election "at the earliest possible date" following dissolution. That came on April 10 and Johnson set voting day for June 12.

The ensuing campaign was bizarre. Both the Liberals and the Conservatives treated the triumphs of the late Coalition as their own. Johnson, still feeling the effects of his accident, regaled the province with tales of rising prosperity and government restraint. Anscomb took credit for the booming economy and promised to dump compulsory hospital insurance and reduce taxes. Neither party dwelt upon the report of a board of inquiry into the hospital mess. The commissioners said the lower-paid income groups should have free insurance, that premiums should be trimmed, that co-insurance was needless and injurious, and that the bureaucracy be slashed.

The result of the election was even more peculiar than the campaign. For starters, it took almost a month to count all those transferable ballots. When every preference was finally tallied, the Social Credit League of B.C. had the most seats, with 19. The CCF finished second with 18, but with the most votes cast for it. The Liberals elected only 6 members and the Conservatives, 4. Both Johnson and Anscomb lost their seats.

Ironically, while the votes were still being counted, Johnson announced that the hospital plan had a surplus of $3,165,062.27 for the preceding twelve months. He said it "was fit and proper" that he tell the public the good news before he left office. "It's gratifying to me that our policies have been vindicated by such a satisfactory financial statement," he said.

When the extent of the election debacle became apparent, Johnson was ready to step down and make room for a new premier. It wasn't until August 1, however, that Lt.-Gov. Clarence Wallace accepted his resignation and invited Socred leader W.A.C. Bennett to form a government.

Johnson withdrew from public life. In April 1955, he suffered a cerebral haemorrhage and became a semi-invalid. Byron Ingemar Johnson died January 12, 1964. Premier Bennett and Lt.-Gov. George Pearkes were among the 700 at the funeral three days later. His remains were cremated and the ashes interred at Ross Bay Cemetery.

William Andrew Cecil Bennett

(August 1, 1952–
September 15, 1972)

I
t was a moment of high hoopla and low comedy. There, on the marge of
Lake Okanagan, Premier W.A.C. Bennett awkwardly fitted a flaming arrow
to his bow. Floating just in front of him was a barge full of government
bonds saturated with a "special chemical preparation." They were supposed
to signify British Columbia's debt-free status, and Da Preem had organized a
big party in his home town of Kelowna to celebrate the fact.

The day was August 1, 1959, exactly seven years after "the undisputed
ringmaster of B.C.'s four-ring political circus" had been sworn in as premier. By
some legislative legerdemain earlier in the year, the government had provided
enough assets in its sinking fund to match its bonded debt. Some $70 million
in cancelled bonds had been ostentatiously transported to Kelowna in an
armoured truck. The celebration marking this retirement of B.C.'s direct legal
debt (to be replaced by "contingent liabilities") was, just coincidentally, scheduled
for the anniversary of Bennett's ascension to the corner office.

But before the "bond-fire," there were all the usual trappings of a carnival.
One of the highlights was a swimming race in the lake, with contestants
representing the leaders of the four political parties. The swimmer who was
supposed to be Bennett won—because he was attached to a towrope. As evening
fell, the premier's launch approached the barge, which had its load of bonds,
straw and other combustibles secured by chicken wire. Bennett aimed his flaming
arrow, fired...and missed.

The arrow hit a strand of chicken wire and sizzled out harmlessly in the lake. Fortunately, a lurking RCMP officer had some ignition ready and fired up the bonds. This was the kind of Bennett extravaganza that earned him the label "Wacky." But like the hidden rope attached to the Socred swimmer, there was much more to Bennett than appeared on the surface. And as the Fifties expired in a blaze of glory, "Cece" Bennett hadn't even got warmed up yet. Still to come were the artifacts of his hegemony: the Columbia River treaty, the Two-River Policy, the B.C. Electric takeover, pipelines, dams, ferries and hundreds of miles of blacktop.

The man who grinned delightedly at everything and everyone around him that August day was rapidly approaching his 59th birthday. William Andrew Cecil Bennett was born September 6, 1900, in the hamlet of Hastings, New Brunswick, to Andrew Havelock and Mary Emma Burns Bennett. He was one of five children in the devout Presbyterian household. Young Cecil went to church twice on Sundays and attended Sunday school in between. In 1911, he got his first taste of politics when he was taken to a Conservative rally. This was during the "no truck or trade with the Yankees" election, and Bennett was hooked by the oratory and excitement.

When he was fourteen, the family moved to St. John, where the bustle of the big city was a huge change from a pious life in the country. In high school now, Bennett became interested in commerce as well as politics. He worked on Saturdays for a local hardware store, then quit school and accepted a full-time job before he was seventeen. Bennett kept the books and accounts as he slowly learned the financial side of the hardware business.

When the Great War was winding down in 1918, Bennett became old enough to enlist and promptly joined the Royal Flying Corps. However, he was never called to duty and spent the remainder of his short military "career" at home in St. John, studying higher mathematics. In 1919, Bennett and his father went west. Andrew started farming in the Peace River country, but the younger Bennett gravitated to Edmonton. He secured a position with Marshall-Wells Ltd., a wholesale hardware firm, and continued his education by way of correspondence courses.

Bennett lived in a rooming house kept by Arthur Meighen's sister, and the future prime minister's visits sharpened the appetite for politics that had been whetted back in St. John. Meanwhile, religion had never strayed far from Cece's mind. He became involved in church affairs and joined the Tuxis movement. This organization was a staple of Christianity on the Prairies in the Twenties and Thirties, as was the Tuxis Parliament, a mock legislative body for youngsters. Bennett loved the boys' parliament and was heavily involved until he reached the cutoff age of 21.

During this impressionable period, Bennett also came under the influence of Orison Swett Marden, a noted American author who had published several books on the theme of success. His message was positive thinking, larded with maxims that were ready-made for a budding politician. Two of them were: "The world makes way for a determined man" and "Seize common occasions and make them great."

Later in the Twenties, Bennett seized the initiative in three important facets of his life. First, his commitment to religion made him seriously consider joining the clergy. But after much thought, he rejected the collar in favour of a secular career. This decision led to his second major step—going into business for himself. And thirdly, Bennett fell in love and decided to get married.

Early in 1927, Bennett and a partner acquired a hardware store in Westlock, 50 miles north of Edmonton. The partner put up most of the money while Bennett supplied the expertise. With that step taken, Bennett married Annie Elizabeth May Richards on June 11, 1927. He and May would have three children. In June 1930, Bennett sold out, and he and May bravely motored off to British Columbia. They went to Victoria to visit May's aunt, but a restless Cece was soon on the mainland scouting for opportunities. He found the ideal business, a hardware store, for sale in the Okanagan Valley community of Kelowna and bought it.

It seemed a curious time to get back in the hardware game, with the effects of the Great Depression already being felt. But the business was large and established, and Bennett didn't lack confidence in himself. So he survived, although "every day was not sunshine in business." Shortly after establishing Bennett's Hardware, W.A.C. became involved in the wine business. Pasquale (Cap) Capozzi was struggling to establish a winery and needed additional capital. Bennett, the non-smoking teetotaller, was one of those who bought in. The Capozzi venture would become Calona Wines Ltd., and Bennett was made president in 1936. (He severed his relationship and sold his shares when he was elected to the legislature in 1941.)

Despite struggling to make ends meet at the store, Bennett somehow found time to indulge his other passion: politics. "I only went into business in order to acquire enough money to go into politics," he said in a 1962 interview. "Politics is the most important thing in any country." A long-standing Conservative, Bennett sought the nomination for the South Okanagan riding in 1937, but lost out. He was more successful in 1941 and then went on to win the South Okanagan seat.

Bennett's chamber-of-commerce smile quickly became a recognizable feature around Victoria. More than one reporter wrote about the "exuberant young businessman from Kelowna." Although he had deep Tory roots, Bennett was a

Coalitionist and claimed later that he was offered a cabinet seat in the first Coalition government. This appears to be a case of convenient remembrance, because the Conservatives only had three seats in the cabinet and the talent available was somewhat more experienced than the green MLA from the Okanagan.

In any event, Bennett's main contribution to that first session was a spot on the Post-War Rehabilitation Council. Its mandate was to forge a blueprint for B.C. to follow in future years. Although the council did not feel called upon to "adopt any particular hypothesis or prognostication about the character of the next peace," it nevertheless explored the subject thoroughly. The interim report was released in 1943 and a final one the following year. Among the many recommendations were creation of a steel industry, northward extension of the Pacific Great Eastern, provincial park development, public ownership of the hydro-electric authority and further development in forestry and mining.

The report fell with a mild thud on the government's front benches. Nothing much would be done, but W.A.C. Bennett did not forget the council or the good points it raised. Still a stout supporter of the administration as late as 1945, Bennett's "face came near to splitting ear to ear with pleasure" when Attorney-General Pat Maitland extolled the benefits of Coalition during a debate in the legislature.

Within a short time, though, the Happy Coalitionist became increasingly disenchanted with the structure of the government. After Maitland died in March 1946, Bennett made a run for the Conservative leadership but lost badly to Herbert Anscomb. He resorted to attacking the Coalition during the 1947 session, then resigned his seat to run in a federal byelection for the Yale riding. He again lost badly. Later in the year, he tried to run in the general election but couldn't get nominated.

This sloppy, ill-fated excursion into federal politics appears to be the product of an unfocused mind, for Bennett briefly was making a hash of his decision-making process. But in the provincial election of June 15, 1949, he got back on track by getting re-elected in his old riding of South Okanagan.

With Anscomb and Premier Byron Johnson glowering, Bennett once again flayed the Coalition during the 1950 session. In a 90-minute harangue to the House, his "whole-hearted attack" included the demand that the single transferable ballot be instituted for the next election as a way to give Liberal and Conservative candidates an identity with the electorate.

Later in the year, Bennett claimed the Coalition had "slipped more in the last 15 months than in the previous nine years." Furthermore, "if some of our people hadn't been quite so stupid (in the early years of the Coalition)," the Conservatives would have had the premiership by now. Bennett made another grab at Anscomb's leadership, but was again routed by convention delegates. After this second rejection, Bennett prowled the Coalition backbenches until he finally pulled the plug. On March 15, 1951, Bennett informed Speaker Nancy Hodges that "I now disassociate myself from the present cabinet and the Coalition government..." He would, he said, sit as an independent. Three months later, Bennett admitted in Kelowna that he was considering a "people's party based on genuine free enterprise." Although he floated some possible names for this new party, he was in fact thinking hard about Social Credit. On December 6, Bennett announced that he had quit the Conservative party to "join the Social Credit movement."

Social Credit began as an economic theory, developed in the Twenties by Major C.H. Douglas, a Scottish engineer. He reasoned that, because the purchasing power of the consumer never matched the production power of industry, an interim step was needed. He suggested that governments set a "Just Price" on goods and issue new money to reimburse retailers who suffered losses. He also advocated a "National Dividend" to bridge the difference between prices and purchasing power.

His theory acquired a certain cachet in monetary circles (although it was basically unworkable) and was seized upon by "Bible Bill" Aberhart, a podium-thumping cross between a politician and fundamentalist preacher in Alberta. During the Depression Thirties, any pitch that claimed it could end the desperate years was welcomed with sunburned arms. Aberhart added some religious touches and rode Social Credit to an astonishing victory in the 1935 provincial election.

By the Fifties, the "funny money" aspect of Social Credit had disappeared, as had much of the evangelical overtone. When embraced by Bennett, it had become a middle-class, free-enterprise alternative to the traditional brand of power politics in Canada. Nevertheless, Bennett's decision was roundly ridiculed. The basic question asked, between giggles, was: Has the man gone mad? Even within the Social Credit League, the reaction was mixed. There were more than a few who regarded him as an opportunist who had parachuted into their ranks.

Bennett was exactly that. His conversion was classic Orison Swett Marden doctrine: grab the golden ring. And he was definitely not mad. A little desperate, perhaps, with his links to the old-time parties severed for good. It could be reasoned that his future was even more empty without Social Credit, so there was no harm in giving it a stab.

To employ a cliché that exactly defines the situation, the election of 1952 was a watershed in B.C. politics. On April 18, 1951, the legislature had approved an amendment to the Election Act providing for the single transferable ballot. Bennett had got his wish, although the outcome was far removed from what he or anyone else had foreseen. Proponents of alternative voting expected the method

W.A.C. Bennett envisions a future for B.C. that is as rosy as these Okanagan apples.

to give voters a sure-fire one-two choice between the Liberals and Conservatives, giving one of the parties enough ballots to control the government.

Social Credit was such a dark horse that hardly anyone noticed it was even in the race. During the 1952 campaign, the coverage of Social Credit in the mainstream press was either perfunctory or negative. In retrospect, only the voters seemed to be paying attention. The newspapers' reluctance to take this strange new political animal seriously was understandable, given the disjointed structure of the B.C. version.

At the league's convention in New Westminster that April, this curious movement got even curiouser. It decided not to elect a party leader, but rather a "campaign leader." Bennett was nominated, but declined after pledging his support "hook, line and sinker." He would bide his time while the task of guiding the Socreds temporarily fell to Rev. Ernest G. Hansell, an Alberta MP who had been seconded to B.C. to help the new folks get their act in gear.

The Social Credit campaign was low-key. While the other parties rushed about, denigrating each other (and the Socreds), Hansell pottered along, emphasizing the movement's main points. These were: free enterprise and individual incentive; government integrity; development of natural resources; and the "elimination of compulsion." Hansell called this compulsion the reversal of democracy, stressing that governments should not impose their will on the people. Meanwhile, Bennett stuck to attacking the "Johnson-Anscomb-Wismer crowd" and concentrating on his receptive audience in the hinterlands. At one Social Credit meeting, he was described as "a sheep among wolves." Some sheep, some wolves.

Lt.-Gov. Clarence Wallace (left) and Premier W.A.C. Bennett
attend the opening of the legislature in 1953.

Attorney-General Gordon Wismer had called for a "one-two vote for free enterprise" (meaning Liberals first, then the Tories), but after the agonizing suspense of counting the ballots was over, the party of Hansell and Bennett had nineteen seats to eighteen for the socialists, although the CCF led in the popular vote.

While the votes were still being tallied, the Socreds met again in Vancouver on July 15 and picked Bennett as their permanent leader. It took just one ballot. The *Sun* promptly anointed Bennett "premier-elect," not bothering to wait for Lt.-Gov. Clarence Wallace to swear him in. And Wallace did not make his choice right away. He dithered for a spell between CCF leader Harold Winch's claim of the most votes and the Socreds' undeniable nineteen seats. But Wallace, a wealthy industrialist who had been appointed on the advice of a Liberal prime minister, definitely leaned rightward rather than leftward. Finally, after seeking advice from several quarters (and getting conflicting opinions), he invited Bennett to Government House on August 1.

Just five weeks before his 52nd birthday, W.A.C. Bennett was premier of British Columbia. An admiring *Sun* reporter noted later that evening that Bennett's "thick shock of hair is well-silvered but his cheeks are rosy, his eyes bright and his manner quick and alert." He also wrote that the new premier hid

The province's first Social Credit cabinet meets in 1952.
Premier W.A.C. Bennett is at the head of the table.

the "budding paunch" on his five-foot-nine, 190-pound frame with a well-tailored suit.

Bennett's first order of business was the structure of his cabinet. Only he and Tilly Rolston among the Socred caucus had legislative experience. The rest of the cabinet were raw rookies, from a talent pool that was probably as thin as any available to a new premier. Bennett even had to go outside the House to fill two key slots. He gave the post of attorney-general to Robert Bonner, a bright young lawyer, and the finance portfolio to Einar Gunderson, a respected chartered accountant. In this first cabinet, Bennett also made a big mistake in assessing character. He made Robert Sommers, a school principal from the West Kootenays, the minister of lands, forests and mines.

During the months before the first session of the House, Bennett and Gunderson (who officially became an MLA along with Bonner via two November byelections) struggled with the budget left behind by Johnson and the Coalition. Bennett decreed there would be no new borrowing and started trimming the fat. He also fulfilled a campaign promise by reducing hospital insurance premiums and grabbed a photo op when the first PGE train rolled into Prince George on November 1. But while he busied himself with all these tasks, the new premier never lost sight of his next major coup: a majority government.

When the House sat in February 1953, Bennett struck by getting Education Minister Rolston to introduce controversial amendments to the Public Schools

Act. This bill radically restructured education financing in favour of rural schools over urban ones. It was a red flag waved in front of a frustrated, snorting herd of opposition members. At 11:25 p.m. on March 24, the bill was defeated on second reading, 28-17. Just as Bennett had choreographed it, the government had fallen.

Although Winch and the CCF sought leave from Wallace to form a new administration, the Liberals refused to support them and the vice-regal representative was having none of it anyway. After the legislature passed a caretaker budget that included an interim supply bill and education grants, Wallace dissolved the House and the election was called for June 9.

The result was precisely what Bennett had manoeuvred to obtain. After every ballot choice had been transferred and counted, Social Credit (no longer listing itself as a league) had 28 seats and a clear working majority in the 48-seat House.[1] During a brief session later in the year, the Bennett government promptly legislated the alternative voting system out of existence and returned to the good old frontrunner-friendly plurality method. The only other significant piece of legislation passed was a new Liquor Act, which swept away generations of archaic booze regulations.

In the years ahead, Bennett would become an election junkie. With one exception (1960), he took his government's record to the people every three years. But as the 1954 session unfolded, the present was more on his mind than the future. Shortly after the election, Bennett had announced "a firm resolve to get on with the business of the province." So he did. The 1954 budget was the biggest in B.C.'s history—$204 million. Hospital insurance premiums were abolished and the sales tax was boosted to 5 percent to pay for the plan. Although business and labour objected (along with the press), the public's response to the elimination of premiums was gratifying. (Most people obviously hadn't figured out that the extra tax was a premium in another form.)

Bennett presented the budget. He had assumed the finance portfolio after Gunderson failed to win a seat in the general election and a subsequent byelection arranged for him by the premier. Bennett was the best man for the job anyway. It is doubtful any other minister could have kept up with his singular approach to fiscal matters. On March 19, the budget was passed without a single dissenting vote. The same would not hold true for a contentious Labour Act passed at the same session. It gave the labour minister sweeping powers in the field of labour disputes as well as tightening controls on union checkoffs, certification and strikes.

The loss of Bennett's good friend Gunderson was a minor irritant compared with two major embarrassments to come. One was the Robert Sommers affair. In February 1955, Liberal MLA Gordon Gibson, the tough-talking "Bull of the Woods," told the legislature that "money talks" in the issuance of forest

Pushing the line north from Prince George in the winter of 1956-57, Pacific Great Eastern construction workers struggle with harsh winter conditions.

management licences. The imputation was that Sommers, the forests minister, was on the take.

Sommers, a nobody from the Rossland-Trail riding, had problems with drinking and gambling, which, it transpired, led to his involvement with a small-time logging operator named H. Wilson Gray. It took Bennett a long time to accept that his judgment of Sommers was wrong. But the evidence presented by Charles Eversfield, Gray's bookkeeper, was so compelling that Bennett finally had to ask for Sommers' resignation.

In his farewell speech to the legislature in February 1956, a bitter Sommers dwelt upon "the most dirty and slanted news coverage in the history of B.C., conducted principally by Mr. Stuart Keate, publisher of the *Victoria Daily Times*." He claimed the charge against him was "as phoney as the man [Eversfield] who makes it," but on November 21, 1957, Sommers was charged with conspiracy and accepting bribes. Another year went by before he was convicted and sentenced to five years in prison. Sommers was the first minister of the Crown in the history of the British Empire to serve time for bribery.

Amidst all this, Bennett called an election for September 19, 1956. Although it may have been regarded as a referendum on the honesty of Bennett's government, it also served as a showcase for the progress being made under Social Credit. The PGE had added some more track, the new Toll Highways and Bridges Authority was throwing up spans all over the place and there was lots and lots of new blacktop. Phil Gaglardi, the highways minister appointed in 1955, appeared intent on paving every square inch of rural British Columbia.

His announcement of a tunnel under the Fraser River didn't hurt either, nor did Bennett's homeowners' grant, which was set at $28 to offset a portion of a family's property taxes. Despite being dismissed by the *Sun* as a "political poultice," it would become one of Bennett's most popular legacies. With all these goodies to ponder, the electorate returned the Socreds to power with 39 seats in the expanded 52-seat legislature.

The Social Credit movement never seemed quite so innocent after the Sommers furore. Even though Bennett was not personally tarnished, it became clear to many that his party was as capable of producing dishonesty as the next one. Bennett might have deflected much of the opprobrium by confronting Sommers the moment the accusations were made. Instead, he stalled and dissembled out of some stubborn sense of loyalty to a minister he had personally accepted as honest.

While this case was still simmering nicely in the press, the premier sprang Axel Wenner-Gren on an unsuspecting British Columbia. On February 12, 1957, he announced to the House that Wenner-Gren, a wandering millionaire gadfly with a truly shady past, was going to develop the Rocky Mountain Trench in northeastern B.C. as part of a billion-dollar development scheme.

Revelations in the papers about the Swedish industrialist's shadowy career, including his possible Nazi leanings, ignited a public storm that forced Bennett to back off in embarrassment. The premier's dream of sharing development of the north with private industry faded away and the Rocky Mountain Trench slumbered on.

In March 1959, the government passed the Trade Unions Act. Described as the "toughest labour laws in Canada," the new legislation sharply curtailed picketing and further restricted other union activities. Union reaction was predictably negative. "When you have growth, you have growing pains," Bennett later told a Vancouver audience. "What we need in labour relations is a reasonable attitude, a willingness to bargain in good faith, so that we can buckle down without interruption to the business of building British Columbia." The unions, of course, were not as sanguine as the premier.

But enough of this negativity and confrontation. A mere seven years earlier, when Social Credit took over, B.C. was mired in debt. Now, by the diligent application of sound economic policies and mushrooming revenues from resource development, the province was in a position to retire its direct legal debt. Bennett got a declaration from a compliant comptroller-general to that effect and threw his August bond-burning party on the Kelowna waterfront.

In actuality, there were two sets of books. While the direct debt had been paid off, the indirect debt was still there and growing. Crown corporations and public agencies were responsible for their own borrowings. This method of separating "contingent liabilities" from the daily financing of government activities has, by now, been widely accepted and copied by other jurisdictions.

"Frankly, the Premier's theatrical pyrotechnics leave me cold."

The Sixties were the years of breathtaking progress in British Columbia. Or, for those with strong opinions about the environment, the years of rapine and pillage. Hydro-electric power was a big component of Bennett's blueprint for the future. Without dams generating enough juice to run the industries of the Pacific Northwest, there could be no progress. For some time, the Peace had been on the premier's mind. The Wenner-Gren pipe dream of a few years back had shone a spotlight on the Peace River canyon and what a dandy spot it was for a dam. At the other end of the province, the Columbia River had long been the subject of Canada-U.S. discussion regarding dams for electricity generation and flood control.

Out of these muscular watercourses came Bennett's "Two-River Policy." It was simple enough: The rivers would be developed simultaneously; exploitation of the Peace by B.C. would be a lever forcing the senior governments to reach a deal on the Columbia that was acceptable to Bennett; a cash payment for downstream rights would help pay the costs of the Peace project.

Although Ottawa and Washington were in the final stages of a deal authorizing joint development of the Columbia, Bennett remained adamant that B.C. should retain control of its own resources. The initial agreement on the Columbia River Treaty was signed January 17, 1961. Bennett didn't climb aboard. Eventually, he got his own way through a hard-bitten combination of haggling, threat and bluff. Meanwhile, there was one little loose end.

Teetotalling W.A.C. Bennett (standing second from the right) braves
the porch of a Barkerville saloon to do some schmoozing.

B.C. Electric had long been opposed to government meddling along the
Peace, regarding the supply of power as its exclusive prerogative. On August 1,
1961, Bennett convened a special session of the legislature and introduced a bill
called the Power Development Act, 1961. It transformed B.C. Electric into a
Crown corporation, at a cost to the taxpayer that would eventually reach $197
million. Canada's largest remaining privately owned power company had just
been expropriated and replaced by something called the B.C. Hydro and Power
Authority. The *Sun* was so taken by this display of CCF-style socialism by the
free-enterprise Socreds that it published a late-afternoon "Extra" edition to report
the startling news.

The revised Columbia River Treaty was signed January 22, 1964. Under its
terms, B.C. would receive a cash payment and in return was committed to

Beaming with delight, Premier
W.A.C. Bennett rides in the cab of
an earth mover as he dedicates the
Bennett Dam on the Peace River in 1967.

build three storage dams to control the flow of the Columbia. The Americans
got to keep all the downstream power U.S. plants could produce for the next 30
years. On September 16, Bennett, Prime Minister Lester Pearson and U.S.
President Lyndon Johnson participated in a brief, largely symbolic ceremony at
the Peace Arch on the B.C.-Washington border.

As heavy rain turned the seaside Peace Arch park into a glum landscape,
they each signed "an agreement of accord." The actual payment to B.C. had
been made earlier in the day at a downtown Vancouver bank. A cheque for
$273,291,661.24 from the Government of Canada payable to the Government
of British Columbia was deposited in the Canadian Imperial Bank of Commerce.
The U.S. had paid Canada in U.S. funds, and the Bank of Canada had added a
premium of nearly $20 million in converting it to Canadian funds.

There would eventually be four dams in B.C. relating to the treaty. Bennett
opened the first one, the Duncan Dam, in August of 1967; a few weeks later, on

September 12, he did the same at the W.A.C. Bennett Dam on the Peace by briefly operating a machine carrying the last load of earthen fill.

Years of hindsight have led observers to conclude that Bennett let the Americans off far too cheaply. They are quite probably right, but in the Sixties the $274 million figure, which included later flood-control benefits, was the rather imposing end product of several years of intense political negotiations. That one country was selling its "birthright" (water) to another also generated international attention and some degree of criticism.

While he was arm-wrestling with the big guys on both sides of the border, Bennett also had a province to run. There was more to life than earthmoving and brinkmanship, obviously. The premier went to the voters four times—in 1960, '63, '66 and '69—and received the required mandate each time. There were a few racing pulses in 1960, when the CCF made good gains, but not enough to worry the Socreds. Bennett's approach to the opposition in the House was to "let them talk...sooner or later the division bells will ring [meaning a vote will be taken] and the problem will be over." So far, there was no problem with the electorate.

In October 1961, the cabinet authorized the purchase of the Black Ball ferry line for $6,795,467. It was a key investment that laid the groundwork for the extensive B.C. Ferries system—as vital a transportation link in seagirt British Columbia as any collection of bridges and highways. Another goal of Bennett's was the Bank of British Columbia. His somewhat radical proposal was for a provincial bank with 25 percent of the shares held by his government. The idea got a rough ride from the Senate banking committee (banks are federally chartered), and when the enabling legislation was passed in the Commons in December 1966, the key 25 percent provision was absent. (The bank failed in 1986 and its assets were acquired by the Hongkong Bank of Canada.)

On the health front, the B.C. legislature passed a bill on March 19, 1965, which provided government assistance to low-income persons paying monthly medical premiums. The B.C. Medical Plan was a forerunner to federal legislation passed in December 1966. Under it, Ottawa promised to pay approximately half the costs of provincially organized and operated medicare plans. On the effective date of the federal plan, July 1, 1968, B.C. and Saskatchewan were the first two provinces to participate.

About this time, *Time* magazine discovered W.A.C. Bennett. His enigmatic visage graced the cover of its international edition following the 1966 election. Inside, the magazine gushed about Bennett as the linchpin of "machine-tooled pioneering" evident in Western Canada. It called him a full-time politician and part-time prophet who was responsible for "Bennett's Boom." The premier, who was embarking on a trip to Europe to do some schmoozing with the continental set, tried to appear humble.

Bennett's façade of determined joviality did sprout a few blemishes, despite all the gung-ho adjectives and backslapping. One of them involved "Flying Phil" Gaglardi, who got the nickname because of his speeding tickets and his habit of jetting around B.C. in government planes. Gaglardi was getting roasted by the opposition over alleged patronage and misuse of highways department resources when it was revealed that his daughter-in-law had used a government jet to fly to Dallas. Gaglardi resigned as highways minister March 21, 1968, not because of the casual use of the jet but because he had fudged when Bennett asked him point-blank who was aboard. He was the second minister, after Sommers, who had violated the premier's trust.

Nevertheless, the Sixties concluded with a landslide at the polls. "The people of British Columbia have stopped the socialists in their tracks," Bennett crowed after the 38-seat victory. "This one is sweeter than them all."

With the 1969 election safely in the books, Bennett seemed as entrenched as ever in the minds of the voters. The new industries, flourishing resource sector and all the dams, bridges and highways were, if you'll pardon the expression, concrete examples of what the Post-War Rehabilitation Council was talking about back in the Forties. On the home front in Kelowna, May ran the family's sprawling house while W.A.C. tended to business in Victoria, Ottawa, or elsewhere. Their two sons, Bill and R.J., were in charge of Bennett's Hardware, which by 1970 had expanded into a chain of stores.

Bennett's alleged wackiness generated more headlines at a constitutional conference in Ottawa in 1969. While the press, the other premiers and Prime Minister Pierre Trudeau gaped in surprise, he unveiled his five-region map of Canada. Boundaries of the existing provinces, he said, should be altered "so as to provide five viable and effective political units consonant and in conformity with the five economic regions of Canada."

Bennett's proposal made a whole lot of sense, given the geographical diversity of Canada, and he was serious about it. Naturally, after the headlines and the head-shaking subsided, nothing happened. Political events of the Nineties, however, indicated that the premier was ahead of his time. Quebec's hand-wringing about separation had the rest of the country talking about regional concerns and priorities.

Quebec demonstrated its pathological intransigence toward the idea of Canada in 1971, when the next conference was held in Victoria. The gathering was part of B.C.'s centennial as a province, but Premier Robert Bourassa was not in a festive mood. He promptly torpedoed the Victoria Charter, which was supposed to settle Quebec's status once and for all.

Bennett, however, had more serious concerns crowding his plate. A century after union with Canada, B.C.'s mood was neither constitutional nor sociable. Rising unemployment, inflation and Bennett's stiff-necked approach to unionism contributed to a January 21 confrontation at the legislature. Jeering demonstrators, organized by the B.C. Federation of Labour and the New Democratic Party (formerly the CCF), invaded the assembly on the opening day of the session and drowned out the proceedings with curses and catcalls. Smiling bravely through his stiff upper lip, the premier tried to ignore the sinking feeling that his love affair with the masses was coming to an end.

In 1972 (on Bennett's timetable, an election year), he tabled a staggering budget of $1.4 billion and prattled on about building "the finer things in British Columbia." After the session, he and his cabinet embarked on a hokey ramble throughout the province. It was a huge mistake. While it gave the government a chance to massage the locals and dispense goodies, the tour also served as an easy target for demonstrators.

The ugly climax came outside a New Westminster hotel on June 8. An angry mob of 500 flailing unionists attacked the cabinet upon its arrival, and several ministers suffered cuts, bruises and at least one broken bone. Bennett called it a "black day for labour" and its NDP co-conspirators. Pressing ever onward, he called an election for August 30.

Wacky Bennett was getting tired. After all, he was 71 going on 72. The easy affability and control of any situation had been replaced by a certain degree of crankiness. Dave Barrett, the bouncing new leader of the NDP, demonstrated the vitality that once belonged to Bennett. The Social Credit cabinet was getting old and tired, too. There never had been many bright sparks in it. Bennett was a one-man band, and with the exception of Bonner and a few others throughout the years, his cohorts were unremarkable.

The result was a fluke election victory for the NDP. The socialists had finally stormed the gates, electing 38 MLAs in the 55-seat House. After two decades, Bennett's deft combination of lofty enterprise and man-in-the-street savvy had succumbed to the decay of age. He resigned as premier on September 15, 1972, and briefly played his part as opposition leader before resigning as the member for the South Okanagan on June 5, 1973. In the ensuing byelection, his son Bill Bennett won the seat, then became party leader.

Bennett the elder now became an ambassador and organizer for the party. He was still loved in many parts of the hinterland, and he used this to help build up the party membership. In the words of Dan Campbell, a former MLA, Bennett always "saw the world in terms of blowing walls down." Now he had to help reconstruct the party's edifice. Largely through the efforts of Grace

McCarthy, a tireless Socred veteran who had been a cabinet minister for many years, there were 75,000 members on the rolls for the next election.

Cecil and May Bennett, two distinguished senior citizens, watched with pride as their son became premier of B.C. in 1975. Then Bennett slipped easily into the persona of elder statesman. He kept a finger in both party and provincial affairs, but also played a little gin rummy and enjoyed the time he spent with May and the grandchildren. He suffered a heart attack in 1976, but had recovered nicely when stricken by viral pneumonia in 1978. The old battler hung on for almost a year before the ravages of age caught up with him.

William Andrew Cecil Bennett died of heart failure at 10:30 p.m. on February 23, 1979, in Kelowna General Hospital. Tributes poured in from around the world. His son, Premier Bill Bennett, summed up his contribution to B.C.: "He took his vision and he took his knowledge, and he had the nerve that it took to make things happen."

Funeral services were held simultaneously in Victoria, Vancouver and Kelowna. Ed Schreyer, the Governor General of Canada, was among the host of dignitaries and lesser folk at the Victoria services. In Kelowna, the Old Man's coffin was draped with the provincial flag he had introduced.

David
Barrett

(September 15, 1972–
December 22, 1975)

They called him the Little Fat Guy. To the notoriously irreverent found-ins at the legislative press gallery, the blossoming rotundity of Dave Barrett, first as opposition leader, then as premier, was a phenomenon not to be ignored.

Social worker, social drinker and a socialist in a hurry, Barrett was the exact opposite of W.A.C. Bennett, his predecessor in the corner office. In stature, demeanour and competence, the gallery was quick to note, this first minister couldn't hold a candle to the previous one. He would also fail miserably to match his predecessor's longevity.

The guy many legislative reporters treated so cavalierly grew up as a working kid in a working-class neighbourhood. David Barrett was born October 2, 1930, in East Vancouver to Samuel and Rose Hyatt Barrett, whose Jewish marriage was arranged and loveless. Nevertheless, David was one of three children. His father peddled fruit and vegetables. First, Sam sold them off the back of a truck, then from a store he purchased on Powell Street. Growing up, young Dave helped his father hawk his produce every Saturday. He also squeezed in a part-time job in the mail room of the *Vancouver Sun* while attending Britannia High School. It was at the East End school that wee Dave fell in with the rugby crowd. His devotion to the game during his political years led to the inevitable press coverage of the premier kicking a ball.

After graduating, Barrett enrolled in Seattle University, where he earned a degree in sociology in 1953. On October 16 of that year, Dave Barrett married Shirley Hackman, whom he had met two years earlier while home on a visit. They would have three children. After university, Barrett went to work for the Children's Aid Society in Vancouver before joining the young offenders' unit at Oakalla prison as a program officer. Accepted by St. Louis University in Missouri, he graduated with a master's degree in social work in 1956. After a year working as a probation officer in the St. Louis juvenile court system, he and Shirley returned to Vancouver.

Dave went to work at the Haney Correctional Institute, joined the CCF and went after a nomination as an MLA so that he could work politically to improve the flawed correctional system. Because Barrett was a civil servant attacking the status quo, his bosses were not pleased. In July 1959, he was fired for "being actively engaged in politics." On October 16—the Barretts' sixth wedding anniversary—he won the CCF nomination for Dewdney on the first ballot.

When polling day came on September 12, 1960, the rookie CCF candidate defeated the Social Credit incumbent, Labour Minister Lyle Wicks, 12,637 to 10,713. This was the election that saw the socialists seat sixteen MLAs in the House, trimming the Socred majority substantially and throwing a brief scare into the Bennett government.

During the Sixties, the CCF was a party in transition. First of all, it changed its name in 1961 to the New Democratic Party. The leader was Robert Strachan, who had held the position since 1954. When Barrett joined the caucus, it contained such left-wing stalwarts as Alex Macdonald, Gordon Dowding and Leo Nimsick.

While the rookie from Dewdney kept a low profile, the party lost some ground in the 1963 election, then rebounded slightly in 1966. Barrett ran and won in Coquitlam after his old riding was carved up by redistribution. A veteran member by now, he welcomed two promising newcomers to the NDP benches: Tom Berger and Bob Williams. The party that would eventually form the government of B.C. was beginning to take shape.

Strachan retired in 1968. The tussle for the leadership was a messy three-way affair between Barrett, Berger and Williams. Berger won on the second ballot, and Barrett found himself shut out of the inner circle. He contemplated quitting politics to concentrate on a doctorate in sociology. However, Berger fared badly in the 1969 election (even losing his own seat), while Barrett piled up an impressive majority in Coquitlam. Berger, one of the fastest fading blooms in the history of B.C. politics, promptly resigned. Barrett was made interim leader, then was endorsed in the position on a permanent basis at a party convention in Chilliwack in June 1970.

Dave Barrett and Bob Williams (left) lost out to Tom Berger (right)
in the 1968 NDP leadership race.

Up to this time, the former social worker had been a lightweight opposition performer, buzzing around the Social Credit cabinet ministers like a bumblebee trying to find a juicy landing place. Now, with the added weight of leadership, his in-your-face style gained more credence. At 1:10 a.m. on March 4, 1971, he was escorted from the legislature after asking the same question—about compensation for the widow of an accident victim—67 times. The media loved it. They reported that it was the first time in the history of the Commonwealth that an opposition leader had been ejected.

The Little Fat Guy kept his name in the papers by suing Bennett for libel and slander over a remark the premier made after 500 unionists attacked the Socred cabinet outside a New Westminster hotel in 1972. Bennett blamed the ugly incident on collusion between the unions and Barrett. The suit was quietly dropped after an election was called later in the year.

The campaign waged during the summer of '72 was one election too many for Wacky Bennett. He appeared tired, negative and defensive, while Barrett bounced around the province, bubbling over about hope and new beginnings. The NDP slogan, "Enough is Enough," struck a chord with the electorate. It had been dreamed up in March when Barrett and a few leftist cronies were sitting around, trying to come up with a strategy that would bring them in from the cold.

Barrett used the catchy phrase as the cornerstone of his campaign. The result was 38 of 55 seats won by the NDP on August 30—a sweep that the

Victoria Times called "brutal" and "stunning." The voters had indeed decided enough was enough—for the present. Wacky was in no hurry to hand the keys of the counting house to the socialist horde, however. He waited two weeks before resigning on September 15.

Before Barrett was sworn in as premier the same day, Bennett made sure the public knew the state of B.C.'s finances. He reported at a press conference that current reserves were $574.8 million and that the fixed, paid-for assets totalled $1.42 billion. Bennett also reminded everyone that B.C.'s net debt was $224.5 million when his Socreds took over, with assets of only $188.7 million.

Barrett immediately started tinkering with that legacy. He convened a short, sharp legislative session in mid-October and started spending money. In eleven days, the House passed thirteen pieces of legislation. These included a bill guaranteeing $200 a month for the elderly and handicapped (passed with the hope that Ottawa would pick up some of the tab).

The first NDP cabinet was smaller and younger than Bennett's. There were a number of double portfolios, because Barrett would only select experienced MLAs. The ministers had diverse occupations ranging from lawyer to storekeeper. "For the working man...this government looks like it was made in heaven," rhapsodized the *Edmonton Journal,* somewhat inaccurately. Although the B.C. Government Employees Union promised to help the fledgling cabinet get on its feet, the unionized working stiffs were never totally comfortable with bouncing Dave.

Barrett decided to emulate his predecessor and retain the finance portfolio for himself. This surprised everyone (and dismayed a good many), because the former social worker had never displayed a head for figures. He may have had no choice. His cabinet, like many of Bennett's, lacked real talent, even after it was shuffled in May of 1973. The premier was reluctant to demote loyal supporters, although he had to fire Frank Calder, the first aboriginal MLA and cabinet minister in B.C.'s history, after an incident in July 1973 involving drinking, a woman and a car parked in the middle of an intersection.

Barrett led a secretive cabinet that kept even its caucus in the dark. Although an overachieving public relations staff started flooding the media and an eventual 40,000-name mailing list with a daily gush of press releases, they seldom said anything. Even Barrett's autobiography, which is self-serving, often inaccurate and poorly written, offers little real news. According to the B.C. Archives, records dealing with Barrett's years as premier have inexplicably gone missing. The records service surmises that they may have been destroyed or given to someone outside the government rather than be archived.

A few nuggets have been left lying around, however, to give us a sense of the brief Barrett years. The NDP did take some positive steps. It introduced a full

The province's first NDP cabinet prepares to go to work in 1972.
Dave Barrett sits in the middle in the front row.

Hansard transcription of debates and an oral question period. (Opposition leader W.A.C. Bennett asked the first question, on March 5, 1973. It was ruled out of order by Gordon Dowding, the highly partisan Speaker, who kept threatening the press gallery with dire consequences if it insisted on reporting the news.)

The Throne Speech on January 25, 1973, promised 1,000 new government jobs. This vow was more than exceeded, as the civil service payroll ballooned from 30,600 in 1972 to more than 40,000 in late 1975. The size of the legislature didn't increase, but its pay packet did: Barrett doubled his own salary and those of the MLAs. He also began spending money on acquisitions. The government set up a Crown corporation called B.C. Petroleum as a way to peddle natural gas for profit, snapped up several minor players in the resource sector, then sat back and watched the deficits pile up. Why was the NDP getting into public ownership? "Because," Barrett told an interviewer, "industry is incompetent in making social decisions that are necessary for geographic areas."

Barrett's budgets were lacklustre and totally missed the mark on curbing rising expenses. Ministry overruns were common, while Barrett routinely overestimated revenues. One high-profile example of departmental profligacy was health and welfare. In early 1974, the ministry had overspent its budget by $106.8 million. Barrett tried to dismiss the red ink by claiming it was "a clerical error" in the budget. It wasn't.

Some NDP legislation was more controversial than others. The bill setting up the Agricultural Land Reserve sought to dictate the disposition of all property—public or private—in B.C. The Mineral Royalties Act imposed such stiff fees and royalties that this important resource industry was virtually crippled. The decision to create an automobile insurance monopoly via the Insurance Corporation of B.C. was quickly beset by problems and rising premiums. Government employees, meanwhile, gained full bargaining powers, including the right to strike.

On the health and welfare front, Pharmacare was introduced in 1974. Welfare rates were raised twice during Barrett's watch. As a social worker, he placed a high priority on welfare. But it was costly—$516 million budgeted for 1975 alone.

In contrast to Bennett's measured pace of a sitting every spring, legislative sessions now consumed much of the year. The workload was formidable. For 1973, 162 acts were registered in the statute books. Over a three-year period, the number of bills exceeded 400. To some, this breakneck pace was "legislation by thunderbolt."

Then there were Barrett's problems with the press. Among the large *Vancouver Sun* staff assigned to cover the legislature in 1974 was Marjorie Nichols, a highly regarded reporter and columnist who regularly and skilfully skewered the government. On the afternoon of March 12, Marjorie and her bureau chief encountered Barrett in a corridor of the legislature. The premier was in a foul mood. Spying his tormentor, he screamed at her, "F— you! F— you! F— you!" before storming off. It may have been the defining moment of his premiership.[1]

By 1975, B.C. was being described as the Chile of the north because of the government's left-wing agenda. That summer, more than 50,000 workers were on strike in various sectors of the economy. Barrett was forced to call an emergency House session on October 8 to pass back-to-work legislation. The B.C. Federation of Labour, which had refused to back Barrett during the NDP's leadership squabbles, cried betrayal and vowed revenge.

It didn't have to wait long. Emboldened by his self-image of strong leadership, and fearing the future power of a reborn Social Credit party, the premier called a snap election for December 11. Secret ballots being what they are, we'll never know how many unionists voted against Barrett and his cohorts after that campaign. While the NDP had only Barrett's raucous style going for it (and a new slogan, "Don't let them take it away"), the Socreds' new leader, Bill Bennett, wisely avoided confrontation with silver-tongued Dave and concentrated on organizing votes.

Bill, who replaced his father as party leader in 1973, was a stiff, awkward opposition leader who had to endure Barrett's taunts and parliamentary parlour

"Stop worrying ... I'm sure his interpreter will clean it up."

tricks. However, Bennett the Younger learned fast. During the spring session of 1974, he predicted in an interview that not only would the NDP lose the next election, the premier would lose his own seat as well. When the votes were counted, Social Credit was back in power with 35 seats to the socialists' 18, and Barrett had been defeated in Coquitlam by a Socred car dealer. He resigned December 22.

The one-term revolution of the masses had turned into a historical footnote. The NDP did not have a blueprint when it took office. Its management of B.C.'s affairs was slipshod, and Barrett was too weak a leader to translate his colleagues' enthusiastic forays into a meaningful policy. In the words of one political insider, he let too many lieutenants "run his ship on to the rocks."

Barrett was back in the legislature in 1976 thanks to a byelection in Vancouver East. Bob Williams resigned as MLA to make room for the ex-premier, receiving in return an $80,000 party sinecure. As opposition leader, Barrett fought elections in 1979 and 1983 that trimmed the Socred majority, but otherwise didn't change much.

At 4:35 a.m. on October 6, 1983, during round-the-clock debate on Premier Bennett's restraint initiatives, Barrett was physically dragged from his chair and out of the legislative assembly after challenging the Speaker and then refusing to obey an order to leave. Although this forcible ejection was another first for

B.C. and gathered its share of headlines, Barrett was left on the sidelines during the Operation Solidarity campaign against Bennett. He resigned as party leader and MLA in 1984.

Barrett became a talk-show personality on Vancouver radio station CJOR, but left in 1987 because of poor ratings. After a year of lecturing and research, he became MP for Esquimalt-Juan de Fuca in the federal election of November 21, 1988. The following year, he ran for the federal leadership of the NDP and lost. He also lost his seat in the 1993 election.

Although not actively involved in politics during the Nineties, the ex-premier managed to keep his hand in. In 1996, he and Williams were named in an RCMP search warrant connected with the Nanaimo Commonwealth Holding Society bingo scandal. The warrants contained allegations of wrongdoing involving the Vancouver East byelection of 1976. No charges were ever laid.

In March 1998, Barrett repudiated one of his former government's most sacred environmental undertakings. The issue at the NDP's Kamloops convention was the removal of some prime farmland from the Agricultural Land Reserve so that a tourist resort could be built. Barrett shocked many by backing the cabinet's decision to overrule its own commission, which concluded the land should be left in the ALR. "Let's dispense with the hokum" about saving land, he said.

Perhaps as a reward, Barrett then chaired (for a generous daily stipend) two separate government commissions inquiring into the shoddy construction of condominiums. Although Barrett had hinted in a newspaper article early in 1998 that non-union workers might be to blame for many of the leaky condos, his first report contained mostly fatuous recommendations and conclusions.

In 1999, when Premier Glen Clark was facing increasing pressure to resign over a gambling scandal, Barrett tried to dissuade Attorney-General Ujjal Dosanjh from getting involved in the leadership crisis. The social worker who had entered politics to improve the system had turned into an "old ghost" who just wouldn't fade away.

William Richards Bennett

(December 22, 1975–
August 6, 1986)

"I am my own man."

T hus spoke the youngest son of the Bennett clan on the night of November 24, 1973. Bill Bennett was informing his party, the government and all British Columbians that the last name may be the same, but the game had changed.

The occasion was the first Social Credit leadership convention in 21 years. Bill's father, W.A.C. Bennett, had resigned both as MLA and party leader after losing an election to the New Democratic Party in 1972. He was still a force in the party, however, and many wondered whether this dynastic progression meant the Old Man would still be pulling the strings.

Bill Bennett had won the leadership on the first ballot. It was the climax to a boisterous, modern-style political convention that had attracted 1,500 delegates to a Vancouver hotel. Beyond all the balloons and bunting was the added realization that Social Credit was alive and thirsting for victory. When and if that victory came, young Bennett pointed out in his acceptance speech, it would be his and not his father's. "Let it be clearly understood by friend and foe alike that as your new leader I am my own man," he declared.

The father had not yet entered politics when his second son came along. William Richards Bennett was born April 14, 1932, in Kelowna to William Andrew Cecil and Annie Elizabeth May Richards Bennett. Bill was nineteen when his father assumed the premiership in 1952 and, like W.A.C., was a recent convert to Social Credit. By then he had completed high school before dropping out of the educational loop in order to work in the Bennett hardware business. Bill Bennett married Audrey Lyne James on April 16, 1955. They would have four children.

When the elder Bennett became a full-time politician, spending much of his time in Victoria, he turned his hardware empire over to Bill and the eldest son, Russell. In addition, the brothers became entrepreneurs, branching out into retail appliance and furniture businesses of their own.

Politics was always part of Bill's subconscious, however. It had to be, what with the press, the sycophants and the politicos regularly intruding. The young Bennett even groomed himself for a possible political career of his own. He worked on his shyness and his public speaking as a member of the Toastmasters Club and joined the Kelowna Chamber of Commerce. But he was 41 when Dad finally stepped aside. Bill's shelf life as a fresh, young political face had almost expired. Nevertheless, he decided it was his duty to enter public life.

Bill Bennett truly believed Social Credit was a bastion of private enterprise and individual rights—two philosophies he strongly supported. He felt the party was not dead, despite the dismal result of the 1972 election, just hurting a little bit. There was some family pride mixed in there, too. Bill wanted to erase the rebuke B.C.'s voters had handed his father.

The first step back for Social Credit and the first step forward for Bill Bennett was the Okanagan South byelection of September 7, 1973. Bill ran for the seat vacated by the elder Bennett and won. The next step was the leadership. The fact that so many delegates had shown up for the convention in the wake of W.A.C.'s retirement was one sign that Social Credit was still ticking. That Bill amassed more than three times as many votes for the leadership as his closest rival also showed that the party was still willing to march to the Bennett beat.

"Daddy's boy" then headed off to the legislature to face the scornful gibes of Premier Dave Barrett and his NDP government, while W.A.C. hit a campaign trail of his own. With Grace McCarthy and Dan Campbell, two accomplished string-pullers in their own right, he trolled the back roads of B.C., trashing the NDP and signing up new Socred members. The delicate balance of father working in the background and son learning his trade as opposition leader apparently had been achieved.

While serving his brief stint in opposition, Bennett received an education somewhat different from that obtained at Kelowna High or in retail merchandising. Although he had matured at the feet of a master, Bennett had a hard time adjusting to the bizarre political arena that was the NDP-dominated legislature. Not a first-class opposition leader, he was tighter than a drum in public and in the House, despite his Toastmasters training.

Grace McCarthy (left) and Dan Campbell, Social Credit stalwarts,
helped revitalize the party for the 1975 election.

Many of his stumbling, convoluted utterances reminded listeners of his father. His seemingly perpetual five o'clock shadow gave him a Nixonesque aspect that was not exactly comforting. He was as confrontational with the press as he was with his political foes—until he realized an opposition leader needed all the positive ink he could get. In the words of one dismissive NDP cabinet minister, Bill Bennett "was a hick." Perhaps. But he was one tough hick.

Bennett did his homework, too. The rube from Kelowna could read a balance sheet—a faculty that was perhaps unappreciated on the government side. In Bennett's own well-thumbed, annotated copy of the 1974-75 budget estimates, he made note that the Ocean Falls mill, one of the NDP's acquisitions, lost $850,000 in 1973. He suspected that the NDP had a long-range plan to take over most of B.C.'s forest industry, beginning with the smaller operators. Bennett also questioned the need for a $20,000 advertising budget for transit services and decided the government "really doesn't trust the people."

As the Barrett cabinet stumbled through 1975, Bennett started attracting support from outside the party. Liberal and Conservative politicians climbed aboard. One was Bill Vander Zalm, a Liberal supporter and the popular mayor of Surrey. In September 1975, Liberal MLAs Garde Gardom, Allan Williams and Pat McGeer joined the Socreds. The triple defection dealt a fatal blow to the provincial Liberal party and, not incidentally, to Barrett's hopes for re-election. There was now an organized, polarized right to confront the NDP left. Furthermore, Bill Bennett was quite comfortable with the politics of polarization.

Barrett's ill-timed election call of December 11, 1975, was predicated partly on the notion he could catch the "lightweight" Bennett II "with his pants down," but insiders suspected he was also fascinated by the elder Bennett's habit of going to the polls every three years or so.

Bill's pants were securely fastened, by the way. In a brochure issued during August he urged everyone "to work with Bill Bennett for a government that cares about the real needs of the people." While the Social Credit and NDP forces trooped through the slush of a November campaign, the New Democrats showcased Barrett as their prime election asset. Bennett, meanwhile, avoided debating the mercurial premier and lobbed long-range salvoes at easy NDP targets: red ink, labour unrest and a bureaucracy gone wild.

While Bennett's supporters whooped it up in Kelowna and Vancouver on election night, Barrett sat glumly in a Port Coquitlam motel room and watched his government drain away on the TV screen. And as Bennett had predicted eighteen months earlier, Barrett was one of the victims of a Social Credit rebound that elected 35 MLAs to 18 for the NDP.

Barrett resigned December 22, 1975, and Lt.-Gov. Walter Owen swore in Bennett the same day. The new premier had an instant message to B.C.'s civil service: "Lock the cash box. The honeymoon's over." However, Bennett's first year as premier was on the quiet side. Although he started working on some of the Barrett excesses, he didn't stop expanding the government. B.C. was still growing and changing, and the man in the corner office knew this.

Among the first items of business was reorganizing the structure of government. A set of more efficient ministries replaced the vaguely defined "departments" from previous years. This would be followed by a cabinet shuffle late in 1978. Its aim, Bennett announced in a press release, was to give a "new look" to many ministries.

The detritus of the Barrett years also shaped Bennett's agenda. On October 22, 1976, his keynote speech to the Social Credit convention spoke of hidden ICBC losses and a large deficit from a budget that was "irresponsible and unattainable." "We pulled the rug out from under the NDP, we lifted the rug and found the mess that had been swept there," he said.

But the premier didn't mind borrowing a leaf from his socialist opponents' playbook. That same month, GAIN (Guaranteed Available Income for Need Act) went into effect. The plan expanded benefits for poor people.

The Throne Speech of January 13, 1977, was notable for some juicy morsels not usually found in a government's bland laundry list of promises and banalities. It warned of an "unacceptably high" jobless rate and called for restraint and the lessening of expectations as the B.C. economy slowed. This early deployment of the R-word was mostly ignored at the time, perhaps because another megaproject harvested a few headlines. This was the government's plan for a Coquihalla Highway between Hope and the Interior. Finally, the speech called for a "flexible union" of the five regions of Canada—an echo of W.A.C. Bennett's vision several years earlier.

By the third year of his mandate, the younger Bennett was experiencing some negative vibes. Speaker Ed Smith was forced to resign because of an influence scandal over a government job for a young woman. There would be further resignations, too, involving fraudulent use of airline tickets and other expense account items.

"Gracie's Finger" also popped up in 1978. Gerrymandering—the structuring of electoral districts so as to favour the government in power—always makes the opposition apoplectic. This time, a redrawing of cabinet minister Grace McCarthy's Vancouver-Little Mountain riding gave it a digit-shaped appendage that just happened to be populated by Socred supporters. Attempts to prove something illegal had occurred were fruitless.

Bennett recovered somewhat by taking on big, bad Canadian Pacific. When the eastern-based transportation and resources icon sought to add the province's own MacMillan Bloedel Ltd. to its stable, the premier thundered that "B.C. is not for sale." He followed this up in January 1979 by offering everyone "a piece of the rock." This piece was five free shares in the B.C. Resources Investment Corporation, which had been established in 1977 as a private-sector repository for several resource-industry assets left over from the NDP regime. (The "rock" turned out be a brick. Thousands of ordinary folk invested their own money in BCRIC, raising $487 million for the company. They ended up losing everything. Rash investments and unwise decisions eventually led to the failure of this experiment in people's capitalism.)

The temporary high of January soon dissipated as 1979 became one of Bill Bennett's most taxing years. First, his father died on February 23. Then came the election of May 10, which Social Credit very nearly blew. The party that so dramatically re-invented itself for the 1975 campaign had degenerated into a collection of amateurs. The NDP took 26 seats to the government's 31, leaving it with an uncomfortable operating margin in the 57-seat House.

The campaign later came to be known as the "Dirty Tricks" election. Media reports of fake letters to the editor and $1,000 handouts by campaign chairman Dan Campbell tarnished the narrow victory. In his unpublished memoirs, Campbell strongly denied involvement in any part of the Dirty Tricks campaign. Nevertheless, he resigned his job in the premier's office, believing that his name had been sullied.

After the 1975 election, Campbell had warned about the disarray in the party. In a long memo to Bennett, he had suggested a plan of rejuvenation.

Campbell's warnings were ignored until the near-disaster of 1979. It was then that Bennett took personal responsibility for the efficiency of the Socred organization. His reconstruction of the party (which had unmistakable overtones of Ontario's Big Blue Conservative machine) replaced the pure political amateur with a highly professional structure for both the party and the premier's office.

On the financial end, he was greatly aided by the emergence in 1980 of the Top 20, a shadowy group of business leaders who provided the party with enough financial support that it did not have to worry about funds during the Bennett years. (The Top 20 was a reference to the 20 swing ridings in B.C., which would be matched by "20 guys" with money who would help finance the fight to win those ridings. There were actually several dozen members of the club over the years.)

In the early Eighties, inflation was increasing and resource prices were falling. With Patrick Kinsella, his political adviser, at one elbow and Norman Spector, his in-house policy guru, at the other, Bennett went on the attack. First, he used the occasion of a premiers' conference in Ottawa in early 1982 to bash the feds over high interest rates. Then he went on television February 18 to announce a government restraint program. This comprised various economies—not the least of which was applying the brakes to runaway civil service pay increases. As the situation worsened and an unprecedented budget deficit appeared unavoidable, layoffs began. The grumbling in the union ranks increased in intensity.

However, restraint would really hit the fan in 1983. The twin burdens of a deepening recession and inflationary pressures forced Bennett into a draconian scenario that had echoes of Duff Pattullo's Special Powers Act of 1934. It would lead to the Summer of Solidarity and confirmation that Bill Bennett was one tough guy. In the meantime, an election was due and the premier called it for May 5. This time, the Social Credit party—now properly organized and in control—won 35 seats to the NDP's 22.

On the morning of July 7, 1983, legislative reporters and analysts were segregated so they could ponder the entrails of the government's latest budget. This is called the "lock-up." The media digest the material and prepare their stories, though they cannot release them until the finance minister begins his speech after lunch.

The budget offering was a little meatier than usual. A record deficit of $1.6 billion was projected, the sales tax would be increased, the civil service would be reduced and its wages remain frozen, and so on. However, the real substance of budget day was contained in the deluge of tough legislation that followed Finance Minister Hugh Curtis's speech.

In a sweeping fusillade of restraint measures contained in 26 bills introduced that afternoon, Bennett eliminated rent controls and the human rights branch, dissolved a number of boards and commissions, gutted regional districts and tinkered with pension plans. He also put the civil service squarely in his sights.

Two pieces of legislation—the Public Service Labour Relations Act (Bill 2) and the Public Sector Restraint Act (Bill 3)—severely restricted collective bargaining and ended job security for civil servants. A third bill provided for wage rollbacks. The bedlam in the House was followed by howls of outrage. Led by the B.C. Government Employees Union and the B.C. Federation of Labour, the wave of protests coalesced into the Operation Solidarity movement.

All that summer and fall, while Bennett tightened the screws in the House with round-the-clock sittings, mass rallies and marches in Victoria and Vancouver demanded withdrawal of the offending legislation. But Bennett suspected the public wasn't buying it. He pointed out that 100,000 people in the private sector lost their jobs during 1982 "and nobody held rallies for them."

The BCGEU legally went on strike November 1. Other unions followed until 80,000 workers had walked out in the public sector. Liquor stores, highway maintenance, the courts, schools, government offices and crown corporations all felt the impact. Twelve days later the famous (or infamous, depending on your disposition) Kelowna Accord was reached. On Sunday evening, November 13, Bill Bennett, Norman Spector and Jack Munro ended up in the premier's home in Kelowna. Munro, the tough-talking, profanity-spewing president of the International Woodworkers of America and vice-president of the B.C. Fed, had inserted himself into the situation because he felt Operation Solidarity was careering out of control; talk of a general strike meant his IWA would be hitting the bricks over someone else's issues.

When Bennett and Munro emerged four hours later, a deal had been reached. Bennett agreed to scrap Bill 2 and exempt the BCGEU from some provisions of Bill 3. The 80,000 workers were told by their union bosses to go back to work. The crisis was over, although the rest of the July legislation package remained virtually in place. While the unions bickered over Munro's "sell-out," tough Bill Bennett rode the crest toward Expo 86.

Bennett had announced Expo in 1980. It would be a world-class fair with a transportation theme and would mark Vancouver's centenary. Super-efficient, super-rich industrialist Jimmy Pattison was put in charge. During construction of the site on a strip of land along False Creek, unions demanded that all non-union labour be banned from the site. No way, said Bennett, that's against government policy. He proceeded to introduce labour code amendments that made the Expo site a "special economic development project," which exempted it from any union harassment or action.

Whizzing past the site of Expo 86, SkyTrain begins fulfilling the promise of rapid transportation between downtown Vancouver and New Westminster.

With Prince Charles and Diana, Princess of Wales, on hand, along with Prime Minister Brian Mulroney and other lesser lights, Expo 86 opened in the rain on May 2. Magically, the weather was fine for the rest of the summer, and the fair was a huge success. It put Vancouver on the map and gave it the "world-class" label it so desperately wanted.

Exactly two weeks later, Bill Bennett sped along the Coquihalla Highway in an open convertible. As he had wished, the first phase of the project had been completed in time for Expo. But it cost a bundle: $414,718,454 for that Hope-Merritt stretch of blacktop. In 1984, Bennett had realized that the highway, which was years in the making, was well behind schedule. He ordered accelerated construction so that it wouldn't miss the Expo deadline.

Estimates of the overtime and other expenses involved with the fast-tracking ranged from $40 million to $160 million. The findings of an official inquiry accepted the $40 million figure. But as commissioner D.L. McKay pointed out, the highways ministry's bookkeeping was so "haphazard and incomplete" that the additional cost could virtually be any figure.

On May 22, 1986, six days after he climbed into that convertible, Bill Bennett announced that he was stepping down as leader of the Social Credit party and premier of British Columbia.

"He can't retire yet … what about the Sky Train extension to Kelowna …
Okanagan Expo 87 … the Hawaii-Penticton tunnel. …"

The province was stunned, for the premier was at the apex of his career. He had beaten back the unions. Expo 86 was obviously a glittering success. The Coquihalla Highway was in place and generating toll revenue. SkyTrain, a rapid-transit link between downtown Vancouver and New Westminster, had opened earlier in the year. B.C. Place, a covered stadium, was a new adornment to Vancouver's skyline. The Tumbler Ridge coal development was another megaproject that would have made Daddy proud.

What was not to like about such a record? Well, there were some embarrassing hiccups escaping from the well-oiled Socred machine. Scandals and resignations arising from such misdeeds as patronization of an escort agency, improper financial transactions and a domestic triangle had gutted Bennett's cabinet. He knew his government, after almost eleven years in office, had become stagnant—a fact of political maturation that Bill's father never fully appreciated.

Besides, Bennett was itching to get out. As Dan Campbell later put it: "He told me from day one: three times, no more." Bennett the Younger had won his three elections and had been in public life for thirteen years. That was a long time for someone as intensely private and guarded as Bill Bennett. He and Audrey had discussed his departure as early as 1984—"subject to certain things happening."

Among those "things" was the need for renewal of the party, which he felt could best be accomplished by somebody else. To the press, Bennett simply said: "I'm retiring from public life." His message was that change must come when things were good. "And things are good," he said. "There must be political renewal." Bennett made his farewell address to the legislature on June 17. "I am pleased to have served with all of you," he said with a reasonably straight face. "I appreciate your contribution and especially the criticism of the opposition."

Bennett then relaxed to await the result of a hastily convened leadership convention in Whistler. On July 30, he was on stage congratulating a beaming Bill Vander Zalm, the freshly anointed head of the Social Credit party. A week later, on August 6, 1986, Bennett tendered his resignation to the lieutenant-governor, and Vander Zalm was sworn in as premier.

Vander Zalm was not Bennett's personal choice as successor, but he went along with the delegates' choice because it fitted his desire for an infusion of fresh blood. (Insiders later reported that Bennett was involved with a failed attempt to oust Vander Zalm in 1988.) True to his word, Bennett removed himself from public life, but not from the headlines.

On May 12, 1989, he, brother Russell and lumber baron Herb Doman (a former member of the Top 20) were cleared of insider trading charges by a Vancouver court. The three had been charged after the Bennetts sold Doman company shares in November 1988 for $2.1 million shortly before trading in the shares was suspended. However, the B.C. Securities Commission later found the trio guilty of substantially the same charges and imposed penalties of its own in October 1999, after a lengthy legal battle.

For William Richards Bennett, the case was an annoying distraction. Now a respected senior citizen, he divides his time between Kelowna, where he still has business interests, and his retirement home in Palm Springs.

William Nick Vander Zalm

(August 6, 1986– April 2, 1991)

N o occurrence so defined Bill Vander Zalm's premiership as the circumstances of his leaving it. On April 2, 1991, Vander Zalm was forced from office, his thousand-watt smile obscured by a fog of lies and evasions.

Premier Vander Zalm's 56 months in power were so filled with turmoil, scandal and controversy that his resignation seemed no more than a fitting denouement. The brash Dutch immigrant from the sand dunes of the North Sea coast had progressed from garden plants to politics to Fantasy Gardens to disgrace in a career that had more than one reincarnation.

Wilhelmus Nicholaas Theodores Maria Vander Zalm was born May 29, 1934, to Wilhelmus and Agatha Warmerdam Vander Zalm in Noordwykerhout, Holland, which is not far from Amsterdam, toward the sea. His mouthful of Christian names did not long survive emigration to British Columbia in 1947. Vander Zalm is listed by Elections B.C. and some biographical sources as William Nick. He is known to sign his name "Bill Vander Zalm," and that is how he is most widely known.

The Vander Zalms were into plants, bulbs and other nursery offerings. Young Bill completed Grade 12 in Abbotsford, then took control of his father's bulb business at the age of seventeen after the elder Vander Zalm suffered a heart attack. This entailed peddling the family product from B.C. to the Lakehead. He acquired Art Knapp's Nurseries, a Lower Mainland company, in the mid-Fifties. About this time, romance also flowered. Bill Vander Zalm married Lillian Beatrice Mihalik in New Westminster on June 27, 1956. They would have four children.

Vander Zalm concentrated on the world of wholesale gardening until he entered municipal politics. He first ran for a seat on Surrey council in 1964 and finished last. But in the 1965 election, Vander Zalm led the polls and was elected to a two-year term. He repeated this success in 1967 and made the step up to mayor in the 1969 election. During his three terms as mayor, the press started adding the adjective "controversial" to any account of his antics.

Municipal issues being low on the scandal scale compared with what raises eyebrows inside the big House on Belleville in Victoria, Vander Zalm's Surrey shenanigans are little more than locally relevant. However, they did portend the future: Mayor Bill, in no particular order, trashed "lazy" welfare recipients, greedy hospital boards, the Social Credit government and even his own council. On the other end of the stick, he had to survive allegations of conflict of interest involving real estate development in the growing municipality.

A card-carrying Liberal, Vander Zalm took a shot at the leadership of the provincial party in 1972. Despite an exhortation that government should crack down on welfare deadbeats, drug pushers and wife-deserters, he was easily brushed aside by David Anderson. Within two years—on May 29, 1974— Vander Zalm dumped the Liberals and joined Bill Bennett's Socreds. All that was needed to propel him onto a larger stage was a provincial election.

That came in December 1975. Vander Zalm was elected MLA for Surrey and joined Bennett's cabinet as human resources minister. For a hard-nosed politician who once suggested "welfare hippies" be forced to pick berries, it was perhaps too sensitive a portfolio. Nonetheless, Bennett later praised him for bringing "sanity and responsibility to the public conscience" and for running an efficient department.

Putting the Surrey wolf in among the welfare chickens was, of course, Bennett's response to the much-publicized haemorrhaging of ministry funds under the NDP. In some circles, Vander Zalm became "the most hated man in B.C." for his uncompromising attitude. You want attitude? How about this quote: "If anybody is able to work but refuses to pick up the shovel, we will find ways of dealing with him."

On June 22, 1978, a cartoon by Bob Bierman in the *Victoria Times* depicted the human resources minister as a grinning sadist pulling the wings off flies. Vander Zalm won a $3,500 libel judgment that was later overturned by the B.C. court of appeal. In December of 1978, he was moved to municipal affairs.

His four years in that portfolio were somewhat less controversial than those in his previous job. He started off with a grand plan: rapid transit for the Lower

Mainland. On December 6, 1980, Vander Zalm announced that an Advanced Light Rail Transit line would be built between Vancouver and New Westminster. It would cost an estimated $650 million and run on an elevated track system. Problem was, Greater Vancouver politicians weren't consulted, nor were the taxpayers. Everyone, from the press to the NDP opposition pooh-poohed the cost, the design and the concept. Nevertheless it was built, at a cost of $854 million plus interest for the first phase. Christened SkyTrain, the line was, as Vander Zalm predicted, an instant hit. It also generated billions of dollars in development along its corridor.

In 1981, Vander Zalm proposed a Land Use Act that would shift power away from municipal and regional officials to a central authority. Spooked by cries of fascism and Stalinism, the cabinet stalled the bill and finally shelved it in July 1982. "The government was not strong, but gutless," Vander Zalm told the press, adding that dropping the bill "was a gutless measure."

Shortly after, Vander Zalm was shifted to the education portfolio. Some have suspected that Bennett threw the tough, persistent streetfighter at the teachers partly because of his "gutless" quotes and partly as a plank in the government's restraint program. Bennett needed tough guys like Vander Zalm to help fight off the recession.

The new education minister immediately irritated everybody concerned by criticizing the low quality of B.C.'s education system. He then took on the B.C. Teachers Federation and was branded "Public Enemy #1" after he warned school boards that the government would not necessarily honour negotiated salary increases. Vander Zalm was actually carrying out a policy that had been put in place beforehand, but his inimitable style turned the cabinet's restraint measures into a personal crusade.

Thankfully for all concerned, Vander Zalm stayed only eight months on the education beat. On April 1, 1983, he announced that he was taking a "sabbatical" from politics. He would not run in the forthcoming election, he said, because Lillian needed him back to help run the family business. The real reasons were more complex. Vander Zalm still considered the cabinet a flock of sheep for not endorsing his confrontational style; he knew he was out of the loop as an MLA whenever a successor to Bennett was discussed; and he was among the multitude who expected the government to be toppled over its restraint program. Best to take a step back and await developments.

The comparison to a rat leaving a sinking ship was obvious. The thing was, the ship didn't sink in the 1983 election and the "rat" was as far from the centre of power as ever. Vander Zalm went to work for radio station CKNW, published a book on gardening, and for a time wrote a garden column for the *Vancouver Sun*. In the summer of 1984, he and Lillian bought the Richmond property that would become Fantasy Garden World.

A strong Roman Catholic, Vander Zalm was also one of the key organizers of Pope John Paul II's visit to B.C. that year. After the Pope departed, Vander Zalm entered the Vancouver mayoralty race and suffered a humiliating defeat at the hands of incumbent Mike Harcourt, who ran on a peace platform.

Bill Bennett's surprise decision to step down as premier in 1986 propelled Vander Zalm back to the provincial stage. By the time the Social Credit party convention was held in Whistler at the end of July, he was the frontrunner in a crowded field of leadership candidates. This support came despite the enmity of several cabinet ministers who deeply resented his desertion of the party in 1983. "Faaantastic," said Bill as the polls gave him the best chance to win the next election.

Among the lesser lights on the list of candidates was Kim Campbell, a Socred MLA who would later join the federal Tories and become Canada's first female prime minister. Although Campbell finished dead last at Whistler, her leadership speech defined William Nick Vander Zalm for all time. "It is fashionable to speak of leaders in terms of their charisma," she said. "But charisma without substance is a dangerous thing. It creates expectations that cannot be satisfied. Then comes bitterness and disillusionment that destroy not only the leader but the party."

Despite Campbell's shrewd assessment, Vander Zalm won the leadership on the fourth ballot over Brian Smith, 801 votes to 454. It was 8:13 p.m. on July 30. Within days, B.C. would have a new first minister. "I need a shower," said Lillian Vander Zalm.

Wrote *Vancouver Sun* columnist Marjorie Nichols: "The neo-Conservative Social Credit machine built by Bill Bennett is dead, the victim of a freakish head-on collision with a grassroots bulldozer driven by an unelected, rampaging populist." Vander Zalm was sworn in August 6, 1986. The job he had wanted since he first lifted his sights from municipal to provincial politics was his. Barely a week later, the new premier was asked how things were going. "So far, it's a piece of cake," he replied.

But Vander Zalm had some hard decisions to make. One was the composition of his cabinet. It would be a relatively weak bunch, because several of Bennett's capable, experienced ministers refused to serve. Another decision was the timing of the provincial election, which was necessary to validate Vander Zalm's ascension to the corner office. Finally, he set the date for October 22.

The NDP leader was Bob Skelly, who had replaced Dave Barrett in 1984. Skelly was an earnest, awkward, jittery champion of the left. His campaign, which opened with a disastrous television appearance, abruptly proceeded downhill. While Skelly attempted to cut through B.C.'s post-Expo euphoria and debate issues and policy, Vander Zalm cranked up his smile and turned on the dangerous charisma that Kim Campbell had reminded everyone he had. The result was an overwhelming Social Credit victory of 47 seats to the NDP's 22 in the expanded legislature.

Bill Vander Zalm was not a leader of men. Or of women. Or of the province. His stewardship of B.C.'s affairs would be marked by raucous debate, controversy, moral thuggery and malfeasance.

The structured administration that Bennett had crafted over eleven years was replaced by an ad hoc caliphate. While Vander Zalm bounced from issue to issue and camera to camera in public, he was centralizing power in the premier's office, estranging himself from his caucus and becoming obsessed with minutiae. More tellingly, his cabinet was kept at bay by Vander Zalm's closest adviser, David Poole.

The Throne Speech in March 1987 was superficially positive, optimistic and ambitious. With the recession fading away, it concentrated on such social reform issues as increased spending on welfare and education. The budget, fiscally cautious and adhering to the government's "Investing in People" theme, was a soft-nosed prelude to some tough legislation to come.

The most important and contentious piece of legislation during the Vander Zalm years was Bill 19, a hastily written and extensively amended revision of the labour code. The Industrial Relations Reform Act replaced the Labour Relations Board with an Industrial Relations Council and a new administrative framework. Although criticized as being "the product of too few and too narrow minds," it was actually more complex and radical than onerous. Labour, not really understanding it, feared the worst and demanded that the bill be withdrawn. Vander Zalm demurred, and a one-day general strike shut much of the province down on June 1, 1987.

A companion bill challenged the B.C. Teachers Federation's control over education, sparking a separate, brief walkout by teachers. Like his predecessor, Vander Zalm had little time for union breast-thumping. "As a duly elected government we are not prepared to capitulate" to illegal acts, he told the press.

It was a wonder any actual governing got done, especially that first year, what with a succession of resignations from Vander Zalm's cabinet. That awkward but pregnant phrase "conflict-of-interest" accounted for three of them in 1987 alone. By 1991, twelve ministers of the Crown had blotted their copybooks for one reason or another. (One of them, Attorney-General Bud Smith, resigned July 12, 1990, after a taped conversation indicated that he was tampering with the administration of justice. The tapes came from illegally intercepted cellular telephone calls and fell into the hands of the NDP. They were released publicly and gleefully by MLA Moe Sihota, who has a rather low ethical threshold.)

Then there was the Peter Toigo affair. Businessman Toigo, a close friend of the premier and an important Socred fundraiser, wanted a piece of the action when the Expo lands went on the block. Vander Zalm and David Poole went out of their way to further Toigo's interests, to the extent of interfering with the Crown corporation charged with unloading the site. Grace McCarthy, the minister responsible, was infuriated, but persevered until the land was eventually sold to Hong Kong billionaire Li Ka-shing in 1988.

The meddling of Vander Zalm—and of Poole, his principal secretary—widened a rift that had been growing in cabinet. Concerns about impropriety voiced by some ministers helped fuel a secret RCMP investigation of the relationship between Vander Zalm and Toigo. Although the Mounties found no evidence that Toigo conferred a financial benefit on his friend the premier, the episode unsettled many Socred MLAs.

Within a week of each other, Attorney-General Brian Smith and Economic Development Minister McCarthy walked out the cabinet door because they felt the premier was listening to his advisers more than to his ministers. McCarthy specifically told Vander Zalm (and reporters) on July 5 that she could not serve as long as unelected officials such as Poole were free to interfere with her ministry. Although Vander Zalm assumed that Smith and McCarthy were in cahoots, they weren't. Both had decided independently to disassociate themselves from a premier who placed style above governance. (Poole was finally forced to quit also, carting away a sweetheart severance package that caused another rumpus.)

Meanwhile, Vander Zalm was getting buffeted on the national scene. The redneck politician who once complained about French language on cereal boxes was having problems with the Meech Lake accord in 1987. This constitutional accommodation, which recognized Quebec's "distinct society" status, was finally signed after the B.C. premier climbed aboard. Vander Zalm then expected some reward for being so accommodating, and when the financial largesse was not forthcoming from Ottawa, he warned in 1988 that "we will monitor and evaluate British Columbia's standing within the federal system." The century-old cry of separation had raised its seductive head once more, although nothing came of it.

Also in 1988, Vander Zalm harvested national headlines by interpreting a Supreme Court decision on abortion as a licence to proscribe the practice in B.C. An ardent pro-lifer who considered abortion to be morally repugnant, the premier announced that his government would no longer pay for these operations except in emergencies. The ban, he added later, also applied to rape and incest victims. The public's unease at Vander Zalm's high-handed self-righteousness was shared by most of his caucus. Although the B.C. Supreme Court upheld a court challenge of the government's action, the abortion issue caused deep disaffection in the party.

Following the unsettling events of 1988, Vander Zalm didn't seem to have the same pizzazz anymore. He drifted through 1989, erratically alternating flashes of his old, outrageous behaviour with indifference. His civil service privatization plan, announced with appropriate fanfare in 1987, had petered out by now, with only about 5,000 workers shed from government payrolls. When 1990 dawned, Vander Zalm had fewer than 24 months left of the electoral mandate handed him in October 1986. He had to call an election eventually, and friend and foe alike were of the opinion that he was now unelectable.

"I remember the good old days when Social Credit
just went in for things like 'funny money.'"

Vander Zalm saw things differently. Convinced he could win, the premier was preparing for a fall election when the press started peeling away the deceit surrounding Fantasy Gardens, which had been sold to Taiwanese billionaire Tan Yu the previous summer for $16 million. The critical turning point that would nudge him toward political disgrace came when the *Sun* revealed Vander Zalm still owned 83 percent of the Richmond tourist attraction, despite his oft-repeated claims he had turned control over to wife Lillian. Reports of misconduct surrounding the sale became so persistent that Vander Zalm was forced to ask conflict-of-interest commissioner Ted Hughes to conduct an inquiry.

Hughes' report, made public April 2, 1991, was brutal. In it, he said Vander Zalm breached his own conflict guidelines by combining government affairs with the sale of what was widely believed to be his wife's business. Among these breaches of proper conduct were the premier's granting of special privileges and the "red carpet" treatment to Yu—including a luncheon hosted by Lt.-Gov. David Lam at Government House.

The second major breach, Hughes said, was Vander Zalm's acceptance of $20,000 in U.S. hundred-dollar bills from Tan Yu early in the morning of August 2, 1990, when they were negotiating the sale of Fantasy Garden World Inc. "Irrespective of the purpose for which Tan Yu provided the premier with that money, I have no doubt reasonably informed persons could properly conclude the premier's ability to exercise his duties and responsibilities objectively in the future might appear to be compromised given the bizarre circumstances in which the money was given to the premier and the lack of any reasonable explanation," he said.

Vander Zalm had long maintained that the media were conducting a vendetta against him and that their allegations were no more than "misinformation." Hughes put that notion to rest. "With due respect to the premier, it was what went on that was wrong, not the media's discovering and publicizing those events," his report said.

The portrait painted by Hughes was of an evasive, dissembling premier who was completely out of touch with certain ethical considerations. "The premier's problem stems not just from his inability to draw a line between his private and public life but in his apparently sincere belief that no conflict existed so long as the public wasn't aware of what was going on," Hughes concluded.

Vander Zalm resigned the day the report was released, offering no defence or apology and refusing to answer questions from the press. He attributed his resignation to "politics," but the press had a different view. It was best put by *Sun* columnist Vaughn Palmer, who observed that Vander Zalm was a premier who simply kept on lying.

Rita Johnston, one of Vander Zalm's dwindling band of supporters, was sworn in as premier a few hours after Vander Zalm tendered his resignation to Lt.-Gov. Lam. She had been chosen by a secret caucus vote after the Hughes report was released. Vander Zalm was subsequently charged with criminal breach of trust, but found not guilty on June 25, 1992. According to Judge David Campbell, his actions may have been "foolish, ill-advised and in apparent or real conflict," but fell short of criminal behaviour.

The former premier's political career lay fallow for a few years, while the Social Credit party he had tried to remake in his own image shrivelled up and died. Bill and Lillian got back into the flower business, becoming Canada's largest producers of lilacs. In 1995, Vander Zalm joined the B.C. Reform party and muscled his way into its presidency in 1998.

He was acclaimed party leader November 12, 1999, at a Vancouver convention, although Zalm-watchers concluded that his commitment would not be permanent. True to form, the born-again Reformer had kicked off his leadership campaign by suggesting that B.C. could solve its illegal immigrant problem by shipping the Chinese boat people who had arrived in the province that summer off to Ottawa.

However, the premier from Fantasyland could not persuade the voters of Delta South to endorse his resurrection. William Nick Vander Zalm failed in his bid to return to the legislature when he decisively lost a byelection to the Liberal candidate on December 7, 1999.

Rita Margaret Johnston

(April 2, 1991–
November 5, 1991)

R ita Johnston, British Columbia's first female premier, was the wrong
person in the wrong place at precisely the wrong time. The whiplash
effect (not uncommon in our political jungle) that accompanied
the loud thud of Bill Vander Zalm's premiership hitting the dust
was enough to relegate her to the footnote category of provincial history.

Never mind that Johnston toiled unselfishly for almost twenty years to
serve her constituents—first as a Surrey alderman and then as a Social Credit
MLA. The fact she was closely linked with the erratic Vander Zalm for so many
years was more than guilt by association in the minds of the voters. It also
identified her as a member of a party that had abused its mandate.

The result? After being sworn in as premier April 2, 1991, to replace Vander
Zalm, Johnston lasted only seven months before losing an election to the New
Democratic Party.

The woman who briefly broke through the all-male cordon surrounding
the premier's office was born Rita Margaret Leichert in Melville, Saskatchewan,
on April 22, 1935. Her parents were John and Annie Chyzzy Leichert. Rita
came to B.C. with her family in 1941 and was educated in North Vancouver
and Vancouver schools. On April 28, 1951—six days after her sixteenth
birthday—Rita Leichert married George Johnston, a millwright. They would
have three children.

George lost a leg in an industrial accident in 1964. A few years later, the

Johnstons built the Johnston Villa Mobile Home Park in the Newton district of Surrey and operated it from 1967 to 1980. At this time, Rita was also immersed in municipal politics. Following the December 1969 Surrey election, she was a rookie alderman on a council whose star was Bill Vander Zalm. She fell into Bill's slipstream right away and rode it all the way to Victoria.

When Vander Zalm abandoned his legislature seat in 1983, he nominated Johnston to take his place. Except for 1975-77 (when she made a bid for the mayoralty and lost), Johnston had served the municipality at the local level. Now, after winning the Socred nomination and the subsequent election, she represented Surrey as an MLA.

When Bill Bennett announced his retirement in 1986, Johnston joined the convention committee that would organize a leadership vote. As soon as Vander Zalm declared his candidacy, she withdrew and joined his campaign. She was one of only three backbenchers to back Vander Zalm from the beginning. The others were Bill Reid and Jack Davis. All three would be given cabinet posts when Vander Zalm became premier—emphasizing the importance he put on personal loyalty.

Johnston was awarded the municipal affairs portfolio, then transportation and highways. On August 10, 1990, she was named deputy premier. During those chaotic years, no whiff of scandal attached itself to Johnston, but she was clearly identified as a Vander Zalm loyalist.

When the caucus met to choose an interim premier on the day Vander Zalm was nailed for conflict of interest, Johnston won on the fourth ballot. She immediately told reporters she would not discuss the report of Commissioner Ted Hughes. "I'm here to talk about Rita Johnston and the new government...and where we go from here," she said, indicating that the new start would be "not quite as—exciting would be the word—as what we have witnessed in the past."

A leadership convention was called for July, and Johnston decided to be a candidate. During the campaign, which was marked by more Socred infighting, she tried hard to haul her baggage out of the Vander Zalm camp. When chosen interim leader, Johnston had defended the former premier's record. In mid-July, she admitted that "there was little or no discipline in the last five years." It wouldn't have happened under Bill Bennett, she said, and it won't happen under Johnston.

During the summer, she jetted about B.C. on a plush Cessna Citation aircraft, but claimed she didn't know whose it was. "It's a private arrangement," she told reporters—and delegates who wondered where the money was coming from. Nevertheless, Johnston won the leadership July 20 on the second ballot, 941-881, over Grace McCarthy. The *Vancouver Sun* called it the "night of the long knives."

After candidate Mel Couvelier crossed the floor to join Johnston's camp, a McCarthy supporter screamed at him: "Judas! Judas!" A key McCarthy aide added: "No, no! You jerk! You double-crosser! You killed the party! You lost the election!" (He was right about that part. Opposition leader Mike Harcourt later admitted he was glad he drew Johnston as an election opponent. Had McCarthy won the leadership, he knew he would be in for a tough fight.)

Sounding like every other winner who just survived a tough battle, Premier Johnston denied there was a serious split in the party and suggested a healing process should begin. "The solidarity and the great fun that we've enjoyed in the last couple of days suggests to me it's not an overwhelming problem," she told the press.

Johnston's victory preserved the status quo—which was perhaps the wrong direction for the party. When Vander Zalm won, he was an outsider. McCarthy, despite her long years of service in the Social Credit cause, was another outsider, one who had abandoned the government in 1988.

One of Johnston's points was that unity was needed to fight the imminent election. As events transpired, it would take rather more than that. In the week following the convention, the premier and her cabinet went on a BC Rail tour of the Interior—where they ran into an Indian blockade. Other protest incidents gave a fairly good indication of the depth of B.C.'s disgust with the post-Zalm Social Credit party.

For Rita Johnston, it seemed she had concluded one campaign only to start on another. Mindful that her party's five-year window was rapidly closing, Johnston swallowed hard and plunged into an election she called for October 17. Winning the hearts of B.C.'s voters, she discovered, was a little harder than capturing the attention of a bunch of delegates.

Right from the beginning, things didn't go well. Protesters dogged her footsteps at almost every campaign stop and her press coverage was uniformly negative. Forced to discuss Vander Zalm's excesses and other scandals, she had no time to get her message of renewal across. Her campaign was wooden and her performance flat.

Harcourt had no such problems. From the beginning, he promised that the NDP would be different, that its government would be open and that there would be no special deals for insiders. If the Socreds got back in, he said, "they will take that vote as a blank cheque to do anything they want." He promised the NDP would end the Socred style of patronage. (Fat chance, but that's the stuff of another chapter.) Otherwise, Harcourt won the election by staying out of the way. He let the voters digest the lies, patronage and corruption of the Vander Zalm years, then decide for themselves.

Johnston was forced to campaign with a "V" for Vander Zalm upon her bosom. Like Hester Prynne, the adulteress in Nathaniel Hawthorne's *The Scarlet Letter,* who was forced to wear the scarlet "A," Johnston's sin of association with a disgraced premier was there for everyone to see.

On election night, the New Democrats were swept into power with 51 seats in the 75-seat House. The surprise second-place finisher was Gordon Wilson's Liberal party with 17 seats, while Social Credit could manage only 7. Wilson came into prominence during a televised debate between the party leaders. While Johnston scolded and Harcourt ducked and weaved, Wilson stood apart from their bickering and came across as a calm, rational alternative.

Johnston was stoic in defeat. Asked how she felt about losing her own seat in Surrey-Newton (by almost 2,400 votes), she replied: "There's more to life than politics." Earlier, she had admitted, "I never dreamed it would turn out the way it did."

For George and Rita Johnston, there was indeed more to life. They moved to Abbotsford and lived there for two years before settling in Vernon in 1995. Usually they spend their winters in Indio, California. After retiring, Johnston's two new activities were "golf and computers." She spends little time pondering the demise of the Social Credit party she once served so loyally, but does keep up to date on political events via the Internet.

Michael Franklin Harcourt

(November 5, 1991– February 22, 1996)

Mike Harcourt and the New Democrats are committed to open and balanced government that deals fairly with ordinary men and women instead of playing favourites with political friends and insiders. A New Democratic government will put an end to secret deals and special favours for political friends.

This paragraph was part of the NDP's election platform of 1991. It is one of the most breathtakingly false promises ever penned by a political party. Within one month of Harcourt's swearing in as premier on November 5, 1991, insiders of high and low caste were flocking to the NDP's patronage trough.

One of the most prominent was Bob Williams. At $112,000 a year, the former cabinet minister in the Dave Barrett government was made chief of the Crown Corporations Secretariat, which was created to oversee all government-owned corporations. It was Williams who resigned his Vancouver East seat in 1976 to make room for his defeated leader, Barrett.

At the other end of the pay scale, a review of NDP appointments in the spring of 1992 turned up a litany of failed NDP candidates, party hacks, left-wing academics and privileged hangers-on. The glut of NDP job-seekers became so overwhelming that the cabinet had to make a special patronage appointment of a patronage coordinator to handle all the patronage appointments. His name was John Pollard and he was married to an NDP MLA. One of his qualifications, apparently, was that he was head usher at the party convention in 1988.

The stampede to spoils engendered a classic *Vancouver Sun* headline in June 1992. "Oink, Oink," it said in huge type over a story about the NDP's pork barrelling. Premier Harcourt defended the appointees as part of the party's progressive approach to hiring. "There are some appointments that were made to substantial positions that were controversial, that we can agree to disagree with," he told a reporter.

For bland, middle-of-the-road Mike Harcourt, all this fuss was not what he expected after becoming the first NDP premier in sixteen years. Life at the top was a little rockier than he had envisioned on the way up.

Michael Franklin Harcourt was born a long way from the cauldron of B.C. politics, in Edmonton, Alberta, on January 6, 1943, to Frank and Stella Louise Good Harcourt. The family moved to B.C. when Mike was three, and he grew up comfortably in Victoria and Vancouver. In Vancouver, the Harcourts lived in the respectable Kerrisdale district. Frank Harcourt, a top-drawer insurance salesman, and Stella were Liberals, so Mike got some early exposure to what he later called "cocktail party revolutionaries."

After completing high school, Harcourt studied political science at the University of B.C. While working one summer as a waiter on the CPR, he experienced a sort of social democratic epiphany. Mike Harcourt met Tommy Douglas, the venerable national NDP leader, on the train and was greatly impressed. By this time, Harcourt had started studying law. He graduated from the University of B.C. law faculty in 1968 and became a storefront lawyer in Vancouver's inner city. He joined the NDP the same year.

In 1970, Mike met Mai-Gret Wibecke Salo at a party. More popularly known as Beckie, she was a Swedish-born teacher. He pursued her for a year until she succumbed. Mike and Beckie were married June 26, 1971. They would have one son.

Harcourt's activism on behalf of the downtrodden led inevitably to his political career. He was elected a Vancouver alderman in 1972 and mayor in 1980. Harcourt defeated the incumbent, Jack Volrich, in that election, then won again in 1982 and '84. In his final campaign for the mayoralty, Harcourt grabbed 62 percent of the vote to humble a Surrey carpetbagger called Bill Vander Zalm.

With his third term as mayor winding down, Harcourt started getting broad hints that he should run for the legislature. So Harcourt did, although two previous tries had ended in failure. In 1986, he was elected MLA for Vancouver Centre, one of the few NDP candidates able to withstand the charismatic campaign of Vander Zalm, who was now the Social Credit premier.

As expected, Bob Skelly promptly resigned as party leader following the election, and Harcourt quickly became the favourite to replace him. Harcourt won the post by acclamation in April 1987, after expounding his "Eleven

Hundred Days of Action" strategy to resurrect the party and overthrow the Socreds. Under the strategy, Harcourt planned to defeat Vander Zalm at the polls and win at least two terms of office as head of the government. He was bang-on about the two terms, except he wouldn't be around for the second one.

Vander Zalm, of course, had also disappeared by the time an election was called in October 1991. When Harcourt was sworn in as premier on November 5, it was after overwhelming the unfortunate Rita Johnston on election day. Part of Harcourt's pitch to the voters was the NDP election manifesto containing 48 promises. But election vows are crafted to be broken, although the NDP's attitude in this regard is more cynical than that of other parties.

The ink was not long dry on the *Sun*'s "Oink, Oink" headline when Harcourt's government started doing other things to upset the taxpayer. A new labour code passed later in 1992 favoured the unions so much that B.C.'s business community erupted in outrage. The code followed the introduction of a corporate capital tax in Finance Minister Glen Clark's first budget, which every company official rightly assumed was a repudiation of "Moderate Mike's" message about getting along with big business.

His first year as premier was not a good one for Mike Harcourt. Along with the patronage, the company-bashing and the flak about a surging bureaucracy, he also made a fool of himself on the federal scene. Tall and balding as he is, the label of "Premier Bonehead" seemed to fit Harcourt perfectly after a constitutional conference in August. Like a rube signing a contract without reading the fine print, Harcourt agreed to a version of the ill-fated Charlottetown accord without realizing it would leave British Columbia under-represented in the Commons. Although a face-saving compromise was later stitched together, it wasn't enough to salvage Harcourt's reputation.

Environmentalists protesting the cutting down of trees on the shores of
Clayoquot Sound forced a reversal in policy by Premier Mike Harcourt.

Clayoquot was the designer issue for 1993. The government's decision to allow logging in a portion of Clayoquot Sound—a temperate rain forest on the west coast of Vancouver Island—transformed it into one of the province's great environmental battlegrounds. While celebrities and meddling MPs tut-tutted Harcourt's decision, protesters demonstrated on the lawn of the legislature and then blockaded roads leading to the logging area. The issue split the NDP, with those concerned about preserving jobs lined up against the vocal "green" faction.

In June 1993, Harcourt bowed to the environmental wing of the party and created Tatshenshini-Alsek wilderness park in northwestern B.C. In doing so, the government summarily cancelled the Windy Craggy copper-gold mining project. Sued by the mine's owner, B.C. agreed in 1995 to cough up $166 million in compensation and investment funding.

Meanwhile, Harcourt was pulling a Barrett and flooding the House with legislation. Much of it was useful and progressive. Health care reform was introduced, as well as human rights and land-claims legislation. A so-called "anti-hate" bill, however, amounted to an abridgement of free speech, while a "freedom-of-information" act often produced just the opposite effect, as reporters, researchers and ordinary citizens would discover.

Despite some positive feedback about the government's accomplishments, Harcourt decided in September 1993 that his hands-off management style was not really working. So he dramatically shuffled not only his cabinet and the top echelons of the bureaucracy, but also the way things were done. The premier would become more hands-on, and the ideological "cowboys" in his cabinet would be reined in.

It was all for naught, really. While the next two years featured feeble attempts to rejuvenate the timber industry through the poorly conceived, poorly managed and inordinately expensive Forest Renewal B.C. and Forest Practices Code initiatives (and a backdown in 1995 on Clayoquot Sound logging), the revenue-friendly pastime of bingo captured everyone's attention.

The scandal had been bubbling since 1992, when the *Sun* revealed that the NDP-controlled Nanaimo Commonwealth Holding Society had been stealing money from charities. After the police got involved and made a few raids, four smaller societies politically linked to the party and the complex NCHS apparatus pleaded guilty to breaching the Criminal Code 27 times. Still insisting there was no official connection between the NDP and the criminal activity in Nanaimo, Harcourt consented to a forensic audit of the society's books, to be carried out by auditor Ron Parks.

Dave Stupich was revealed as the mastermind behind the Nanaimo bingo scandal.

While Parks audited, Harcourt plodded through 1994, hoping that the NCHS bogeyman would go away. His government made progress on aboriginal claims and land-use planning. One opinion poll actually showed the premier had gained in popularity. But in early 1995, his government reneged on a Kemano Completion Project deal that had been struck with Alcan, triggering an expensive settlement.

A leaked finance ministry report in February announced to the world that the province was even more awash in red ink than anyone had suspected. B.C.'s spending on capital projects was out of control, it said, with the NDP adding $7 billion to the provincial debt since coming to power in 1991. Harcourt's response: "What we've been doing these past two years is catching up on ten years of Social Credit cutbacks, ten years when schools weren't built [and] hospitals weren't built..."

A few months later, just before the Parks report hit the cabinet table, Harcourt had to fire Environment Minister Moe Sihota after the Law Society of B.C. found him guilty of professional misconduct. Then he dumped Housing Minister Joan Smallwood for publicly questioning his handling of the Nanaimo Commonwealth scandal.

On Friday the 13th of October 1995, after the government sat on it for four months, the Parks report was released to the public and the press. Like Ted

Hughes' report on Bill Vander Zalm's Fantasy Gardens sale, Ron Parks' disclosures were crushing. He reported that the NDP and the Nanaimo Commonwealth organization had long collaborated on diverting charity funds for political purposes.

The money, proceeds from bingo games, was funnelled into party coffers instead of to the charities involved. Parks described the NCHS as a "bank," from which the NDP drew funds to finance its activities. Furthermore, he said, the party tried to cover up its involvement by secretly returning $60,000 to the society in 1993. (David Stupich, a former MLA, MP and NDP president, was later convicted of fraud and running an illegal lottery scheme. At the end of 1999, almost $1 million of diverted bingo proceeds were still unaccounted for.)

After first professing that Parks' revelations had nothing to do with him, Harcourt later admitted that he knew he had to quit as soon as he read the report. "I couldn't see any other way of resolving it because I knew the lynch-mob mentality that was around at that point wanted blood now," he told an interviewer.

The "lynch mob" was not only being formed out in front of the Legislative Buildings. Inside the cabinet room in the west wing, a posse of anti-Harcourt ministers was testing the noose and looking for a suitable tree. If not exactly pushed, Harcourt was the recipient of a few well-placed elbows. The provincial NDP has been riven by power struggles through much of its history, and the Harcourt era was no exception.

There were several members of the caucus who wanted him to go because he was too soft, too centrist and not nearly rabid enough. And despite all his government had done for the unions, the B.C. Federation of Labour never cottoned to Harcourt. Only days after the Parks report was made public, the word out of the Fed was that he had to go.

Finally, he did. Mike Harcourt announced November 15, 1995, that he would step down as premier and party leader as soon as a successor was chosen. On February 22, 1996, Glen Clark was sworn in as the new premier and Harcourt formally resigned.

In the end, Harcourt had to leave not because he failed to govern B.C. properly, but because he failed to control his own party. Although he blamed the media for his demise, Harcourt's hand on the tiller was too tentative to steer the good ship NDP on a proper course. That strong hand would come from his successor, who could certainly steer—right toward the rocks of oblivion.

After retiring from politics, Harcourt wrote his memoirs (with the help of a co-author) and became a senior associate at the University of B.C.'s Sustainable Development Research Institute.

Glen David Clark

(February 22, 1996–August 21, 1999)

I n the words of a *Province* editorialist, Glen Clark looked "like a deer caught in the headlights" when the opposition party sprang the B.C. Hydro investment scandal on him. Clark was supposed to savour the publicity surrounding his ascension to the premiership on February 22, 1996, but instead had to answer a barrage of media questions about his role in the Hydro affair.

The day before, the Liberals had alleged that New Democratic Party and Hydro insiders were major shareholders in the Raiwind power project in Pakistan. Clark, who had been minister responsible for B.C. Hydro when the private sector deal was put together in 1995, promptly (and precipitately, it turned out) fired President John Sheehan and ordered chairman John Laxton to resign.

Apparently the cosy deal was legal, although it involved offshore tax havens and, in the words of the *Vancouver Sun,* "tax avoidance, secrecy, fabulous deals to friends—all under the usually watchful eye of Mr. Clark." The Raiwind revelations provided the rockiest launch ever for any B.C. premier, but the scrappy, cocky Clark managed to divert the voters' attention long enough to win a critical election. The Hydro mess never completely faded from view, although it had to jockey for attention with other scandals during Clark's administration.

Clark always liked to polish his image as a streetwise, card-carrying unionist who battled his way to the top. In real life, the road to the premiership was a mite smoother. Glen David Clark was born November 22, 1957, in Nanaimo to James and Barbara Hamilton Clark. His father was a painter and the family soon moved to Ladysmith for a spell, then to Vancouver's East End.

Educated in the Roman Catholic school system, Clark ended up at Notre Dame High School. As a second stringer on the football team, the diminutive Clark was a hard-nosed fullback and linebacker. He also did some acting and was elected student president in Grade 12. At Simon Fraser University, Clark earned a degree in Canadian studies and political science. Then he took his master's degree in community and regional planning at the University of B.C. Glen Clark married Dale Babish on March 29, 1980. They would have two children.

While at SFU, Clark worked part time as a machine operator and joined the Iron Workers local. Then, while writing his master's thesis, Clark became a union organizer for a Richmond plant. In 1985, when he was 27 years old, Clark won the NDP nomination in Vancouver East (later to be renamed Vancouver-Kingsway). He was elected in 1986 and joined the young, aggressive group of opposition critics yapping at the heels of the Vander Zalm government.

With Mike Harcourt at the helm, the NDP won the 1991 election and Clark joined the cabinet as finance minister. Although the New Democrats reckoned they had inherited a $1.8 billion deficit from the Socreds, Clark was in no hurry to pay it down. He would rather spend money. Clark's two budgets, in 1992 and '93, introduced some $1.5 billion in tax increases in order to fund the party's agenda. This included sweetheart deals with unions, greatly increased welfare spending and infrastructure projects (including a wage-fixing bonanza for Clark's labour pals in the construction industry). The provincial debt blossomed dramatically, but not before Clark took a run at the bad guys in suits. In 1992, he introduced a corporate capital tax, which quickly soured the business community on the government.

Then in 1993, Clark ran afoul of a bunch of little old ladies. His budget that year attempted to levy a surtax on owners of homes worth more than $500,000. Many of these "wealthy" homeowners turned out to be revenue-poor but house-rich widows who had no other assets. The response was so negative that the tax was junked, and so was Clark. He was dumped from finance as part of a major realignment of Harcourt's cabinet later that year and ended up in the employment and investment ministry.

By this time, the Nanaimo Commonwealth Holding Society scandal was eating away at the NDP. Harcourt finally took the bullet for the party after the links between it and the society's bingo scam were established beyond a doubt. In November 1995, the premier announced his intention to step down, and Clark became the favourite to replace him. At a Vancouver convention in

February 1996, which generated little debate or outward evidence of any schisms, Clark won the leadership on the first ballot. He cruised to victory with 802 out of 1,132 delegate votes.

After bobbing and weaving around the Pakistan bomb crater, Premier Clark got all his promises lined up and called an election for May 28. Prevailing wisdom was that the newly minted premier, with his hard-spending, hard-taxing reputation, didn't stand a chance against Gordon Campbell's Liberals. Boy, was everybody surprised.

Clark conjured up fake balanced budgets—not only for 1995-96 but also for 1996-97—and projected the image of a take-charge battler in contrast to the meek Harcourt. Campbell, who ran a negative campaign second in futility only to the NDP's Bob Skelly in 1986, was forced on the defensive. His murky economic platform and mud-slinging were no match for Clark's fiscal fabrications and class-warfare rhetoric.

Still, the Liberals captured 41.82 percent of the vote, compared with 39.45 percent for the NDP. With more than 60 percent of the electorate voting against it, the NDP somehow held on to government with 39 seats to 33 for the Liberals in the 75-seat House.

The Clark juggernaut, with its load of chutzpah and little else, started going off the rails shortly afterward. Treasury board documents leaked to the press confirmed that the "fudge-it budgets" were not only unbalanced but would show huge deficits. Clark was accused by the opposition of "relentlessly lying." Maintaining that the budget lies weren't lies at all, but simply "variances," the premier went on TV in October to try to explain why the government's rosy forecasts were so far off the mark. He couldn't.

After the budget fiasco, hardly anyone was inclined to accept a Clark promise as genuine. He was quickly pegged as a leader lacking in integrity, with almost every word he uttered being discounted. A poll disclosed that 75.4 percent of B.C.'s voters believed Clark deliberately misled them about the budget and was less trustworthy than his political opponents.

Earlier in October, Clark donned a hardhat, climbed aboard a forklift and symbolically opened the first stretch of the Island Highway. It reminded folks how much this new link between Victoria and Campbell River was costing them. When he was employment minister in 1994, Clark had decreed that the $1 billion project would be built by union workers exclusively. Accountants estimated that this closed-shop provision added $73 million to the bill.

A weak effort by the Liberals helped the government escape the 1997 legislative session without major damage, but a little black cloud of controversy had no trouble following the premier around. A report released in March by Brian Smith, a former Social Credit attorney-general, laid most of the blame for the Pakistani power deal on former Hydro chairman John Laxton, but took a passing slap at Clark.

Smith, who was simultaneously named as Laxton's successor by Clark and ordered to probe the Hydro mess, said the premier was at fault for "enabling" some of the problems associated with the scandal. While the critics labelled the report a whitewash, a lawsuit launched by former president John Sheehan loomed in the background.

As the economy sagged and timber companies started failing, another report revealed in April that the NDP's much-touted Forest Practices Code had increased the cost of cutting down trees by 75 percent.

Clark then unwrapped his Jobs and Timber Accord, one of his grandest fantasies. In the "biggest announcement that I've ever been involved with," Clark said 40,000 forestry jobs would be created through a partnership of government and the industry—although the forest companies hadn't agreed to anything. The phantom "accord" never produced a single job.

"Glendoggle" became the preferred term to describe the premier's schemes aimed at massaging special-interest groups and party insiders. It was the most descriptive epithet since "Bowserism" was coined early in the twentieth century as a synonym for the excesses of William Bowser's Conservative machine.

One instance was Clark's willingness to spend the public's money on an aging, uneconomic pulp mill in Prince Rupert. Late in 1997, the NDP government bailed out Skeena Cellulose for $240 million in order to save a bundle of union jobs. It was more than a coincidence that the mill was in Deputy Premier Dan Miller's riding.

In the kitchens and wheelhouses of coastal B.C., families dependent on another resource industry were more worried about the salmon than forests. As the number of fish dropped, the Pacific Salmon Treaty became a major source of friction between Canada and the United States. It also provided Glen Clark with a handy diversion.

Like a Stephen Leacock hero riding off in all directions, he simultaneously blamed Ottawa, Alaska and the U.S. government for the dwindling catches of B.C. fishermen. "Canada has been undermining B.C.'s position at every front," he proclaimed in August while attending a premiers' bun-toss in New Brunswick. If the senior governments couldn't reach a deal acceptable to B.C., he warned, he would cancel the federal lease on the Nanoose Bay torpedo testing range. (Ottawa retaliated by expropriating the site.)

The reason for all this fed-bashing? Optics. Clark's approval rating went from 30 to 42 percent that summer. The popularity blip was short-lived, however. By the spring of 1998, the party's rating was back down to 28 percent. Then, in a poll taken in the summer, it reached 15 percent, on the way down to 11 in

October. These were the lowest numbers for a government since Brian Mulroney's Conservatives hit 15 percent in 1991.

The numbers followed another disastrous year for the forest industry, with huge financial losses and layoffs dominating the headlines. The stormy legislative session also did little to enhance the NDP's credibility. Few people paid attention to the budget and its modest tax breaks, expecting that the projections and forecasts were a sham anyway.

On the bill-passing front, the NDP continued its Pecksniffian attack on the tobacco industry, passing three tough anti-smoking measures while continuing to collect major tax revenue from the sale of cigarettes. It also downloaded the cost of running B.C. Transit and the West Coast Express commuter line to Greater Vancouver municipalities, and passed watered-down amendments to the labour code. The code amendments, which still favoured union organizing, and Bill 50, in which the government retroactively declared itself immune to gambling-related lawsuits, triggered all-night debates in the legislature.

Because of the opinion polls, the deepening financial morass and Clark's erratic despotism, demands that he step down became more than a background mutter. His doomed Jobs and Timber Accord—one analysis showed B.C. actually lost forest jobs rather than gaining any—and growing concerns over another pet scheme promised to make 1998 a hot year for the hands-on premier.

One of the issues that moved to the front burner was the fast-ferry project. As the cabinet minister responsible, Clark had committed the Harcourt government in 1994 to building three super-speedy catamarans. The objectives—all quite laudable—were threefold: upgrade the aging B.C. Ferries fleet; give the province's moribund shipbuilding industry a boost, and then peddle the aluminum-hull technology around the world.

Clark's concept went adrift right from the get-go. First, the contracts were cost-plus, which meant the shipyards could virtually charge whatever they wanted to complete each vessel. There was no formal business plan, no firm designs, no proper supervision, no local expertise and no trained workforce.

The first ferry was scheduled to be launched in early 1996, at a cost of $70 million. It didn't go into service between Horseshoe Bay and Nanaimo until mid-1999, and the price by then approached $120 million. The cost of all three ferries, firmly set by Clark at $210 million, reached the $460 million plateau by the end of the year.

More nails thudded into Clark's political coffin on March 2, 1999, when the RCMP knocked on the front door of his East End home. With a lurking BCTV news crew rolling its cameras, the cops searched the premier's house as part of an investigation into the issuance of a provisional casino licence to a

The fast ferry, Pacificat, was already sailing into trouble
when it cleaved the waters of Howe Sound.

friend and neighbour. Clark protested his innocence and hired a high-priced mouthpiece (at taxpayers' expense).

On March 17, Auditor-General George Morfitt, after a lengthy investigation, concluded that the phoney 1996 budget that helped get Clark elected was incomplete and unreliable and suffered from unjustifiable political interference. He stopped short of saying Clark just plain lied. Two days later, forensic accountant Ron Parks (who blew open the bingo scandal in 1995) reported that the premier's office was directly involved in a "dirty tricks" campaign directed against attempts to recall three NDP MLAs. One of the targets of the disgruntled voters was cabinet minister Paul Ramsey.

Meanwhile, the legislative session droned on. On April 22, the House gave final passage to the controversial Nisga'a Treaty. The vote, after the government invoked closure, was on straight party lines. The treaty, B.C.'s first modern-day land-claims settlement, was opposed by the Liberals (and some constitutional experts) because it created a new level of government and established a disturbing precedent for future treaties.

Finance Minister Joy MacPhail's budget was the usual borrow-and-spend model. The forecast deficit—$890 million—was the ninth straight for the NDP. Net debt for 1999-00 was calculated at $26.2 billion, which didn't include the billions owed by Crown corporations.

The government's string of unbalanced budgets can be traced directly to the desk of deputy minister Tom Gunton, a left-wing academic on leave from SFU. Gunton was Clark's thesis adviser in the Seventies and the pair had been closely associated for years. As the resident pedant in Clark's inner circle, Gunton headed the cabinet policy and communications secretariat, or CPCS (known as "Cupcakes" around the legislature). CPCS could do anything it wanted in the field of policy. As far as the budgets were concerned, Gunton's influence was virtually unassailable. The auditor-general identified him as a key architect of the overly optimistic 1996 election budget.

Clark's credibility took another jolt in June when the B.C. Supreme Court ruled that John Sheehan was wrongfully dismissed in 1996 following disclosure of Hydro's dubious venture into offshore investment. Judge Donald Brenner chose not to believe Clark's testimony that he knew nothing beforehand about insiders buying shares in the project.

By this time, even core NDP supporters were among those alienated by Clark's performance as premier. Some caucus and cabinet members began considering a palace putsch. MacPhail resigned from cabinet and an NDP backbencher bolted. The premier, once regarded as the party's brightest spark, was now a grinning albatross draped around its neck.

Attorney-General Ujjal Dosanjh delivered the fatal blow on August 20 when he revealed that Clark was a police target in a major investigation into corruption. "The premier is under criminal investigation in the context of the information released by the court today," he said.

That information included the details of the warrant used to justify the search of Clark's home. Police were looking for evidence the premier had received a benefit in the form of discount home renovations or had used his influence in connection with an application for a casino licence by his friend, Dimitrios Pilarinos.

On August 21, Clark announced he would resign as soon as the caucus selected a replacement. Dan Miller was chosen the same day and was sworn in as premier August 25.

During his years in government, Glen Clark became noted for making wildly inappropriate comments. As employment and investment minister, for

instance, he heralded the inauguration of commuter rail by boasting, "Gawd, we're shovelling money off a truck." In 1994, he vowed that the cost of his three fast ferries was a firm $210 million, "right down to the toilet paper."

The day after his election in 1996, Clark allowed that "I want to reserve a tiny, little wriggle room" regarding validation of the "balanced" budget that helped keep the NDP in power. And in 1998, as he desperately tried to find someone to invest in B.C., he boasted that "three, count 'em, three aluminum smelters" were on the way. None were built.

So it is not surprising that the ex-premier's take on his forced resignation was not exactly in touch with reality. "I would say the problems for the NDP have not been particularly me, my leadership or even the mistakes I made," he said. "The real problem has been the psychology of the province and the sense by a lot of people that we're not doing as well (in terms of the economy) as we should have."

Glen David Clark promised he would be back.

Arthur Daniel Miller

(August 25, 1999– February 24, 2000)

I t's Miller Time in B.C.! So went one of the witticisms exchanged by habitués of the B.C. legislature during the final months of 1999. There were other variations—Miller Draft and Miller Lite—with the same beery theme, because Premier Dan Miller had been known to inhale a brew or two in his home town of Prince Rupert.

And after Miller replaced the autocratic Glen Clark on August 25, the notably relaxed character of provincial politics indicated it was indeed time for some lightness of being. The NDP stalwart getting much of the attention once reserved for Clark was a sad-faced, chain-smoking, stoop-shouldered former pulp mill worker with a reputation for bluntness and salty language.

Arthur Daniel Miller was born December 24, 1944, in Port Alice, B.C., to Arthur William and Evelyn Estelle Lewis Miller. The family moved to North Vancouver, and young Dan finished high school there before drifting north on his own. Aged nineteen, he went to work at the local pulp mill, saved up his money and then took off for Europe. He came back with a British wife and an infant child and started learning the millwright's trade at the mill.

Active in the Pulp, Paper and Woodworkers of Canada, he served briefly as the local's president before going to work for Graham Lea in Victoria in 1973. Lea had become the MLA for Prince Rupert in 1972. After the Dave Barrett government was defeated in 1975, Miller returned to his millwright's job. By this time, his marriage had failed.

During the late Seventies and early Eighties, Miller served as an alderman on city council. Elected to Lea's old seat of Prince Rupert (now called North Coast) in 1986, Miller became the New Democrats' forestry critic. On February 19, 1987, he married Gayle Ballard. They are parents to five children.

When the NDP formed the government in 1991, Miller was given the forestry portfolio. He also handled the labour, municipal affairs, and employment and investment ministries before being made deputy premier and energy and mines minister by Premier Clark. In 1992, Miller was suspended from cabinet for three months for conflict of interest after keeping his seniority rights at the Prince Rupert mill even though it was affected by one of his cabinet decisions.

That same year, Miller, Premier Mike Harcourt and another cabinet minister, David Zirnhelt, made a secret deal with the Nemiah band that gave the Indians veto power over any logging in their traditional territory west of Williams Lake. This promise was made after Indians blockaded a road and despite the fact that a forest firm, Carrier Lumber of Prince George, had a valid licence to cut down trees in the area.

When the government abruptly cancelled its licence, Carrier sued. On July 29, 1999, the B.C. Supreme Court ruled that the government had breached the terms of its agreement with Carrier. Describing government officials as arrogant, deceitful, duplicitous and unethical, Judge Glenn Parrett said the government had sacrificed Carrier in order to make peace with the Indians, then tried to cover it up. He awarded punitive damages to Carrier that some experts said may reach $150 million. Even before he was sworn in as premier, Miller said B.C. would appeal the decision.

In 1997, when his old employer, Skeena Cellulose, drifted into bankruptcy, Miller was the lead negotiator in government attempts to bail it out. Despite his boast at the time that "I understand business, these guys don't" (and his premature announcement that a deal had been made), Miller and the NDP cabinet had to come up with $240 million to stop the banks from closing down the money-losing mill.

Miller managed to keep out of harm's way during the final months of Clark's self-destruction. However, he was privately distressed at the government's refusal to deal honestly with a wide range of issues. After the police raid, he was the first to tell Clark he had to go.

When it was revealed that Clark was the focus of a criminal investigation involving the issuance of a provisional casino licence, Miller was back home in Prince Rupert. He hastily returned to Victoria for the August 21 emergency caucus meeting following Clark's resignation and was chosen interim leader and premier. Miller was the obvious choice, sources said, because of his stability and his low-key approach to governing.

One of Miller's earliest moves was to clean out the nest of Clark advisers and political appointees in the premier's office. The cabinet policy and communications secretariat was disbanded, leaving Clark's top aide, Tom Gunton, without influence. Still troubled by being shut out of the inner circle along with the rest of Clark's cabinet, Miller quickly emphasized that centralized control was over. "People who are elected represent the public best and they should be the principal policy makers," Miller told *Vancouver Sun* columnist Vaughn Palmer. To his own cabinet, the premier stressed that his ministers must "assume the responsibility for which they have been given a mandate."

Several sins of the Clark administration didn't make Miller's life any easier during his first months in office. The 1999-2000 deficit was officially pegged at $1.5 billion by Auditor-General George Morfitt—millions more than the figure touted by Finance Minister Gordon Wilson earlier in the year. ("Flip" Wilson, former leader of the Liberals and then his own party, the Progressive Democratic Alliance, before joining the government, was assigned to another portfolio after he started positioning himself for a run at the NDP leadership.)

Miller ordered a review of the SkyTrain expansion to Coquitlam, which was ramrodded through by the former premier in 1998. As the minister responsible for B.C. Ferries while the fast-ferry fiasco unfolded, Miller was well versed in the runaway economics of a Glen Clark project. As for the fast ferries themselves, Morfitt's October 28 report on the controversial program confirmed that it was one of the most massively mismanaged initiatives ever undertaken by a B.C. government.

Clark got most of the blame for the political interference, improper management and premature construction that led to a trio of costly, overweight and inefficient vessels. But Miller, who was made minister responsible for ferries on April Fool's Day 1996, had to take his share of the heat for being Clark's stooge during most of the botched exercise. He accepted Morfitt's report with the terse observation that he personally accepted responsibility for his role in the disaster.

Miller had to cancel another "Glendoggle" (at a cost to the taxpayer of $70 million) that never advanced much further than a lot of Clark posturing. This was the proposal to build a $1 billion convention complex on the Vancouver waterfront. After failing to get the federal government or anyone else to act as partners, Clark had boasted that B.C. would build the facility by itself. Miller wasn't prepared to spend that kind of money.

Although a caretaker premier, Dan Miller had to consider the future. "The public will forgive you lots but they won't forgive much if they think you're trying to put one over on them," he told Palmer. Compared with the previous occupant in the corner office, Miller Time had started out with a refreshing example of straight talk.

Ujjal
Dosanjh

(February 24, 2000–   )

A ttorney-General Ujjal Dosanjh was chosen party leader February 20, 2000, at an NDP convention in Vancouver. Later that week, on February 24, Dan Miller formally resigned and Dosanjh was sworn in as premier of B.C.

Dosanjh won over Agriculture Minister Conrad (Corky) Evans on the final ballot, 769 to 549. Evans' laid-back attitude drew unexpected support during the leadership campaign, which turned into a two-man race after candidates Gordon Wilson and Len Werden withdrew prior to the voting.

The Dosanjh victory marked the end of a pitched battle within the NDP following Premier Glen Clark's resignation in August, 1999. Dosanjh had triggered Clark's downfall by publicly identifying him as the target of a criminal investigation.

Clark's animosity toward Dosanjh turned the lengthy campaign into an intense struggle for control of the party. The Clark loyalists, who included former premier Dave Barrett and cabinet minister Moe Sihota, gave their support to Wilson. However, several thousand "instant" NDP members had been signed up by Dosanjh's backers during the campaign — which translated into pro-Dosanjh delegates at the convention — and this helped the attorney-general win the leadership. By the time the delegate selection process had ended in mid-February, Dosanjh had built up a strong lead.

He also had the support of former premier Mike Harcourt and former cabinet minister Joy MacPhail, who had earlier declared her candidacy but then withdrew.

242

"We are kicking, gouging and scratching and using whatever is at hand," Harcourt said of the campaign on the day he announced his support for Dosanjh. Harcourt said the politics of confrontation practised by Clark and Wilson must be replaced by Dosanjh's cool leadership.

Ujjal Dosanjh was born September 9, 1947, in the Punjab territory of India. He and his wife Raminder have three children. Educated at SFU and UBC, Dosanjh practised law in private life and was first elected as an MLA in 1991. In 1985, he was severely beaten with an iron bar during an attack believed to be connected with Indo-Canadian community politics.

Dosanjh came into prominence as attorney-general during the Gustafsen Lake standoff in 1995. The month-long crisis involved a land dispute between a rancher and a group of natives claiming the land was aboriginal territory. While the RCMP and the armed forces confronted the group at its camp, Dosanjh kept his cool and behaved "fairly and firmly in the face of immense pressure," Harcourt said later.

A high-profile Indo-Canadian, Dosanjh polished his image of competence and reasonableness, in contrast to the bullying tactics of Clark. However, a revelation that Dosanjh for several months during 1999 had private knowledge of the investigation into Premier Clark's affairs brought his integrity into question. Enemies within the NDP portrayed him as a self-centred turncoat who knew this information would destroy Clark, and thus began manoeuvring for the leadership before other candidates entered the race.

Wilson, despite support from the Clark faction and some union delegates, had too many enemies within the party. The fact he had been a member for only 13 months weighed against him. Evans, despite removing himself from the bitter polarity of the Dosanjh-Harcourt and Wilson-Clark cliques, could not garner enough support to come up the middle.

From First to Worst: Rating the Premiers

Any attempt to design the perfect politician very quickly falls prey to reality. There ain't no such animal. However, if it was possible to clone the ideal premier from bits and pieces of the previous incumbents, these are the attributes we should consider:

The leadership of Duff Pattullo, the integrity of John Oliver, the vision of W.A.C. Bennett and the financial acumen of John Hart. This ideal first minister would also have the patience of William Smithe, the toughness of Bill Bennett and the charm of Richard McBride.

At the other end of the scale, the premier from hell would display the lack of leadership manifested by Amor De Cosmos, the pettiness of John Robson, the amoral loutishness of Joe Martin, the slippery ethics of Bill Vander Zalm and the financial incompetence and two-bit tyranny of Glen Clark.

That said, our real premiers can be ranked from the very best to the very worst by using a common set of criteria. That we expect more from our premiers now than 50, 75 or 125 years ago is obvious. The electorate is better educated at the dawn of the 21st century than ever before, and it is kept better informed. A complicating factor is that we also expect *different* things from the corner office.

From the early 1870s to the arrival of the CPR in 1886, a premier had to concentrate on the need for responsible government, free from the shackles of Ottawa. British Columbia came into existence as a province because its citizens wanted to direct their own destiny. The man in the premier's chair forgot this at his peril. When the railway arrived, the next several decades were devoted to progress and prosperity—almost to the exclusion, one might think, of rational thoughts about the future.

Issues come and go. Railway development was once an important yardstick by which a premier was measured. So were relations with Ottawa (which even now are trotted out whenever a beleaguered first minister needs a red herring).

Voters today worry about lies, conflict of interest, scandals, class warfare and government policies that are designed to reward or placate special-interest enclaves.

The handling of the public purse is still of great concern. While premiers over the years have messed up their financial obligations more often than not, the situation in Victoria at the end of the twentieth century was almost beyond comprehension. Like lying, which was expected and accepted in the past, fiscal ineptness seemed to come with the territory. But when these two negatives were combined, as they were in the late 1990s, what were merely irritating traits connected with past administrations reached the level of outright malfeasance.

The integrity of a premier goes beyond charisma, style, party label or high-priced mouthpieces. The reasonably honest ones tend to be around for a while. The economy is another issue that never goes away, and the bottom line has carried off more than one premier.

So integrity and fiscal responsibility are two of the benchmarks. Others include leadership of the party and the province; the quality of a premier's vision, whether it is long-range or politically motivated; and the level of communication between the leader and the citizenry. An added, intangible factor is the feel-good level the public has about the premier, which can be more (or less) than the sum of his or her accomplishments.

Applying these considerations to the political life of each premier, I produced a scoring system with which I ranked all 31 first ministers to determine whether they are Good, Bad or Transient. Just like an old-fashioned civics exam, the scores are based on a maximum of 100 points.

John Foster McCreight

Score: 52. McCreight held two of the most important positions in British Columbia—premier and Supreme Court justice. He adhered to solid Victorian values, but his legal erudition made him an acknowledged authority on jurisprudence, not politics. Uncomfortable in the glare of the legislative assembly, he remained too aloof to inspire a following. Nevertheless, McCreight left a foundation of statutes for his successors to build upon. If McCreight had lasted longer, he could have played a more prominent role in our history. Colour him **Transient.**

Amor De Cosmos

Score: 42. De Cosmos can be celebrated for his vision and drive in dragging B.C. into Confederation, but not for his contribution afterward. Even when he reached the highest office in B.C. politics, his heart belonged to Ottawa. De Cosmos's fame as a pioneering journalist has clouded perception of his worth as a premier. Self-conceit was a large part of his makeup (as his name change suggests). De Cosmos never took the office of premier seriously, nor did he try to ease the growing pains of a young province. He provided little leadership, preferring to concentrate on his commitments as an MP. George Walkem, his successor, characterized him as a man who had "all the eccentricities of a comet but none of the brilliance." In the words of historian S.W. Jackman, Amor De Cosmos always had one foot on the dock and the other in the boat. Colour him **Bad**.

George Anthony Walkem

Score: 61. Beginning with his efforts as attorney-general in 1872, Walkem established a rudimentary political machine that ran B.C. for a decade. He was a canny, pragmatic, no-nonsense professional who was genuinely admired by his constituents. His detractors accused Walkem of "dangling small things" before the people in an attempt to "humbug" them—not an abnormal practice for a politician. Walkem's fiscal record was unenviable. He sank the province into debt by embarking on an ambitious public works project. In dealing with others, he always met his obligations and never forgot a favour. Walkem's lasting legacy, however, is the transcontinental railway. Without his stubborn dedication, the terms of union may well have been altered beyond recognition. Colour him **Good**.

Andrew Charles Elliott

Score: 50. Elliott was a genial soul with generous impulses. A civil servant who served the colony and the province to the best of his ability, Elliott had no more than adequate skills. His brief career in politics demonstrated that he had neither the stamina nor the temperament to decipher the nuances of that rough-and-tumble calling. Elliott's premiership was more an accident of politics than a logical step in his career. Colour him **Transient**.

Robert Beaven

Score: 51. Beaven was B.C.'s longest-serving MLA during the nineteenth century. He was a study in contradictions, managing to get re-elected despite a manner that was not exactly voter-friendly. A skilled debater, Beaven was shrewd and worked hard, but had little personal charm. He had an acrid, cynical attitude that attracted more enemies than supporters. Saddled by the sins of his predecessor, Beaven was given little chance to extend his mandate. That Beaven hung on to power for several months after being repudiated at the polls is a black mark. Colour him **Transient**.

William Smithe

Score: 69. Smithe's premiership was one of stable expansion. Using his oratorical and debating skills, he was able to build on the efforts of previous premiers and lead B.C. out of two decades of rancour into a bright future. Smithe was an attractive figure in an era when politicians had more warts than redeeming features. He communicated well and projected a persona that inspired followers. As the *Colonist* observed at the time of his death, "A good man has fallen." The political landscape may well have been much altered if Smithe had not died so young. Colour him **Good**.

Alexander Edmund Batson Davie

Score: 50. Because the years 1887 to 1889 were tranquil, and there were no legislative crises to test the premier's mettle, Davie's poor health did not materially diminish his governance of the province. He did exhibit an obstinate, jealous nature that was mixed with a degree of personal charm, but his forced absences from the legislature made it difficult to evaluate his historical impact. Like his predecessor, Davie died much too young. Had he lived a longer, more fruitful life, the verdict on his premiership may have been more positive. Colour him **Transient**.

John Robson

Score: 41. Suave, theatrical and often larger than life for much of his career, Robson did not grow in stature while premier. Somewhere along the way, his fiery idealism had been replaced by expediency and the pursuit of power. Although Robson's government took some positive steps—tightening up land-grant procedures was one of them—he was a crotchety old man weary of the game. Imprudent and often not too guarded in his opinions, the journalist and premier made many enemies. Although Lord Stanley of Preston, the Governor General, called Robson's death an "untimely loss" to the Dominion and the province, his many adversaries did not mourn his passing. Colour him **Bad**.

Theodore Davie

Score: 50. A greyness seemed to surround the younger Davie. A gruff and stiff exterior masked a considerable shyness—not positive traits for a premier. His one visionary move was to commission the new Legislative Buildings. Like John McCreight, Davie was a lawyer more than he was a politician. His lofty brow and balding hairline testified to his intellectual rather than his political abilities. Davie was a vigorous opponent, but a run-of-the-mill premier. Colour him **Transient**.

John Herbert Turner

Score: 41. During much of his long life, Turner exhibited all the traits of a shrewd businessman and convivial companion. Out of politics, he was a success. Inside the legislative precincts, Turner was very much less. He rejected any move toward party discipline, but may have functioned better had it been in place. Turner's business acumen deserted him when the province's finances were on the line, and this makes him one of our lesser premiers. Colour him **Bad.**

Charles Augustus Semlin

Score: 51. Semlin was a good man, simple and honest, but lacking the charisma of some of his counterparts. Despite considerable experience in politics, his brief fling at the helm of British Columbia was disjointed and traumatic. An intransigent lieutenant-governor and a shaky coalition kept meaningful legislation to a minimum. At heart, Semlin was a rancher, and history should regard him that way. Colour him **Transient.**

Joseph Martin

Score: 38. There is little good one can say about Fighting Joe. He was a political viper wrapped in a cloak of egocentric brilliance. Martin was a skilled orator, a canny parliamentarian and a dogged fighter. But he was also a devious, amoral, boorish bully whose cynicism infuriated his colleagues. Thankfully, Martin's term as premier was exceedingly brief. Had he lasted longer, this political lout would have poisoned B.C. even more. Colour him **Bad.**

James Dunsmuir

Score: 53. Dunsmuir was a rich man who was honest and reliable in his business dealings but who could never grasp the essence of politics. He entered the legislature out of self-interest rather than any sense of civic duty and may have been the most reluctant of our premiers. Dunsmuir could not adapt to public life and was too obstinate to seek compromises. The minutiae of office bored him and the bigger picture eluded him. Dunsmuir left the premiership when it was decently possible to do so, leaving behind only a faint impression. Colour him **Transient.**

Edward Gawler Prior

Score: 42. Prior was not nearly as rich as James Dunsmuir, but he was another capable, industrious business leader who was naïve as a politician. A genial sort, he never hid his conviction that railway construction meant prosperity. Before he could lead the province further down that roadbed, however, Prior messed up. It was his naïveté, not dishonesty, which led to the contract scandal involving the construction of a bridge. Nevertheless, Prior is the only premier to be dismissed because of malfeasance. Because of that, colour him **Bad.**

Richard McBride

Score: 67. Like Amor De Cosmos, McBride often seemed to be absent when most needed. The impression some voters got was that he spent most of his time in London. Apart from this absenteeism, which was more prevalent in the latter years, McBride was, over all, a positive force. He made British Columbians feel good about themselves and made outsiders feel good about B.C. He introduced party politics, stabilizing the legislative scene, and had the wit and luck to ride an economic boom without falling off. Despite the favouritism, patronage and railway give-aways associated with his regime, B.C. prospered and took giant steps forward. Colour him **Good.**

William John Bowser

Score: 41. Bowser was respected by fellow lawyers and in the business community, but he was cast as Richard McBride's hatchetman early in his political career and couldn't shake the image (even if he wanted to). Bowser was a curious combination of modesty and bravado. He regarded politics as an extension of power, not democracy. The term "Bowserism" came to mean patronage and machine politics, whereby the vested interests overrode those of the ordinary voter. Bowser was grim and taciturn, with a poor public presence. But he was straightforward and never beat about the bush. Colour him **Bad.**

Harlan Carey Brewster

Score: 56. Brewster was honest, conscientious and down to earth. He had none of the charisma or arrogance of his immediate predecessors. A good organizer and fair, Brewster was a very ordinary man who found himself, briefly, in an extraordinary job. He did some good, bringing in legislation creating a treasury board, which would help bring the province's financial affairs under control. Another premier who died too soon, Brewster didn't last long enough to make a mark. Colour him **Transient.**

John Oliver

Score: 67. Oliver was honest to a fault about his personal dealings, carefully paying for all his expenses not connected with the government. Around the premier's office, he was bossy and cranky. Oliver wasn't born a great politician, but made himself an effective one. His homespun persona—the country boy taking on the city slickers—charmed many a voter. He fought hard for British Columbia, scoring a significant victory on the national stage by getting a beneficial change in railway freight rates. Oliver reduced both taxes and the debt, leaving B.C. in reasonable shape for his successor. One hostile editor said Oliver's "brain becomes inflamed with the noise of his mouth," but the farmer-premier's aphorisms always seemed to make a point. Colour him **Good**.

John Duncan MacLean

Score: 51. MacLean was safe, faithful and dull. A good lieutenant but a boring leader, he was orderly, logical and diligent. Known to insiders as "Old Velvet Belly" because of his subtle manner, MacLean was a competent legislator. But after the folksy charms of John Oliver, his dry, unspectacular presence attracted few voters. Colour him **Transient**.

Simon Fraser Tolmie

Score: 39. When he became premier, Tolmie reached the level of his incompetence. As an MP, MLA, backbencher or minor cabinet minister, he was loyal, successful and popular. But once in the corner office, Tolmie lacked the killer instinct and the flair for administrative action. His lack of leadership might have got him by in stable times, but in a crisis his ineffective confusion destroyed both Tolmie and the Conservative party. The Great Depression was a monster far larger than any he had dreamed could be possible, and it devoured him. Colour him **Bad**.

Thomas Dufferin Pattullo

Score: 73. Pattullo was a man of principle and a premier of vision who restored B.C.'s confidence in itself during the Great Depression. He was often charming, elegant and suave on the surface, but obdurate and rock-hard underneath. Pattullo's obstinate pursuit of a better deal from Ottawa was a blind spot that alienated both the voters and his own party. Although he steered the province through one of its worst times, he was out of tune toward the end. Certainly the greatest Liberal in B.C.'s political history, this happy warrior never knew a moment of doubt or fear. Pattullo's impact is matched by few other premiers. Colour him **Good**.

John Hart

Score: 76. Hart believed in orthodoxy but had an Irish twinkle in his eye. That twinkle and that shock of white hair, however, masked a character of chilled steel. He was an astute, able finance minister. As premier, he exhibited a rational, logical style that kept the Coalition on an even keel. Although Hart showed leadership in avoiding Coalition disasters and in reaching a tax deal with Ottawa, this was partly offset by his "me-too" response to the Japanese panic in 1942. He had the vision to realize that B.C. needed a rest from party quarrelling, but also recognized that the Liberals needed to plan for the future. Colour him **Good.**

Byron Ingemar Johnson
Score: 53. Johnson looked like a premier. Charming, handsome and a spiffy dresser, he displayed all the attributes of a successful leader. However, the dogfight that was the Coalition government in its final years of existence was not the place for a sissy, and Johnson was too easy-going. His lack of leadership also showed in the handling of the hospital insurance crisis. Low-cost health care was a noble concept, but the Coalition totally mismanaged it. Johnson's visionary decision to extend the PGE and thus open the north for development is balanced by his endorsement of the fatal alternative-voting scheme. In the end, Byron Johnson was an amateur politician who had no staying power. Colour him **Transient.**

William Andrew Cecil Bennett
Score: 79. To many people, Bennett was as much a charlatan as he was a hero. The *Vancouver Sun* never did cotton to him. "During 20 years under Social Credit, this province's physical face was scarred permanently by the actions of a government intent on pursuing economic growth in the cowboy tradition of the frontier," it growled in 1975. On the other hand, Gordon Shrum, former co-chairman of B.C. Hydro, echoed the thoughts of many when he called Bennett one of the "most courageous and imaginative political leaders I have ever known." Bennett was a huckster, an opportunist and a visionary. He truly wanted B.C. to prosper and believed he was the man to make it so. He ran an autocratic, one-man government and had no patience for the team approach. Because Bennett didn't delegate awfully well, his overall leadership qualities at the cabinet level were less than optimum. Wacky he certainly wasn't; rather, he liked to rattle everyone's cage now and then by making outrageous remarks. Bennett often blurted out his thoughts with a sort of nervous confusion. His jerky syntax and wandering speech patterns robbed his utterances of apparent clarity, but no premier influenced the province's history as much as W.A.C. Bennett. Colour him **Good.**

David Barrett
Score: 42. Silver-tongued as the gregarious, wise-cracking Barrett was, he could not communicate his party's vision for B.C. One wonders whether he even had

a handle on it himself. The hasty, frenetic style of the short-lived NDP government owed much to his poor leadership. Ministerial irresponsibility and financial ineptness must be laid squarely at Barrett's doorstep. He failed to govern. Then, years afterward, he repudiated a key socialist belief—the sanctity of land use. The clever spontaneity of Barrett's garrulous style was not nearly adequate to the task of leadership. Colour him **Bad.**

William Richards Bennett

Score: 67. Much has been made of Bennett's "tough guy" image by fringe political chroniclers. That toughness is equated with leadership was usually glossed over. Bennett had his faults. He depended too much on the politics of polarity and confrontation. Because of his perceived aloofness and insularity, he was not usually a good communicator. But his restraint package, in the context of the Eighties, was a necessary step to keep B.C. on the move. Bennett entered politics to win. In achieving that goal, he revived the Social Credit party and steered B.C. through a rough economic period that was the most daunting since the Great Depression. Colour him **Good.**

William Nick Vander Zalm

Score: 36. Anyone wishing to know why Vander Zalm was one of B.C.'s worst premiers should visit their local library and read the Hughes Report on Fantasy Gardens. Vander Zalm's moral turpitude is amply demonstrated by his conduct during this affair. As a leader, he preferred to give too much power to an unelected aide while leaving his cabinet directionless. Vander Zalm has been called a right-wing, redneck populist, but this populism consisted more of an ad hoc, scattergun approach to issues rather than any serious communication about them. He had no vision except the next headline. Vander Zalm once said that "politics is marketing," as if it was on a par with peddling tulip bulbs. Colour him **Bad.**

Rita Margaret Johnston

Score: 50. Johnston was an establishment politician and a team player. That is to say, the Social Credit establishment and the Bill Vander Zalm team. Her loyalty to her predecessor was her main strength through the unravelling of the Vander Zalm mandate, and it hurt her in the end. Johnston could offer nothing new to the voters during her brief administration and couldn't discard the Vander Zalm shroud during the election campaign. She did no harm as a premier, but lacked the vision to move the party into the future. Colour her **Transient.**

Michael Franklin Harcourt

Score: 52. Harcourt was a premier vastly overmatched by the office. His lack of control over the party "pit bulls" was mirrored by his inability to govern B.C. effectively. The fact that Harcourt stepped down (after a slight shove) for the good of the NDP was probably the noblest act of his premiership. Harcourt presided rather than led. During his administration, the NDP record ranged from appalling patronage to solid achievement, but he never seemed to be in charge—a fence-sitter without strong convictions. As one astute observer noted, "He's no Tommy Douglas." Colour him **Transient**.

Glen David Clark

Score: 30. The cabinet system of government under the British parliamentary system assumes that "gentlemen" will use their enormous power wisely. Clark's predatory use of such power, which included petty bullying, constant dissembling and preference for an inner cadre of non-elected cronies, made a mockery of his office. Under a thin veneer of cocky assertiveness, he was a reckless incompetent who had conned his way into the premiership. Clark abandoned leadership of his cabinet, his party and the taxpayers, preferring to enrich special-interest supporters. At best, his vision was opaque. Apart from his personal addiction to power, Clark's adherence to a left-wing ideology of wanton spending helped drive the province deep into debt. Colour him **Bad**.

Arthur Daniel Miller

Score: 48. Following the sound and fury of the Clark years, the relative calm of Miller's premiership was a welcome break for British Columbians. Miller's low-key style, however, didn't mean he wasn't a dedicated New Democrat with strong ties to the labour movement. This partisanship helped saddle B.C. with the Skeena Cellulose debt. In addition, Miller's integrity comes into question because of the Carrier Lumber and fast-ferry episodes. However, under the time constraints of this book, Miller's administration was relatively benign. Colour him **Transient**.

The List

Throw in a few intangibles here and there, which would affect the evaluations slightly, and this is how our premiers are ranked, from the very best to the very worst:

1. W.A.C. Bennett
2. John Hart
3. Duff Pattullo
4. William Smithe
5. John Oliver
6. Bill Bennett
7. Richard McBride
8. George Walkem
9. Harlan Brewster
10. James Dunsmuir
11. Byron Johnson
12. Mike Harcourt
13. John McCreight
14. Charles Semlin
15. John MacLean
16. Robert Beaven
17. Andrew Elliott
18. Theodore Davie
19. A.E.B. Davie
20. Rita Johnston
21. Dan Miller
22. Edward Prior
23. Amor De Cosmos
24. Dave Barrett
25. John Robson
26. William Bowser
27. John Turner
28. Simon Tolmie
29. Joe Martin
30. Bill Vander Zalm
31. Glen Clark

The Final Word

There is an abiding myth that the voting public determines the fate of governments. Not bloody likely, in most elections. Our archaic plurality system, which favours the frontrunners above everyone else, is responsible for more electoral miscarriages than any other element in a democratic society.

Take the British Columbia election of May 28, 1996. The voters awoke the next morning to marvel at what they had wrought, for the party having the most ballots cast in its favour did not win the most seats. Yes, 661,929 votes—41.82 percent of the total—went to the Liberals and 624,395—39.45 percent—to the New Democratic Party. Yet the NDP laughed all the way back to the legislature with 39 out of 75 MLAs elected.

Clearly, the system isn't working. In a two-party environment, the first-across-the-line method of selecting electoral winners functions adequately. When the multi-party system rules, however, the results often do not reflect the will of the electorate. And B.C. has never offered a simple "Us vs. Them" choice in the voting booth. There is always one "Us" (the party in power), but several fragmented "Thems" seek to bring it down. Before formal party designations were adopted in 1903, the voters faced an equally bewildering array of personal philosophies and ideologies.

There are other ways to elect governments—the transferable ballot (or alternative voting), proportional representation, weighted ballots, run-off elections, for instance—but all have flaws just as disturbing as the plurality system. Before we discuss these, however, and propose a method that would be fair to everyone concerned, an examination of B.C.'s quirky electoral past is needed to put the situation into context.

For the past 130 years, the constitutional entity that is British Columbia has been shaped and reshaped by forces that sometimes seemed out of control. It is hard to imagine, for instance, in these days of the impeccably secret ballot and rigid control of voters' lists, that for a brief period, members of the House were elected by open declaration. During the early 1870s, MLAs were allowed to hold seats in the House of Commons. For more than 50 years, also, a member appointed to a cabinet post had to resign the seat and run for it again in a byelection. This picky requirement was scrubbed in 1929.

For many years, absentee voting was not allowed. And, in a province that took the Imperial shibboleth "God is an Englishman" seriously, discrimination was widespread. Women, of course, were not enfranchised until 1917. Chinese and native Indians were disenfranchised in 1874, Japanese in 1895 and "Hindus" in 1907. None of these ethnic groups were allowed in a voting booth until after the Second World War. Civil servants, schoolteachers and the clergy were also disenfranchised for brief periods. Doukhobors, Hutterites and Mennonites were denied the vote for several years during the Thirties and Forties. Until 1985, voters were required to be British subjects.

As those eligible to cast ballots increased, so did the number of members. In 1871, 25 MLAs from 12 ridings were elected by 3,804 voters. Then, only white males who owned property were handed a ballot. In 1996, the number of MLAs had grown to 75, and they were chosen by 1,592,655 voters of all persuasions aged nineteen and over. (It was not the largest number to ever cast ballots; that was 1,935,453 in 1986).

Redistribution over the years has gradually added seats and redefined electoral boundaries as the population flowed toward the Lower Mainland. Since 1898, the importance of Vancouver and its environs has been reflected in the number of MLAs sent to Victoria.

When Richard McBride wrote his historic letter of June 2, 1903, to the legislature declaring the advent of formal party politics, the groundwork had been laid for some time. The first Labour candidate officially listed as such popped up in 1886. In 1890, there was also a "Farmer's candidate."

Premier John Turner had to resist attempts to introduce the federal system into B.C. in 1898, and Lt-Gov. Thomas McInnes (who fired Turner) was an open supporter of Wilfrid Laurier's Liberal party. Several strange bedfellows were listed for the 1900 election—the last one before formal labels. These included Government-Independent, Liberal-Conservative and Provincial Party. The first Socialist party hopeful also ran in this election.

Among the wannabes who elbowed their way into the 1903 election were Labour, Socialist Labour and Socialist adherents. There were also other permutations of "Labour," with the candidates backed by various union splinter groups. These fringe dwellers got about 16 percent of the popular vote and picked up the three seats that did not go to the Conservatives or Liberals.

While the two main parties lumbered on, swapping promises and governments, those occupying the outer reaches of the voters' consciousness came and went. The Social Democrats chipped in for a couple of elections before disappearing in the Twenties. In 1920, the first election following the Great War, the number of party affiliations set a record that still stands. There were fifteen with formal labels, plus eighteen candidates listed as Independent. Who could not vote for the Grand Army of United Veterans? (5,441 did.) Or the Independent Soldier party, or the Soldier/Farmers, or the United Farmers of British Columbia? Among them, the 68 candidates not allied with the two big parties attracted 31 percent of the vote and won 7 of the 47 seats.

Until the Co-operative Commonwealth Federation showed up in 1933, there was not a third party of any permanent consequence. And the ones on the outer edge got even more creative. In 1937, there was the B.C. Constructive and the Financial Justice parties. The Communist party and the Social Credit League of B.C. also made their appearance in this election.

The Victory Without Debt party fielded one candidate in 1941, and he got 209 votes. The CCF segued into the NDP during the Sixties and the Communists started eating their young. The Revolutionary Marxist Group ran three candidates in 1975, while in 1979 the Communist Party of Canada (Marxist-Leninist) split off from the parent group.

This election also saw a Gay Alliance Toward Equality candidate (126 votes). The Green party appeared in 1983. In 1986, there were the Libertarians, something called the Libertas of British Columbia, the New Republic party and the Western Canada Concept, among others. By now the Social Credit party and the NDP dominated the legislature; the Liberals and Conservatives had been moribund since 1952. In the 1991 and 1996 elections, the voters had other colourful choices: Human Race party, Family Choices, Green Wing/Rhino, Family Coalition, Natural Law and the Reform Party of B.C.

All legitimate political parties, if they are around long enough, drift toward the centre in order to attract as many voters as possible. The broad moral concepts of the original Liberal and Conservative parties—liberalism and social equality vs. traditionalism, elitism and free enterprise—were often suborned by practicalities.

Pattullo's Liberalism of the Thirties was a far cry from that of Laurier. His no-nonsense application of state interventionism smacked more of a far-right regime than anything else. And Gordon Campbell's Liberal party of the 1990s had links to big business that were as strong as any the Tories ever had. The Conservatism of Richard McBride and William Bowser during the Great War became a synonym for greed and patronage.

The desire to cling to power (and keep the godless CCF at bay) led both to the Liberal-Conservative Coalition government of the Forties and to the

Coalition partners' ultimate destruction. An unabashedly right-wing party, Social Credit, arose to do battle with the left-wing CCF-NDP. In the 1990s, the NDP government strayed so far from its CCF roots that its blend of special-interest politics and patronage resembled "Bowserism" more than socialism.

In the first nine elections conducted under party auspices, only three times did the winners surpass 50 percent of the vote. Even when a simple Liberal or Conservative choice was available, the fringe parties nibbled away at the totals. And after the CCF came on the scene in 1933, any chance of a government being chosen by more than half the people went out the window.

The only times since then that an elected government received more than 50 percent were the Coalition amalgams of 1945 and 1949. Social Credit's arrival spread the ballots around even more. During his twenty years in power, Premier W.A.C. Bennett never enticed 50 percent of British Columbians to vote for him. Although it became a two-way race between Social Credit and the NDP, the lingering presence of the Grits and the Tories still had nuisance value.

A fringe party can cause havoc if its popularity spikes at the wrong moment. Just as the Provincial Party siphoned off Liberal support in 1924, the Liberals came to life in 1991 and took away so many Social Credit votes that the NDP formed the government. In 1996, the New Democrats clung to power with their puny 39.45 percent because the Reform party lured away more than 100,000 probable Liberal votes.

But nobody in B.C. ever translated a minority of votes into a majority of seats under the plurality system until the NDP accomplished that dubious feat in 1996. The phenomenon is so rare in Canada that it invariably gets remarked upon at length (as when Quebec's Parti Quebecois easily retained power in 1998, although the opposition Liberals outpolled it). What is far more common is a party forming the government despite having 60 percent of the people turning thumbs down. Unless there were to be a legislated end to minority parties on the ballot, thus forcing the citizen to make one of only two choices, the plurality system is an overripe vestige of a more innocent era. It is time to change the way our representatives are democratically elected. There are several main options. Let's take them one by one.

The first is the single transferable ballot, or alternative voting. Out of strict selfishness, the Coalition government of 1949 decided to change the voting system for the next election. Instead of the old-fashioned plurality method, alternative voting would be used. Under this system, candidates in each riding are chosen in order of preference. Anyone with more than 50 percent of first-choice votes is automatically elected. If this magic percentage is not reached, the last-place finisher is dropped and the second choices in his or her pile are counted. This elimination and transferral continues until a winner emerges.

The Liberals and Conservatives, who coalesced in 1941, had decided to go their own way again, and figured this preferential method would ensure that either party would form the next government. Well, no. The Socreds, of all people, ended up with the most seats. Alternative voting was junked by Bennett in 1953.

So scratch the single transferable ballot and all its permutations. This would include the weighted ballot, on which the candidates are graded. If there were four names on the ballot, you would mark 4 alongside your first choice, then 3,2,1. Sounds good, unless there are, say, eight candidates and six of them are single-issue weirdoes. It wouldn't take very many petulant voters scribbling 8,7,6, etc., alongside the fringe entries to invalidate the legitimate contenders.

Proportional representation is the flavour of the day in electoral reform circles. In fact, PR in one form or another is the preferred method in most of the democratic world. Under it, the electoral map is divided into multi-member districts, the parties present lists of candidates and the ballots are cast. Seats are then allocated according to the proportion each party receives of the total vote.

For instance, a party receiving 40 percent of the votes in a twenty-member district would elect eight members. In some variations, the voters cast two ballots—one for a local favourite and one for the party. The problem with the straight proportional method (apart from the fact percentages are seldom nice, easy round numbers) is that the party, not the voter, decides which of its eight winners gets to sit in the House. There are visions of trade-offs and backroom deals.

To overcome this flaw (the constituent is basically casting a blind vote), a run-off could be held, in which the eight party representatives are chosen. This would seem to require party registration of each voter. Either that or a complicated ballot requiring the poor schmucks in the booth to mark both their party choices and their individual preferences should their party win some seats. One more thing giving PR bad PR is that it encourages single-issue minority candidates and coalition governments. Ask New Zealand, which endured a period of multi-party squabbling after instituting proportional representation.

One theory that has generated some discussion in Great Britain is "PR Squared." This purports to take proportional representation and massage it so that local constituency MLAs are selected, as well as ensuring that a legitimate majority government always wins out. In an overly simplified nutshell, it works something like this: Each party is allocated seats in proportion to the square root of its nationwide vote total. The method favours large parties and penalizes small and splinter ones.

Another avenue is the run-off election. France is the most well-known proponent of this method, and it is one way for the citizenry to get a result approximating what they intended. The simplest version is for the top two finishers on the original polling day to square off again in a second round. This is fine, unless one guy got 24 percent of the vote and the other 23 percent in a multi-candidate race. That would leave 53 percent of the voters wondering why they must choose either of these two losers. A further drawback is that this scenario requires an additional polling date, which means more expense, more bureaucracy and more campaigning.

It is now time to unveil my Plurality Plus formula. Under this method, majority governments are elected according to the real wishes of the people and there are no added costs or extra voting days. Under PP, voters in each riding would mark an "X" alongside their candidate in the normal manner. In addition, however, the ballot would contain a question asking voters to signify whether they want the government returned to power. It would be a simple yes-no choice, requiring another "X" in the appropriate box.

When these additional choices are added up, we would have two provincewide totals that reflect the pro- and anti-government feelings. Divide each total by the number of ridings (75) and subtract the difference. Take 20 percent of that difference and apply this new number to either the government or the leading opposition candidate in all ridings that did not have a clear winner.

If a candidate amassed more than 50 percent of the normal vote, he or she is automatically elected. All the rest are then subjected to the yes-no equation. To illustrate, I applied the PP formula to the voting totals from the 1996 B.C. election. The difference for each riding (rounded off) was 890 and, naturally, it favoured the opposition. Applying this number to the 60 ridings that did not have a clear winner would result in 41 seats for the Liberals and 31 for the NDP. The seats won by the Reform party and the Progressive Democratic Alliance would not be affected.

The beauty of Plurality Plus is that the will of the voters would be concentrated more than ever before. They can cast protest votes for any special-interest party they choose and be assured their ballot could really bring down an unpopular government should circumstances warrant. These fringe parties would still have an important voice on the ballot, but the government could no longer count on being re-elected because of a fragmented opposition.

Whatever new method British Columbia chooses to select its government, a decision should be made early in the new millennium. Otherwise, the wishes of hundreds of thousands of voters could again be thwarted.

Notes

The Corner Office

1. The Conservative party changed its name to Progressive-Conservative in December 1942, at its national convention in Winnipeg. For purposes of clarity, this book refers to "Conservatives" throughout.
2. Up until the year 2000, 30 men and 1 women have served as premier, for a total of 31. Because Walkem was sworn in twice, some sources list the number of premiers as 32.

George Anthony Walkem

1. Some sources list Walkem's given names as George Anthony Boomer, presumably to honour his mother's maiden name. However, his will is in the name of George Anthony Walkem. "Boomer" may be a nickname derived from his boisterous Cariboo law practice.

Andrew Charles Elliott

1. Bulwer-Lytton was an influential British politician and author. As colonial secretary in 1858-59, he took particular interest in Canada. The town of Lytton is named after him. "It was a dark and stormy night," the opening sentence of one of his novels, is widely regarded as the classic example of bad writing.

Theodore Davie

1. Davie's elevation to the bench bitterly disappointed Justice Henry Pellew Crease, who had been lobbying for Begbie's job even before he died. At the funeral for Begbie, Crease theatrically broke down, but to no avail. He resigned within a year of Davie's appointment.

James Dunsmuir

1. Laura had been in love with a poor farmer's son named Lunsford Richardson, but her father rejected him as a suitor. Richardson became a druggist and invented Vick's VapoRub, which became the largest-selling cold remedy in North America.

Edward Gawler Prior

1. The precedent for all land grants was the CPR deal with the Dominion government. The CPR lands in B.C., known as the Railway Belt, comprised a strip of land approximately twenty miles wide on each side of the line. Later, some of the land in the Peace River Block was added to the CPR's assets to replace acreage in the Railway Belt that had already been alienated.

John Oliver

1. John Stewart was a known Liberal supporter who helped bankroll the *Vancouver Sun* in 1912. He also became a partner in the timber firm Bloedel, Stewart & Welch. Why Conservative Premier McBride granted a Liberal sympathizer a patronage railway charter is still a puzzlement.

Thomas Dufferin Pattullo

1. Superintendent James Morrow Walsh of the North West Mounted Police gained a measure of notoriety for his handling of Chief Sitting Bull and his Sioux warriors when they fled to Canada following the Battle of the Little Bighorn. Walsh resigned the Yukon post in 1898 under a cloud because of poor administration.

Byron Ingemar Johnson

1. Under the single transferable system, voters chose alternative candidates on each ballot. See "The Final Word" chapter for full details of how this system works.

William Andrew Cecil Bennett

1. The Socreds called themselves the British Columbia Social Credit League on the 1952 ballot. In subsequent elections until 1975 they were listed with Elections British Columbia as Social Credit. In 1975, "Party" was added to the designation.

David Barrett

1. As Marjorie's bureau chief, the author witnessed this tirade. We decided to let Barrett's obscenities slide, but the rest of the press gallery and the opposition got wind of it. The result was a short-lived cause célèbre.

Premiers of British Columbia

John Foster McCreight	November 13, 1871–December 20, 1872
Amor De Cosmos	December 23, 1872–February 9, 1874
George Anthony Walkem	February 11, 1874–January 27, 1876
Andrew Charles Elliott	February 1, 1876–June 25, 1878
George Anthony Walkem	June 25, 1878–June 6, 1882
Robert Beaven	June 13, 1882–January 29, 1883
William Smithe	January 29, 1883–March 28, 1887
Alexander Edmund Batson Davie	April 1, 1887–August 1, 1889
John Robson	August 2, 1889–June 29, 1892
Theodore Davie	July 2, 1892–March 2, 1895
John Herbert Turner	March 4, 1895–August 8, 1898
Charles Augustus Semlin	August 15, 1898–February 27, 1900
Joseph Martin	February 28, 1900–June 14, 1900
James Dunsmuir	June 15, 1900–November 21, 1902
Edward Gawler Prior	November 21, 1902–June 1, 1903
Richard McBride	June 1, 1903–December 15, 1915
William John Bowser	December 15, 1915–November 23, 1916
Harlan Carey Brewster	November 23, 1916–March 1, 1918
John Oliver	March 6, 1918–August 17, 1927
John Duncan MacLean	August 20, 1927–August 20, 1928

Simon Fraser Tolmie	August 21, 1928–November 15, 1933
Thomas Dufferin Pattullo	November 15, 1933–December 9, 1941
John Hart	December 9, 1941–December 29, 1947
Byron Ingemar Johnson	December 29, 1947–August 1, 1952
William Andrew Cecil Bennett	August 1, 1952–September 15, 1972
David Barrett	September 15, 1972–December 22, 1975
William Richards Bennett	December 22, 1975–August 6, 1986
William Nick Vander Zalm	August 6, 1986–April 2, 1991
Rita Margaret Johnston	April 2, 1991–November 5, 1991
Michael Franklin Harcourt	November 5, 1991–February 22, 1996
Glen David Clark	February 22, 1996–August 21, 1999
Arthur Daniel Miller	August 25, 1999–February 24, 2000
Ujjal Dosanjh	February 24, 2000–

B.C. Election Results

Election Results, 1871–1900

1871   25 MLAs elected
(October 16–December 15)

1875   Government: 8; Opposition: 15; Others: 2 (25)
(September 11–October 25)

1878   Government: 8; Opposition: 15; Others: 2 (25)
(May 22)

1882   Government: 4; Opposition: 18; Others: 3 (25)
(July 24)

1886   Government: 18; Opposition: 9 (27)
(July 7)

1890   Government: 19; Opposition: 7; Others: 7 (33)
(June 13)

1894   Government: 21; Opposition: 12 (33)
(July 7)

1898   Government: 18; Opposition: 19; Others: 1 (38)
(July 9)

1900   Government: 5; Opposition: 11; Provincial Party: 5;
(June 9)   Conservatives: 8; Others: 9 (38)

Results by Parties, 1903–1996

	Cons.	Lib.	CCF/NDP	SC	Others	Total
1903 October 3	27,913 22 Seats	22,715 17			3	60,120 42
1907 February 2	30,871 26 Seats	23,481 13			3	63,205 42
1909 November 25	53,074 38 Seats	33,675 2			2	101,415 42
1912 March 28	50,423 39 Seats	21,433 —			3	84,529 42
1916 September 14	72,842 9 Seats	89,892 36			2	179,774 47
1920 December 1	110,475 15 Seats	134,167 25			7	354,088 47
1924 June 20	101,765 17 Seats	108,323 23			8	345,068 48
1928 July 18	192,867 35 Seats	144,872 12			1	361,814 48
1933 November 2	—	159,131 34 Seats	120,185 7		6	381,223 47
1937 June 1	119,521 8 Seats	156,074 31	119,400 7		2	417,929 48
1941 October 21	140,282 12 Seats	149,525 21	151,440 14		1	453,893 48
1945 Coalition: October 25	261,147 37 Seats		175,960 10		1	467,747 48
1949 Coalition: June 15	428,773 39 Seats		245,284 7	8,464 0	2	698,823 48
1952* June 12	65,285 4 Seats	170,674 6	231,756 18	203,932 19	1	675,654 48
1953* June 9	7,326 1 Seat	154,090 4	194,414 14	300,372 28		659,563 48
1956 September 19	25,373 0 Seats	177,922 2	231,511 10	374,711 39	1	817,397 52
1960 September 12	66,943 0 Seats	208,249 4	326,094 16	386,886 32		996,404 52

Results by Parties, 1903–1996, continued

	Cons.	Lib.	CCF/NDP	SC	Others	Total
1963 September 30	109,090 0 Seats	193,363 5	269,004** 14	395,079 33		967,675 52
1966 September 12	1,409 0 Seats	152,155 6	252,753 16	342,751 33		751,876 55
1969 August 27	1,087 0 Seats	186,235 5	331,813 12	457,777 38		978,356 55
1972 August 30	143,450 2 Seats	185,640 5	448,260 38	352,776 10		1,132,172 55
1975 December 11	49,796 1 Seat	93,379 1	505,396 18	635,482 35		1,290,451 55
1979 May 10	71,078 0 Seats	6,662 0	646,188 26	677,607 31		1,405,077 57
1983 May 5	19,131 0 Seats	44,442 0	741,354 22	820,807 35		1,649,533 57
1986 October 22	14,074 0 Seats	130,505 0	824,544 22	954,516 47		1,935,453 69
1991 October 17 (Conservatives received 426 votes)	Ref. 2,673 0 Seats	486,208 17	595,391 51	351,660 7		1,462,467 75
1996 May 28 (Social Credit received 6,276 votes and Conservatives, 1,002)	Ref. 146,734 2 Seats	661,929 33	624,395 39	PDA 90,797 1		1,582,704 75

* The 1952 and 1953 elections employed the alternative ballot method. The results in this appendix reflect the final count. The preliminary figures varied widely.
** This is the first election contested by the NDP.

Legend: CCF: Co-operative Commonwealth Federation
Cons: Conservative and Progressive Conservative
Lib: Liberal
NDP: New Democratic Party
PDA: Progressive Democratic Alliance
Ref: Reform Party of B.C.
SC: Social Credit

Population of B.C.

1871	36,247
1881	49,459
1891	98,176
1901	178,657
1911	392,480
1921	524,582
1931	694,263
1941	817,800
1951	1,165,210
1961	1,629,100
1971	2,184,600
1981	2,744,467
1991	3,282,061
1999 (Estimated)	4,100,199
2001 (Projected)	4,249,075

A Premier In Waiting

Gordon Muir Campbell

A former occupant of the corner office once called Gordon Campbell the "most dangerous man in B.C." That premier was Glen Clark and he was commenting on the Liberal leader's policies. But the unspoken message was that Campbell and his Liberals were personally dangerous to Clark and his New Democrats.

After going into the dumpster over the casino licence affair, Clark probably stopped worrying about how threatening the opposition leader was. That was for a future premier to handle in a future election. The NDP could only hope that Campbell ran a campaign as bad as the one in 1996.

The man who would be premier was born January 12, 1948, in Vancouver General Hospital to Charles Gordon and Marghret Janet Muir Campbell. After Charles committed suicide in 1961, Mrs. Campbell was forced to get a job as a secretary and Gordon helped raise the family.

Campbell graduated from University Hill school and accepted a scholarship from Dartmouth College in New Hampshire. Returning to Vancouver with a BA degree, he married Nancy Jean Chipperfield on July 4, 1970. They would have two children. After their marriage, the pair went to Nigeria to teach under Canadian University Service Overseas auspices for two years.

Later in the Seventies, Campbell got a taste of municipal politics while working as an assistant to Vancouver mayor Art Phillips. He then became a real estate developer before running successfully for Vancouver city council in 1984. Campbell was elected mayor in 1986 and served for seven years.

It was during Campbell's mayoralty that his pro-development tunnel vision came to the fore. During the battle to save the Stanley Theatre in 1991, for example, Campbell told a reporter that property owners should not have to pay for uneconomic heritage sites. Asked whether something should die if it wasn't profitable, he replied: "Yes, in this community we normally say that."

Campbell wrestled the leadership of the provincial Liberal party away from Gordon Wilson in 1993 after Wilson's adulterous affair with fellow MLA Judy Tyabji became public knowledge. In 1994, Campbell gained a seat in the legislature via a byelection.

The 1996 election was a humbling experience for Campbell. Despite having a huge lead in the opinion polls, he allowed Clark and his financial doubletalk to overwhelm the voters. Campbell's reserved personality made the Liberal leader come across as aloof, condescending and uptight. As one reporter noted, Campbell's smile seemed to be connected to a knot in his stomach.

Campbell's performance as opposition leader was uneven. His party didn't offer much resistance during the 1997 legislative session, but did better in 1998. And, of course, the Liberals did drop the B.C. Hydro scandal into Clark's unsuspecting lap in 1996. Campbell often gave the impression he was speaking down to people from a podium. By 1999, however, he had noticeably improved. His effort before a Liberal convention in Kelowna drew high marks from observers as well as the party faithful.

In that speech, Campbell refined his proposal to reform B.C.'s troubled political system. He advocated free votes in the legislature on all non-confidence matters; more power to House committees; a "citizen's assembly" to review all electoral matters; fixed election and budget dates, and balanced-budget legislation. As an added twist, Campbell said a Liberal government would end cabinet secrecy, even to the extent of holding public cabinet meetings.

In mid-1999, while Glen Clark twisted in the vortex of the casino crisis, Gordon Campbell undertook to climb Mt. Kilimanjaro in Africa as part of a campaign to raise funds for the Alzheimer Society. The symbolism, although unscripted, was obvious: Liberal leader breathes the unpolluted air at the top of the heap while the NDP leader is mired in the muck at the bottom.

With the polls once again strongly in his favour, Gordon Muir Campbell ended 1999 eagerly awaiting an election he felt was just over the horizon.

APPENDIX E

Random Intelligence

Longest-Serving: W.A.C. Bennett, 7,351 days

Shortest Tenure: Joseph Martin, 106 days

Only Female Premier: Rita Johnston

Brother Act: A.E.B. Davie and Theodore Davie

Father and Son: W.A.C. Bennett and William R. Bennett

First B.C.-Born Premier: Richard McBride

Number Born in B.C.: 7; **in England:** 7; **in Ireland:** 4; **in New Brunswick:** 3; in the rest of Canada: 8

Born Farthest Away: Bill Vander Zalm (Holland)

Born South of the 49th Parallel: James Dunsmuir (Oregon Territory)

Youngest to Take Office: Richard McBride (32)

Oldest to Take Office: John Robson (65)

Bachelors: Amor De Cosmos, Charles Semlin

Longest-Living: Charles Semlin (91 years)

Shortest-Living: A.E.B. Davie (41 years)

Premiers Who Died in Office: William Smithe, A.E.B. Davie, John Robson, Harlan Brewster, John Oliver

Most Premiers from One Riding: 4 (Victoria City)

Dismissed by Lieutenant-Governor: John Turner, Charles Semlin, Edward Prior

Largest: Simon Tolmie (300 lbs.)

Tiniest: William Bowser (approximately 5' 2")

Towns and Settlements Named after Premiers: Bowser, Dunsmuir, McBride, Oliver, Robson, Semlin

Selected Geographical Features: Amor De Cosmos Creek, McCreight Lake, Mount McBride, Mount Pattullo, Oliver Lake, John Hart Lake

Acknowledgments

During my odyssey through the byways of British Columbia politics, I spent many hours in Vancouver, Burnaby and New Westminster libraries. I wish to thank the staff at these libraries—especially at the Bob Prittie Metrotown branch in Burnaby—for their help. I also wish to acknowledge the assistance of the personnel at the British Columbia Archives, who did everything they could to furnish material, despite the censorship and red tape imposed by the NDP government's "Freedom of Information" legislation. More thanks go to Vaughn Palmer of the *Vancouver Sun* for sharing some of his insights into modern B.C. politics. Lastly, a grateful nod to Audrey McClellan, my editor at Heritage House, whose keen eye and gentle prodding made this a better book.

Bibliography

Akrigg, G.P.V. and Helen B. *British Columbia Place Names.* UBC Press, 1997

Barrett, Dave and William Miller. *Barrett.* Douglas & McIntyre Ltd., 1995.

Begg, Alexander. *History of British Columbia.* William Briggs/Ryerson Press, 1894/1972.

Carty, R.K. (editor). *Politics, Policy and Government in British Columbia.* UBC Press, 1996.

Creighton, Donald. *Dominion of The North.* Macmillan of Canada, 1957.

Fisher, Robin. *Duff Pattullo of British Columbia.* University of Toronto Press, 1991.

Garr, Allen. *Tough Guy.* Key Porter Books Ltd., 1985.

Harcourt, Mike and Wayne Skene. *Mike Harcourt: A Measure Of Defiance.* Douglas & McIntyre, 1996.

Jackman, S.W. *Portraits of The Premiers.* Evergreen Press Ltd., 1969.

—————. *The Men at Cary Castle.* Morriss Printing Company Ltd., 1972.

Leslie, Graham. *Breach of Promise.* Harbour Publishing, 1991.

Levy, Gary and Peter White (editors). *Provincial and Territorial Legislatures in Canada.* University of Toronto Press, 1989.

Mason, Gary and Keith Baldrey. *Fantasyland.* McGraw-Hill Ryerson, 1989.

Mitchell, David. *W.A.C. Bennett and The Rise of British Columbia.* Douglas & McIntyre, 1983.

—————. *Succession: The Political Reshaping of British Columbia.* Douglas & McIntyre, 1987.

Monet, Jacques. *The Canadian Crown.* Clark Irwin & Company Ltd., 1979.

Morton, James. *Honest John Oliver.* J.M. Dent & Sons, 1933.

Ormsby, Margaret. *British Columbia: A History.* Macmillan of Canada, 1964.

Reksten, Terry. *The Dunsmuir Saga.* Douglas & McIntyre, 1991.

Robin, Martin. *The Rush for Spoils.* McClelland & Stewart Ltd., 1972.

—————. *Pillars of Profit.* McClelland & Stewart Ltd., 1973.

Segger, Martin (editor). *The British Columbia Parliament Buildings.* Associated Resource Consultants, Ltd., 1979.

Sherman, Paddy. *Bennett.* McClelland & Stewart Ltd., 1966.

Twigg, Alan. *Vander Zalm: From Immigrant to Premier.* Harbour Publishing, 1986.

Walker, Russell P. *Politicians of A Pioneering Province.* Mitchell Press Ltd., 1969.

Wild, Roland. *Amor De Cosmos.* Ryerson Press, 1958.

Woodcock, George. *Amor De Cosmos, Journalist and Reformer.* Oxford University Press, 1975.

Woodcock, George. *British Columbia: A History of The Province.* Douglas & McIntyre, 1990.

Also consulted were the *B.C. Historical Quarterly*; the *Vancouver Sun Centennial Edition* (1971); other newspaper records; encylopediae; biographical dictionaries; genealogical databases; provincial and federal government documents, reports, studies and papers; private collections; university archives; and the author's own files and memory.

Photo Credits

B.C. Archives and Records Services

C-06178 (p.8), E-01894 (p.10), F-06738 (p.12), A-01449 (p.16), B-06678 (p.17, ul), A-08291 (p.17, ll), PDP00775 (p.22), C-06116 (p. 24), A-04656 (p.26, l), A-07820 (p.26, r), A-01230 (p.27), F-08478 (p.31), A-02559 (p.33), I-30851 (p.37, t), D-06672 (p.37, b), A-02125 (p.39), A-09064 (p.40), F-08211 (p.41), A-01990 (p.44), H-00153 (p.46), H-00791 (p.48), D-07548 (p.51), E-02200 (p. 52), G-01256 (p.53, t), G-04703 (p.53, b), F-04451 (p.55), G-04699 (p.57), A-01718 (p.59), A-02802 (p.60), E-07841 (p.61), E-01369 (p. 62), C-03718 (p.63), A-06454 (p.65), A-01219 (p.67), D-05994 (p.69), A-03951 (p.70), B-00880 (p.71), G-08302 (p.72), A-03462 (p.73), A-02563 (p.75, t), A-02646 (p.75, b), G-01362 (p.76), A-01645 (p.79), A-03888 (p.80), A 02102 (p.81), D-09313 (p.84), E-01245 (p.89), A-01257 (p.90, l), A-01253 (p.90, m), B-02273 (p.90, r), PDP03503 (p.93), I-21075 (p.94), B-02288 (p.95), D-04426 (p.96), B-04315 (p.98), A-01411 (p.100), B-01159 (p.104), A-04451 (p.107), D-07384 (p.108, b), C-00590 (p.111), E-01194 (p.114, t), A-06826 (p.114, b), A-01105 (p.116), D-00373 (p.118), D-07520 (p.119), B-08188 (p.120), G-07429 (p.122), A-02680 (p.123), I-52341 (p.127), PDP03694 (p.128), F-09918 (p.129), B-08260 (p.130), I-60812 (p.133), A-01425 (p.134), F-07721 (p.136), C-09974 (p.139), I-60825 (p.142), A-04616 (p.143), F-07523 (p.146), C-03115 (p.152), A-00828 (p.153), B-08114 (p.156), B-08419 (p.158), G-00774 (p.163, t), G-04125 (p.163, b), C-05267 (p.165), B-08117 (p.166), B-07943 (p.168), F-07642 (p.170), I-02131 (p.173), F-04428 (p.176), I-60025 (p.181), F-08614 (p.182), B-06613 (p.183), F-03019 (p.185), PDP09149 (p.187), G-04069 (p.188), H-01741 (p.189, b), I-60826 (p.196, l), I-32420 (p.196, r), I-32654 (p.198), PDP09183 (p.200), ZZ-95266 (p.204, l), I-60824 (p.204, r), I-09398 (p.209), PDP09251 (p.210), PDP09265 (p.219), I-32605 (p.229).

The photo on page 181 is from the Jim Ryan Collection at BCARS. The cartoons on pages 187, 200, 210 and 219 are from the Len Norris Collection at BCARS.

Other Credits

B.C. Ferries (p.236)
B.C. Government Photograph (p.194)
B.C. Hydro Information Services (p.189, t)
Bob Bierman (p.214)
Bob Krieger (p.222, 227, 238)
Canadian Illustrated News (p.42)
Dave Roels (p.269)
Government of B.C. (p.231, p.239)
Government of B.C./Visions West Photo (p.242)
Heritage House Collection (p.25)
Dan Murphy (p. 216)
Richmond Review (p.202, p.212, p.221, p.225)
Vancouver Public Library (#1785 p.108, t; #1277, p.155)
Western Canada Wilderness Committee/Mark Wareing (p.228)
William Rayner (p.17, ur, lr, 19, 64, 286)

Index

The Author

William Rayner is an author and semi-retired journalist who has been a keen observer of British Columbia's political scene for more than 40 years. Born in Winnipeg in 1929, Mr. Rayner was educated in that city's school system before joining the Royal Canadian Navy in 1947. After five years' service (including action in the Korean War), he returned to civilian life.

Mr. Rayner's first newspaper job was as a reporter with the *Trail Daily Times* in 1954. Although he also wrote and edited for the *Victoria Times*, the *Vancouver Herald*, the *Montreal Star* and *The Globe and Mail*, Mr. Rayner spent most of his newspaper career with the *Vancouver Sun*. His assignments included the Watts Riot in 1965, posting to the Ottawa bureau in 1969 and chief of the *Sun*'s legislative bureau in Victoria in 1974. In 1971, he edited the much-acclaimed *Vancouver Sun Centennial Edition*. Mr. Rayner served nine years as news editor and five years as editorial systems manager before taking early retirement in 1988.

Since retiring from daily journalism, Mr. Rayner has written a number of articles for magazines and newspapers. From 1990 to 1995, he wrote a biweekly column for the *Vancouver Province*. Mr. Rayner is the author of two previous books: *Vancouver Sun Style Guide* (1976) and *Images of History—Twentieth Century British Columbia Through the Front Pages* (Orca, 1997). To keep abreast of current affairs, he reads at least three newspapers a day and has maintained his contacts on the political front in Victoria.

Although Mr. Rayner has counted the occasional politician as a friend during his career, he is wary of the breed. "Politicians are fascinating," he says. "There's something about getting elected that transforms the thought processes of even the most sincerest, altruistic individual. Their grasp on reality (apart from the imperative of getting re-elected) is often tenuous at best."

Mr. Rayner's hobbies include playing bad chess and passable scrabble, chasing tornadoes each spring and reading. He is divorced but he and his former wife are planning to remarry. They have one son.